The Challenge of Nietzsche

The Challenge of Nietzsche

HOW TO APPROACH HIS THOUGHT

Jeremy Fortier

The University of Chicago Press CHICAGO & LONDON

The University of Chicago Press, Chicago 60637
The University of Chicago Press, Ltd., London

Published 2020
Printed in the United States of America

29 28 27 26 25 24 23 22 21 20 1 2 3 4 5

ISBN-13: 978-0-226-67939-6 (cloth)
ISBN-13: 978-0-226-67942-6 (e-book)
DOI: https://doi.org/10.7208/chicago/9780226679426.001.0001

Library of Congress Cataloging-in-Publication Data
Names: Fortier, Jeremy, author.
Title: The challenge of Nietzsche : how to approach his thought / Jeremy Fortier.
Description: Chicago : University of Chicago Press, 2020. | Includes bibliographical references and index.
Identifiers: LCCN 2019024284 | ISBN 9780226679396 (cloth) | ISBN 9780226679426 (ebook)
Subjects: LCSH: Nietzsche, Friedrich Wilhelm, 1844–1900. | Philosophy, German—19th century.
Classification: LCC B3317 .F593 2020 | DDC 193—dc23
LC record available at https://lccn.loc.gov/2019024284

♾ This paper meets the requirements of ANSI/NISO Z39.48-1992 (Permanence of Paper).

I would rather be an authority on myself than on Plato. In the experience I have of myself I find enough to make me wise, if I were a good student.

Montaigne, *Essays*

Our passions sketch our books, the repose in between writes them.

Proust, *In Search of Lost Time*

CONTENTS

ACKNOWLEDGMENTS

I am indebted to the reviewers for the University of Chicago Press for their exceptionally incisive comments.

Chapter 2 draws on material that appeared in an earlier version as "Nietzsche's Political Engagements: On the Relationship between Philosophy and Politics in *The Wanderer and His Shadow*," *Review of Politics* 78, no. 2 (2016): 201–25. Chapter 4 draws on material that appeared in an earlier version as "Authenticity and the Motives for Political Leadership: Reflections from Nietzsche's *Zarathustra*," in *Leadership and the Unmasking of Authenticity*, edited by Brent Cusher and Mark Menaldo (Northampton, MA: Edward Elgar Publishing, 2018).

A NOTE ON REFERENCES TO NIETZSCHE

When quoting from Nietzsche, I adopt the following convention: words in italics represent his emphasis; words that are underlined represent my own emphasis.

When ellipses (three dots) appear in a quotation from Nietzsche, they represent his own punctuation, not an omission from the text; in quotations from all other authors, ellipses indicate an omission.

References to Nietzsche's works are given using the standard English abbreviations (listed below), along with an aphorism number or section title (and section number, where applicable). I have used the translations listed, but I have sometimes modified these after consulting Nietzschesource.org, which provides a digital version (edited by Paolo d'Iorio) of the critical edition of the complete works of Nietzsche (edited by Giorgio Colli and Mazzino Montinari).

A	*The Antichrist*. In *Twilight of the Idols and The Antichrist*. Translated by R. J. Hollingdale. London: Penguin Books, 1990.
AOM	*Assorted Opinions and Maxims*. In *Human, All Too Human*. Translated by R. J. Hollingdale. Cambridge: Cambridge University Press, 1996.
BGE	*Beyond Good and Evil*. In *Basic Writings of Nietzsche*. Translated by Walter Kaufmann. New York: Modern Library, 1968.
BT	*The Birth of Tragedy*. In *The Birth of Tragedy and Other Writings*. Translated by Ronald Speirs. Cambridge: Cambridge University Press, 1999.

CW	*The Case of Wagner*. In *Basic Writings of Nietzsche*. Translated by Walter Kaufmann. New York: Modern Library, 1968.
D	*Daybreak*. Translated by R. J. Hollingdale. Cambridge: Cambridge University Press, 1982.
EH	*Ecce Homo*. Translated by Duncan Large. Oxford: Oxford University Press, 2007.
GM	*On the Genealogy of Morality*. Translated by Maudemarie Clark and Alan J. Swensen. Indianapolis: Hackett Publishing, 1998.
GS	*The Gay Science*.* Translated by Josefine Nauckhoff. Cambridge: Cambridge University Press, 2001.
HH	*Human, All Too Human*. Translated by R. J. Hollingdale. Cambridge: Cambridge University Press, 1986.
HL	*On the Uses and Disadvantages of History for Life*. Translated by R. J. Hollingdale. Cambridge: Cambridge University Press, 1997.
KSA	*Sämtliche Werke: Kritische Studienausgabe in 15 Bänden*. Edited by Giorgio Colli and Mazzino Montinari. Berlin: Walter de Gruyter, 1980. (I refer to *KSA* for Nietzsche's unpublished notes. In order to facilitate cross-referencing, I cite the volume and page number of *KSA*, followed by the year, notebook number, and entry number in square brackets.)
NCW	*Nietzsche contra Wagner*. In *The Portable Nietzsche*. Translated by Walter Kaufmann. New York: Viking Press, 1954.
RWB	*Richard Wagner in Bayreuth*. Translated by R. J. Hollingdale. Cambridge: Cambridge University Press, 1997.
SE	*Schopenhauer as Educator*. In *Untimely Meditations*. Translated by R. J. Hollingdale. Cambridge: Cambridge University Press, 1997.
TI	*Twilight of the Idols*. Translated by Duncan Large. New York: Oxford University Press, 1995.
TSZ	*Thus Spoke Zarathustra*. Translated by Graham Parkes. Oxford: World's Classics, 2005.
WS	*The Wanderer and His Shadow*. In *Human, All Too Human*. Translated by R. J. Hollingdale. Cambridge: Cambridge University Press, 1996.

*Since the most common English translation of *Die fröhliche Wissenschaft* is *The Gay Science*, the standard English abbreviation is *GS*. I have followed this convention in order to minimize confusion, but when giving the full title of the work, I have opted to use *The Joyful Wissenschaft*, since too much is lost if one does not keep in view the broad pursuit of knowledge that the German word encompasses (including both humanistic inquiry and research in the natural sciences).

INTRODUCTORY REMARKS

Friedrich Nietzsche was the author of no fewer than a dozen books, which have been among the most widely read in the world from the time of his death to the present day. There have also been innumerable books written *about* Nietzsche and his work.

These facts are in need of some explanation—and even a justification. For despite being a prolific author, Nietzsche was something of a skeptic about books. He had once been an academic, making the study of books his profession, but he came to view that period of his life as a great waste, and he claimed that after abandoning his career as a professor, he went for years without reading any books at all. And when Nietzsche did begin to read again, he insisted that he did so only very selectively, and he advised others to do the same: "In the early morning at break of day, when you are at your freshest, at the dawning of your strength, to read a *book*—that is what I call depraved!"[1]

Today one sometimes hears advocacy of "great books" education: that is to say, an education that is not directed toward vocational training or contemporary intellectual trends, but is instead centered on the study of landmark works of the past (for instance, texts by Plato or Shakespeare). Now, Nietzsche certainly expected to have readers who were familiar with the great books (and he stressed the importance of cultivating the "*art* of reading" books of that caliber with the utmost degree of care and reflection).[2] But the *education* that he recommends is less one of immersing oneself in great books than one of seeking out "great experiences." Nietzsche attributed his most important insights to his experience of the world, not to his reading of great books of the past.[3] Thus, his advice to avoid reading in the morning: for Nietzsche, we must always look to our experience of the world for our primary education; books are a supplement to (and in the service of) that primary education. Nietzsche approached the writing of his own books accordingly: for the most part, he dedicated himself to writing only at the end of each day, and his writings amount to a reflection on (and a document of) his experience of the world.[4] Moreover, the books that Nietzsche most enjoyed reading, and which he recommended to his readers, tended not to be books that laid out abstract philosophical principles, but those which either depicted or reflected upon the conduct and psychology of individual lives (for instance, Diogenes Laertius' *Lives of the Ancient Philosophers*, the essays of Emerson and Montaigne, the novels of Dostoevsky and Stendhal).[5] Nietzsche's preference in that regard is consistent with a principle that he asserted near the beginning of his career as a writer: "The only criticism of a philosophy that is possible and that also proves something, is to attempt to see if one can live according to it."[6] And near the end of his career Nietzsche applied that principle to himself by equipping his books with autobiographical commentaries, explaining how they grew out of his life (how each book was shaped by different episodes in his life), evaluating the degree to which he had been able to live out the principles which they proposed, and presenting his life as an exemplary one (a model to inspire and direct the lives of readers). At every turn, then, Nietzsche's books point away from themselves and toward the life that he lived (and the life that readers ought to live).

Nietzsche's books are therefore designed to bring readers to a fuller understanding of the experiences that produced them. What is at issue, however, are not trivial or haphazard events that are scattered throughout an individual's day-to-day life, but more elemental experiences that dominate and define an individual life. Every element of Nietzsche's writings—from his philosophic doctrines ("the will to power") to his provocative aphorisms ("what does not kill me makes me stronger")—is at bottom an interpretation of those experiences. This study of Nietzsche aims to bring readers to a fuller understanding of three of the elemental experiences at issue: the drive for independence; the feeling of love; the assessment of one's overall health (or well-being). The study is undertaken on the basis of my conviction that Nietzsche's work resists exhaustive interpretation: even and especially a reading of Nietzsche that is firmly grounded in the text (as mine aims to be) must recognize that the depth and comprehensiveness of his thought compels different readers to draw together different threads of his thought in different ways, in studies that bring to light possibilities that are contained within his books but that could easily be overlooked without the assistance of diversely equipped guides to such rich but challenging territory (and I think that Nietzsche would have welcomed being treated less as an authority to be admired than as a sort of alien but powerful life form, requiring careful examination and competing interpretations).[7] The justification for this book *about* Nietzsche is, then, that it brings new light to a crucial dimension of Nietzsche's thought that other intrepid explorers have surveyed incompletely (and sometimes overlooked altogether): namely, the way in which—and the *degree* to which—Nietzsche's writings must be related to his life, and read as a commentary on his life. But it should now be evident that the aim of this exercise is not merely to acquire biographical information about Nietzsche, but to understand how his reflection on his *particular* life can contribute to the general understanding of experiences that are fundamental to *all* human life: independence, love, health.

My claims about Nietzsche's thought and its relation to his life require the entire study that follows for their proper elaboration, but my narrower claim that previous surveys of his thought have overlooked something crucial (whether in whole or in part) demands greater justification up front. Let me therefore use the remainder of this introduction to spell out in more detail how Nietzsche has generally been read, and explain why those readings need to be supplemented.

*

Most scholars (and even a few casual readers) are aware that Nietzsche's books must be read in light of his life in at least one important respect: Nietzsche's books reflect an evolution within his thought over the course of his career. And, to a degree that is unique among philosophers, Nietzsche made a point of emphasizing and explaining the evolution of his life and his thought. Thus, late in his career Nietzsche returned to the books that he had published during his first decade as an author, and outfitted them with new prefaces, commenting critically on their content and the process of their composition. Moreover, one of Nietzsche's very last writings is a sort of autobiography titled *Ecce Homo* (Behold the Man), and it includes a series of short chapters discussing his earlier books one by one. Finally, many of Nietzsche's writings include citations to his other books, along with remarks about the relationships among the various texts. All of this reflects the fact that Nietzsche's thought *evolved*: he rejected, revised, or supplemented major elements of his thought throughout his career, and he commented extensively on those changes.

This self-reflexive aspect of Nietzsche's writings demands greater attention than it has so far received. To be sure, most scholars recognize that, given

Nietzsche's evolution as a thinker, some basic framework is needed for understanding how his books relate to one another. But many studies of Nietzsche operate on the basis of presuppositions about how his writings fit together that are left implicit, or alluded to only in passing (and without focusing on what Nietzsche himself had to say about his evolution). Of course, the issue of Nietzsche's development is complex enough that not every study can afford to deal with it in detail. But, for just that reason, a study such as the present one may provide a valuable service by laying out and assessing how Nietzsche explained the development of his thought over the course of his career. This sort of study may be of use to readers who are relatively new to Nietzsche (and who, accordingly, have only a vague sense of the relationships among his books), as well as to readers who are already well versed in his thought (but who may not have worked through all of his self-commentaries).[8]

This book will, then, amount to something of a guide to Nietzsche's writings, by offering an original framework for understanding and analyzing the relationships among his books. I do not claim to be offering a *definitive* or *exhaustive* guide to Nietzsche's oeuvre. What I offer here is a *framework* that others may be able to build on productively, especially since I will highlight and help to interpret something that deserves more attention than it has so far received: namely, what Nietzsche himself had to say about his development as an author.

AN OVERVIEW OF NIETZSCHE'S CAREER

The first detailed study of Nietzsche's work was written four years before his death, but five years after the (to this day somewhat mysterious and debated) mental collapse that left him hospitalized for the last ten years of his life, with only vague memories of his former existence. The study was authored by his old acquaintance Lou Salome (Nietzsche had once hoped that Salome might become a disciple of his, but they knew each other only briefly, and she went on to become accomplished in her own right, forming close associations with Rainer Maria Rilke and Sigmund Freud along the way). Salome's study established a basic scheme for interpreting Nietzsche's career—a scheme that, as one recent study notes, "has become such a commonplace in Nietzsche scholarship that she is rarely credited with it."[9]

Salome divided Nietzsche's career into three major periods, as follows:[10] (1) during his early period, Nietzsche's work has a strong metaphysical and quasi-mystical bent, reflecting the influence of Arthur Schopenhauer's philosophy and Richard Wagner's artwork; (2) Nietzsche's "middle period" is often characterized as "positivist," since the writings from this period advocate the methods of modern science, and adopt an accordingly skeptical temper and moderate tone;[11] (3) the writings of the final period—beginning with his most famous work, *Thus Spoke Zarathustra*—are more radical, and move back toward a "mystical" and poetic/artistic stance (although Nietzsche remains critical of Schopenhauer and Wagner).[12] For many readers (including Salome), the writings of the third period are an object of suspicion (or even outright condemnation): they are generally recognized as containing passages of great brilliance, but they also seem too mystical or artistic or simply intemperate (and even downright fanatical) to quality as properly philosophic.[13]

Salome's "periodization" of Nietzsche's career has exerted a great influence, partly because it has a degree of broad plausibility. There are major features of Nietzsche's works that fit within her schema (for instance, Nietzsche's rhetorical tone is relatively moderate during the "middle period" and becomes more extreme in later works). But there are problems with dividing up Nietzsche's career along the lines that Salome proposed. One problem is that Salome's scheme is not entirely compatible with how Nietzsche judged his own work, and yet her scheme provides a readymade framework that can discourage readers from looking very closely at exactly what Nietzsche has to say about his career. Let me give one significant example: what Salome's scheme refers to as Nietzsche's "middle period" corresponds to a series of writings that he himself identified as belonging together, as part of a series devoted to establishing the ideal of the "Free Spirit." To this extent, Nietzsche's self-assessments support Salome's scheme. But there is a major difficulty here, because Nietzsche also characterized his last two "Free Spirit" writings as "yes-saying" works, together with *Thus Spoke Zarathustra*. So Salome's "periodization" imposes a clear division where Nietzsche himself suggested a cross-cutting categorization, and that complication is often overlooked.[14] And this is no trivial matter, because a cardinal feature of Nietzsche's mature thought concerns the contrast between a philosophy that is "yes-saying" (affirmative or creative) and one that is "no-saying" (debunking or merely critical). Since Nietzsche identified a continuity between *Zarathustra* and his two previous books in this crucial respect (they were all "yes-saying"), Salome's method of categorization implies that Nietzsche is not a reliable guide to his own thought. One wonders if for some readers that may be just the point: to claim (or presuppose) that Nietzsche is basically an incoherent or contradictory thinker, who cannot be trusted to know his own mind (and whose work therefore does not amount to a rigorous intellectual challenge, however engaging his writing may be at times). But it seems to me that Nietzsche's self-assessments show the opposite: they show him to have been exceptionally lucid about the tensions within his thought, and to have worked out a detailed explanation of his own development—an explanation that successfully demonstrates that his oeuvre is more of a coherent and well-integrated whole than its critics have supposed.[15]

In short, I think it is fair to say that in light of the fact that Nietzsche's thought clearly *evolved*, and the fact that he put great effort into *explaining* that evolution, any assessment of his thought that disregards his self-assessments must count as incomplete at best, and liable to serious misrepresentation at worst.[16] What I aim to do here, then, is to use Nietzsche as a guide to Nietzsche. This proposal comes with an important proviso: Nietzsche gives us guides to reading his books, but not instruction manuals. In other words, his self-commentaries offer clues, cautions, and signposts, but they are at the same time calculatedly complex, ambiguous, and puzzling in ways that require no less interpretation than the writings on which they comment.[17] Nevertheless, the self-commentaries do not lead readers down rabbit holes; they illuminate genuine pathways through his work, giving his books a clearer and richer meaning than they would have had without those commentaries. The interpretation outlined in what follows is offered as evidence for that claim.

That being said, in order to make use of Nietzsche's self-assessments, a fairly extensive knowledge of his writings is required. This study will lay out and unpack the complex details that inform Nietzsche's self-assessments. But given all the complexities involved, it may be helpful to begin with two basic points of orientation: first, a chronological summary of Nietzsche's books; second, a provisional outline of how I understand the divisions between those books, and the relationship between them.

Let me begin, then, with the chronological summary. Nietzsche's books have a complicated publishing history, but the basic facts are as follows:[18]

1872: Publication of *The Birth of Tragedy Out of the Spirit of Music*
1873: Publication of *David Strauss the Confessor and the Writer* (conceived of as part of a series titled *Untimely Meditations*)
1874: Publication of *On the Uses and Disadvantages of History for Life* and *Schopenhauer as Educator* (the second and third of the *Untimely Meditations*)
1874: Publication of *Richard Wagner in Bayreuth* (the fourth of the *Untimely Meditations*)

1878: Publication of *Human, All Too Human: A Book for Free Spirits*
1879: Publication of *Assorted Opinions and Maxims*
1880: Publication of *The Wanderer and His Shadow*
1881: Publication of *Daybreak: Thoughts on the Prejudices of Morality*
1882: Publication of *The Joyful Wissenschaft* (which, at this stage, is composed of four books)
1883: Publication of part 1 and part 2 of *Thus Spoke Zarathustra: A Book for Everyone and Nobody* (the two parts are written and published successively)
1884: Publication of part 3 of *Thus Spoke Zarathustra*
1885: Part 4 of *Thus Spoke Zarathustra* is written, but not published (although Nietzsche circulates it to a few friends)
1886: Publication of *Beyond Good and Evil: Prelude to a Philosophy of the Future*. In addition, Nietzsche prepares all of his previous publications to be reissued. For most of these reissues he composes new, autobiographical prefaces commenting on the composition and content of the work (only the *Untimely Meditations* and *Thus Spoke Zarathustra* do not receive new prefaces). Moreover, *Human, All Too Human*, *Assorted Opinions and Maxims*, and *The Wanderer and His Shadow* are now placed under one cover (with the latter two works placed together as a second volume, and with an original preface written for each volume).
1887: Publication of *On the Genealogy of Morality: A Polemic*. Nietzsche also writes a fifth book for *The Joyful Wissenschaft* (the work is therefore reissued in this year with the following new material: the preface written in 1886, the fifth book, and an appendix of songs).
1888: Publication of *The Case of Wagner: A Musician's Problem*. Nietzsche writes *Twilight of the Idols* (which is prepared for publication), and then writes *The Antichrist* and *Ecce Homo* and compiles *Nietzsche contra Wagner* (an amalgam of previously published material). Composition of the last three works overlaps considerably. Nietzsche suffers a mental collapse shortly after completing them, and they are not published for several years.

As this study proceeds, additional details will be added to this basic chronology.

The standard interpretive scheme (derived from Lou Salome) takes the works of 1872–74 as Nietzsche's "early period," those from 1878 to 1882 as the "middle period," and those from 1883 onward as the final period of his career.

In this study, however, I will be operating on the basis of a scheme that divides Nietzsche's writings along the following lines:

1. *The Birth of Tragedy*, and the four *Untimely Meditations*. These are Nietzsche's early works, and can be considered "pre-Nietzschean" (being Schopenhauerian and Wagnerian instead).
2. *Human, All Too Human* (encompassing all three of its installments—originally published separately between 1878 and 1880, and then reissued as a single unit in 1886). This work is Nietzsche's "declaration of independence." It rejects the authorities of his early writings (Schopenhauer and Wagner), and establishes his own ideal of the "Free Spirit" as a model of intellectual and personal independence.
3. *Daybreak* and *The Joyful Wissenschaft*. These works extend the project of *Human, All Too Human*. (Thus, the original back cover for *The Joyful Wissenschaft* stated: "This book marks the conclusion of a series of writings by Friedrich Nietzsche whose common goal is to erect *a new image and ideal of the free spirit*"—and then listed those writings, beginning with *Human, All Too Human*.) But these works also show Nietzsche working out a new and distinctive philosophic position (beyond the more narrowly critical position of *Human, All Too Human*), so these works are not only "destructive" (of old ideas), but also "constructive" (of new ones). As such, these books are simultaneously connected to stages (2) and (4) of this schema.
4. *Thus Spoke Zarathustra*. Here Nietzsche presents (or, rather, has the character of Zarathustra present) the major doctrines that would come to define him in the popular imagination (the will to power and the eternal return). Because the work contains these doctrines, and because it takes a quasi-prophetic tone, this seems to be the one work in which, more than in any other, Nietzsche sought to have a major impact on the world. In later writings Nietzsche emphasizes the singular status of this work by referring the reader to it in the most exalted terms possible.
5. *Beyond Good and Evil*, *On the Genealogy of Morality*, *Twilight of the Idols*. In these writings Nietzsche does not present original ideas so much as he aims to explain and advertise his thought, in order to help prepare audiences to understand *Thus Spoke Zarathustra* (although, to be sure, he does devise memorable new ways of formulating his ideas in these writings). The fifth book of *The Joyful Wissenschaft* can also be included in this category. Near the end of his career, Nietzsche would refer to all

of his post-*Zarathustra* writings as "fish-hooks," as well as calling them "no-saying" works (whereas he labels the writings from the previous two categories of this schema as "yes-saying").[19]

6. *The Antichrist*, *Ecce Homo*, *The Case of Wagner*, *Nietzsche contra Wagner*. These can be considered works of self-knowledge. To be sure, that is true to an important degree of all of Nietzsche's works, but it is especially true here. Like the writings of category (5), these works do not present major innovations in Nietzsche's thought. But these are some of his most personal books, showing what he had to overcome in order to become a philosopher (working through the challenges of cultural authority, religion, and his own nature). The autobiographical prefaces of 1886 can also be included in this category.

This outline of Nietzsche's works is, to repeat, provisional, but it will be elaborated and defended as this study proceeds (although I should acknowledge immediately that I believe reasonable variations on the scheme are possible, particularly with regard to how the post-*Zarathustra* writings are divided up).

That being said, there are two features of the scheme just outlined that I believe are absolutely essential for understanding Nietzsche's career: *Human, All Too Human* and *Thus Spoke Zarathustra* each stand apart from Nietzsche's other writings. These are two landmarks, and turning points, in Nietzsche's career. This is reflected by the fact that each work introduces a major "character" into Nietzsche's oeuvre: the Free Spirit and Zarathustra, respectively. None of Nietzsche's other writings introduces a major character into his oeuvre in a comparable way—and, indeed, none of the numerous other characters that Nietzsche creates is of comparable importance to his oeuvre (with one potential exception, which will be discussed shortly).[20]

After the Free Spirit and Zarathustra are introduced into Nietzsche's oeuvre, there is not a single work in which Nietzsche fails to mention them (and, in many cases, he discusses them prominently and at length). To be sure, there is an important difference between the two cases: Nietzsche regularly refers readers back to the text of *Thus Spoke Zarathustra*, whereas the Free Spirit is not defined by a single work (accordingly, the ideal to some degree develops over time, while the figure of Zarathustra does not). Nevertheless, the Free Spirit and Zarathustra represent essential (and broadly consistent) ideals in Nietzsche's thought, and so the writings that introduce them are of special importance—as this study will demonstrate in detail.

THE FREE SPIRIT, ZARATHUSTRA, AND "MR. NIETZSCHE"

The Free Spirit and Zarathustra are more than simply prominent character types in Nietzsche's oeuvre. These characters represent the major alternatives (of thought and of life) that are presented through his body of work.

To be sure, the Free Spirit and Zarathustra do not represent the whole of Nietzsche's thought. This duality needs to be supplemented by a character who is introduced primarily in Nietzsche's post-*Zarathustra* writings: the character of Nietzsche himself. For Nietzsche very much presents himself *as* a character—"Mr. Nietzsche," as he says at one point. But "Mr. Nietzsche" appears primarily in *Ecce Homo* and the 1886 prefaces, and those writings presuppose readers who are already familiar with Nietzsche's oeuvre. So one cannot properly consider the character of Mr. Nietzsche without first saying a few words about the Free Spirit and Zarathustra, who represent the most prominent alternatives offered by Nietzsche's books.

The Free Spirit and Zarathustra can be thought of as representatives of two different ways of being-in-the-world. Both characters stand apart from the world around them, and view it with profound skepticism. The Free Spirit strives to remain as comprehensively critical and independent of the world as possible. Zarathustra, in contrast, is not merely critical and independent, but also strives to be creative (constructive), and thereby contribute to (help to *change*) the world. So while the Free Spirit finds fulfillment in maintaining a solitary independence, Zarathustra finds fulfillment through engagement with others. This difference entails another: the Free Spirit and Zarathustra represent contrasting postures toward the world because they represent contrasting postures *toward oneself.* The Free Spirit is deliberately self-restrained in a way that Zarathustra is not, finding in love or music dangers to be resisted for the sake of independence, where Zarathustra would find potential to be creatively harnessed. So in each case, the example of the character challenges the reader to consider engaging with the world in a particular way, *and* to recognize how and why that manner of engagement demands cultivating distinctive qualities of soul.

As this suggests, the contrast between the Free Spirit and Zarathustra can be thought of in the same terms that Nietzsche employed to distinguish between his books: the Free Spirit is primarily "no-saying," while Zarathustra is primarily "yes-saying." At the same time, while there is a very significant *distinction* to be drawn between the Free Spirit and Zarathustra, this is not to say that there is a pure *opposition* between the two: they are alternatives, not antipodes. After all, the creation of both characters was part and parcel of Nietzsche's own evolution as a thinker and as a human being—and, accordingly, both characters retained a place in his writings until the end. Determining exactly how the alternatives of the Free Spirit and Zarathustra relate to each other is therefore essential to understanding why Nietzsche's career evolved in the way it did: why was he moved to go beyond the ideal of the Free Spirit by creating the figure of Zarathustra? And how did he assess that development after the fact? Nietzsche shows us the importance of just such questions, and helps us to answer them, through his autobiographical commentaries. These self-reflections show us how the character of Mr. Nietzsche encompasses, but also to some degree transcends, his creations of the Free Spirit and Zarathustra.

In sum: understanding what each of these major characters—the Free Spirit, Zarathustra, and Mr. Nietzsche—represents, and how they relate to one another, can provide us with an essential lens or framework through which to view the evolution of Nietzsche's career. To that end, let me make a broad suggestion (which will be spelled out in more detail in the chapters that follow): the tension between the different dispositions represented by the Free Spirit and Zarathustra is one that Nietzsche wants us to understand as an essential tension—a natural, universal, and unavoidable feature of human life. At the same time, because the Free Spirit and Zarathustra are Nietzsche's self-conscious and artful creations, and insofar as they each serve his own larger project, the tension between the Free Spirit and Zarathustra should be understood as a *unifying* and *productive* tension in his oeuvre: Nietzsche explores each character, and alternates between them, as a way of negotiating a tension in human existence that can never be definitively resolved. This means that while the lion's share of Nietzsche's oeuvre is focused on establishing the Free Spirit and Zarathustra as its major figures, in the end it is Nietzsche's own life that proves to be most exemplary.[21]

NIETZSCHE'S TROUBLESOME LEGACY

With this study, then, I am aiming to understand Nietzsche's project *as he understood it*: to grasp what he was attempting to accomplish through each of his books, and how he retrospectively evaluated the major stages of his career. My inquiry is not addressed only (or even primarily) to readers who may happen to have an interest in Nietzsche's autobiography. Rather, it seems to me that getting a better grasp on how Nietzsche understood his project as an author is indispensable to coming to terms with the influence his work has had—an influence that has been extremely substantial, and, in the judgment of many, extremely negative. I think it is fair to say that, for many readers, Nietzsche's impact—his legacy—is evidence that his thought is fundamentally unsound, and even quite dangerous.

The problem of Nietzsche's influence is summarized clearly, concisely, and combatively in a recent, widely reviewed overview of the contemporary political situation by the academic polymath and public intellectual Steven Pinker. According to Pinker, Nietzsche's thought is the fountainhead for much of what is wrong with the modern world. To begin with, Nietzsche "helped to inspire the romantic militarism that led to the First World War and the fascism that led to the Second"; subsequently, Nietzsche, "an inspiration to relativists everywhere," served as "a godfather to all the intellectual movements of the 20th century that were hostile to science and objectivity, including Existentialism, Critical Theory, Poststructuralism, Deconstruction, and Postmodernism"; and Nietzsche's influence remains visible in contemporary reactionary and neofascist movements, as well as in the willingness of some intellectuals to disdain liberal modernity as weak and decadent while admiring dictators as models of strength and revolutionary vitality.[22] Pinker's assessment is polemical, but not baseless: it is undeniable that Nietzsche's writings have had a special appeal to readers representing a wide variety of radical and rebellious political stripes, and who have in some (though certainly not all) cases been willing to act on their convictions in destructive and even outright bloodthirsty ways. This has been the case around the world and across different generations.[23] Moreover, Nietzsche's unusually captivating writing (whose allure even a severe critic such as Pinker is compelled to acknowledge),[24] combined with his virulent criticism of liberal modernity, seems destined to leave him as an inspiration to radicals of all sorts well into the future.[25]

Scholars have long recognized these objections to Nietzsche, and have addressed them in a variety of ways. The major stages of Nietzsche's reception in the English-speaking world are well known: in the first half of the twentieth century Nietzsche was alternately abhorred or admired for his declaration that "God is dead!"[26] but his reputation suffered the most from its association with militaristic nationalism, including the abominations of German fascism (an association that was encouraged by Nietzsche's sister, whose nationalism and anti-Semitism he had often condemned, but who nevertheless controlled his literary estate, and who welcomed Adolf Hitler into the Nietzsche museum she established).[27] After World War II Nietzsche was rehabilitated almost singlehandedly by Walter Kaufmann, who produced the most widely used

English translations of his writings and who contended that Nietzsche was not properly understood as a political thinker at all. In Kaufmann's words, the "leitmotif of Nietzsche's life and thought" was "the theme of the antipolitical individual who seeks perfection far from the modern world."[28] Subsequently, the most influential readings of Nietzsche were those of Alexander Nehamas, who read Nietzsche primarily as a theorist of self-care and self-creation, and those inspired by Michel Foucault, in which Nietzsche was read as providing tools to help critique and undermine existing social orders rather than offering any constructive proposals of his own.[29] In that context, a scholar such as Bernard Williams could assert, without anticipating any obvious objections, that Nietzsche never arrived at "a view that offered a coherent politics . . . in the sense of a coherent set of opinions about the ways in which power should be exercised in modern societies, with what limitations and to what end."[30] Nevertheless, the "antipolitical" (or, at least, "apolitical")[31] reading of Nietzsche was challenged by a steadily growing number of scholars who argued that, in fact, Nietzsche held to a determinate political position (most concisely described as that of an "aristocratic radical"),[32] which identified liberalism and democracy as late-modern consequences of a soul-enervating nihilism set in motion by Christianity (and, standing behind it, Platonism), which were to be counteracted through the adoption of a martial, hierarchical, and probably quite brutal, political culture.[33] As a result, today many scholars would endorse the judgment that "Nietzsche's political views are integral with the rest of his thought."[34] Thus, in recent studies one can find Ronald Beiner writing that "the *whole* of Nietzsche's philosophy is subordinate to, or in the service of, his politics,"[35] and Michael Gillespie contending that Nietzsche's "task was not merely a task of thinking, but also of doing, deeply practical and political."[36] But whereas Steven Pinker admonishes contemporary intellectuals to "drop the Nietzsche" (whose ideas he dismisses as "repellent and incoherent"),[37] Gillespie concludes that Nietzsche presents a critique of the modern world "in both its starkest and most profound form, and . . . we would be remiss if we did not give it our utmost attention."[38] And Beiner (who echoes Pinker in contending that Nietzsche has a particularly pernicious subterranean influence on the contemporary political far right) cautions that "Nietzsche was a great philosopher," but "great thinkers can be dangerous," so that our only intellectually rigorous and responsible option is to read him "with our eyes fully open" to just how "*intellectually*, *morally*, and *politically*" dangerous his thought really is.[39] Thus, whereas scholars once generally preferred to characterize Nietzsche as an "antipolitical" or "apolitical" thinker, now they are more likely to affirm the following three propositions: (1) Nietzsche *is* a political thinker; (2) his political thought is *dangerous*; (3) his thought is at some level deeply *compelling* (even if not ultimately or entirely correct).[40]

In light of recent scholarship, then, Nietzsche's legacy appears more problematic than ever. For if Nietzsche *is* a political thinker, and his political thought is exceptionally *dangerous*, but his thought nevertheless remains *compelling*, then how can we reasonably justify devoting our serious attention to his work (or, at least, looking to his work as offering anything other than a cautionary tale, with a warning label attached to his books, marking them out as something to be read only as examples of what *not* to think)?

This problem must be faced squarely, for I think there can be no doubt that Nietzsche expected and intended that his thought would have an incendiary political effect. He once notoriously wrote, "I am not a man, I am dynamite,"[41] and he was fairly candid about the fact that his often inflammatory rhetoric amounted to playing with fire—not only metaphorically, on the page, but also in practice, through politics. Thus, in a revealing aphorism titled "*The Explosive Ones*," he remarks:

> When one considers how the energy of young men needs to explode, one is not surprised to see them decide so unsubtly and so unselectively for this or that cause: what thrills them is the sight of the zeal surrounding a cause, and, so to speak, the sight of the burning match—not the cause itself. The subtler seducers therefore know how to create in them the expectation of an explosion and to disregard justifying their cause: reasons are not the way to win over these powder kegs! (*GS* 38)

Nietzsche knew how to provide "the sight of the burning match" and "the expectation of an explosion" far more than the great majority of writers of any sort, let alone any other philosophers, and he knew that his thought would thereby become associated with causes of all sorts, causes that would not necessarily be reasonable. That being the case, it seems to me that the most profitable question we can ask is not whether Nietzsche is best read as "political" or "antipolitical" (much less "apolitical"), but instead: *given* that Nietzsche was concerned with politics, *why* was politics a matter of concern for him. And I think that the answer to this question is implied by the aphorism just quoted: Nietzsche was especially interested in the sort of *spirit* or *character* that drives political action, and so the power of his writing has rested heavily on its ability to describe (and appeal to) what *motivates* politically restless, ambitious, and radical individuals in the modern world. (Thus, it is not entirely incongruous that the anarchist rabble-rouser Emma Goldman was captivated by Nietzsche, even though he himself denounced both anarchism and the rabble.)[42]

Stated differently, Nietzsche's concern is not only with *how to* engage in politics, but even more fundamentally with *why would* someone take part in politics in the first place (in other words, the core of Nietzsche's political philosophy is a political psychology).[43] When Nietzsche's concerns are understood in this way, I think it becomes clear that it would be a false dichotomy to think that we need to choose between "antipolitical" readings of Nietzsche (which emphasize the aspects of his thought that are concerned with self-creation and self-care) and "political" readings (which stress his interest in impacting the trajectory of the modern world). These facets of Nietzsche's thought need to be brought together, not opposed to one another, because his political concerns are always connected to (and *in the service of*) his interest in self-care and self-creation.

As I have already suggested, Nietzsche presents more than one model of how this might work: the Free Spirit and Zarathustra approach politics in different ways, and for different reasons. But although Nietzsche's statements are sometimes inflammatory, I believe that even his most immoderate declarations are qualified by deeply critical reflections about what any engagement with the world could accomplish. Appreciating this fact can help us come to terms with the problematic legacy of Nietzsche's thought: for if the problem we face is that Nietzsche's thought seems to be both *dangerous* and *compelling*, then we might engage with it more productively if we recognize that Nietzsche set out not only to stoke radical ambitions, but also to show the limits those ambitions must confront. In other words, Nietzsche provides an auto-critique of the same dangerous and destructive forces that he has been blamed for provoking. To take one example: that Nietzsche writes unabashedly about "the will to power" as "the fundamental fact" of all life has sometimes been taken as an incitement to brute control, domination, and self-exaltation, but close examination reveals that he is acutely aware of how deeply self-defeating the quest for control and domination can become (as we will see in part 2 of this study).[44] In making this claim, I do not mean to liberalize, democratize, or otherwise "domesticate" Nietzsche.[45] To say that Nietzsche's thought travels along a pathway that ultimately results in reflecting critically upon some of its own most radical tendencies is not to say that Nietzsche winds up as either a liberal or a democrat. But the fact that even an antiliberal and antidemocratic author such as Nietzsche engages in this sort of auto-critique ought to make his thought of interest to liberal democrats looking for forces that might counter the tides of radicalism in an era when commitment to liberal democracy appears to be increasingly precarious.

At the end of the day, however, Nietzsche helps readers to understand problems more than to solve them. That is why I have suggested that the complicated status of his legacy reflects a genuine tension in his work: a tension between (roughly speaking) detached philosophic reflection and engaged worldly activism (as will be seen in the contrast between the Free Spirit and Zarathustra). And if Nietzsche does not resolve all the tensions he identifies, his thought can still help us to better understand those tensions as woven inextricably into the fabric of human life.

THE PLAN OF THIS BOOK

Since this study outlines how to approach Nietzsche's thought, I have written it without presupposing any familiarity with Nietzsche on the part of the reader. Moreover, since I have kept in mind readers who may be new to Nietzsche, and since I am trying to show that Nietzsche can be usefully deployed as a guide to Nietzsche, I have opted to confine discussion of scholarly literature mainly to footnotes. Scholarship on Nietzsche presents both a challenge and an opportunity for any reader: on the one hand, the literature is so vast, diverse, and often so interesting and influential in its own right that one can easily become consumed by it, with one's point of focus drifting away from Nietzsche's own writings as a result; on the other hand, the literature is often an invaluable aid to making sense of the numerous puzzles in Nietzsche's writings, and thinking through the manifold possibilities they raise. I have, therefore, kept the focus on Nietzsche's own writings in the main body of the text, while using the notes to highlight some of the help I have gratefully received from the scholarly literature.

The book is divided into three parts, each of which examines two sets of writings, focusing on a single theme in each case.

In part 1, I examine Nietzsche's project in *Human, All Too Human: A Book for Free Spirits*. I look at what Nietzsche set out to accomplish with this work, how he modified the project along the way, and how he judged the work's shortcomings in retrospect. Taken together, these two chapters outline the challenges that the character of the Free Spirit was designed to meet, and the challenges for the Free Spirit that remained at the end of the *All Too Human* project (especially in the last "installment" of the work, *The Wanderer and His Shadow*). The core of the argument is this: for Nietzsche, a philosopher is one who desires—and through extended effort comes to grasp the true meaning of—independence. This requires that a would-be philosopher go through a long process of rethinking and renegotiating their relationship to broader human community. The Free Spirits acquire independence by cutting themselves off from many of the goods that are characteristic of human community, and they thereby raise the question of whether a life that was more engaged with others might not be more satisfying. This is the possibility that Nietzsche moved on to consider with the creation of his character Zarathustra, who is driven out of solitude and into an engagement with the wider world due to the force of his great *love* for it (a motivating characteristic that distinguishes Zarathustra from the Free Spirit).

In part 2, I look at the challenges addressed by the figure of Zarathustra. I consider the text of *Thus Spoke Zarathustra* in light of Nietzsche's engagement with his former mentor Richard Wagner. Nietzsche's writings on Wagner deal with many of the same problems that are taken up by Zarathustra, including the task of the creator, the longing for redemption, the response to suffering, and the feeling of love. But those writings also suggest the need for a love different from what Wagner was capable of: one that is able to love the world for what it is, rather than for what the lover would make it. The character of Zarathustra thereby aims to go beyond the Free Spirits in his capacity for love, and beyond Wagner in the nature of his love.

With the alternatives of the Free Spirit and Zarathustra established, in part 3 I am able to turn to the assessment of those alternatives provided by "Mr. Nietzsche," in his late autobiographical writings. I contend that Nietzsche finds his greatest degree of independence and self-clarity in the autobiographical writings, but that he is still able to justify the projects of the Free Spirit and Zarathustra as having made essential contributions to arriving at his own distinctive position. The tensions between the Free Spirit and Zarathustra are not perfectly resolved, but they are better understood—and, on my argument, Nietzsche's deepest and highest goal was always that of self-understanding.

Reading Nietzsche in light of his autobiographical commentaries provides evidence for a crucial point: namely, that although Nietzsche may have become famous as the boastful and belligerent advocate of "the will to power," his body of work is ultimately more self-reflective and more self-critical than the writings that have been left for us by any other philosopher.

* 1 *

Independence

CHAPTER 1

The Path to Philosophy in *On the Genealogy of Morality* and *Human, All Too Human*

On the Genealogy of Morality provides an obvious point of entry into Nietzsche's thought. The text is commonly assigned in university courses designed to introduce students to the subjects of philosophy, or political theory, or ethics. In that context, the *Genealogy* offers a number of concepts, formulas, or doctrines for the student to digest: the contrast between "master morality" and "slave morality"; the problem of "*ressentiment*"; the notion of "perspectivism"; the method of "genealogy," and so forth. All these theories can be summarized and memorized by a student, and then compared with the theories of other philosophers. At more advanced levels of scholarship, the theories can be analyzed with greater precision, refined or modified in certain respects, and applied to a variety of puzzles that occupy the scholar's interest.[1]

The *Genealogy* is, therefore, Nietzsche's most user-friendly book: it is accessible to the student, while offering grist for the scholarly mill. And Nietzsche would surely have approved of his book being put to use for diverse purposes, given that the work was conceived as part of a broader effort to make his thought more accessible to the public. It is part of a sequence of writings that he characterized as "fish-hooks" designed to draw readers to his thought, and he advertised the *Genealogy* in particular as "[a] sequel to my last book, *Beyond Good and Evil*, which it is meant to supplement and clarify."[2] The *Genealogy*'s comparatively straightforward, easily digestible appearance is no accident, but it is also, in its way, as partial and misleading as the bait offered on a hook proves to be to a fish. For the *Genealogy* does something more than present the reader with Nietzsche's thoughts on morality (for example, the contrast between "master morality" and "slave morality"); it also provokes the reader to reflect on the conditions that produced those thoughts, and which play an important role in shaping all philosophic reflection. This self-reflexive aspect of the *Genealogy* will be my focus in what follows.

On the reading that I propose, the *Genealogy* presents what has been aptly characterized as an "autobiography of philosophy":[3] it commences with a preface stressing personal, seemingly idiosyncratic details about the process through which Nietzsche came to write the book, and uses those details to point toward generalizable features of the activity of philosophy as such. It thereby exemplifies a movement from the "particular" to the "universal," only the universal features of philosophy that Nietzsche stresses here are not those to be found in the book's famous theories, but in *the process that produced them*. It is this "theory" of philosophy—a theory of how philosophy attempts, and often fails, to ground itself—whose importance is impressed on the reader by the preface to the work. And the preface also shows the reader how to interpret the *Genealogy* (along with the rest of Nietzsche's oeuvre) within the context of that problem—the point here being not that the inquiry into morality is *replaced* by autobiography, but that the autobiographical turn, the turn to self-knowledge, is necessary to complete any inquiry into morality.

Nietzsche's preface to the *Genealogy* is, then, something much more significant than simply an introduction to the three essays that make up the main part of the text. The preface also clarifies how Nietzsche understood the development of his thought over the course of his career, and it ties that development to a series of broader (*universal*) claims about the nature of (and the obstacles to) philosophic inquiry. For all these reasons, the preface to the *Genealogy* serves as an introduction to the whole of Nietzsche's thought.

THE *GENEALOGY*'S BEGINNING: THE PROBLEM OF SELF-KNOWLEDGE

Nietzsche broaches the problem of the ability of philosophy to adequately ground itself (to show that it is not an arbitrary or perverse activity) with the very first words of the *Genealogy*: "We are unknown to ourselves, we knowers." The last words of section 1 of the preface reiterate the point: "with respect to ourselves we are not 'knowers.'" The category of "we knowers" is a broad one, but surely includes potential philosophers.[4] Indeed, these remarks echo and extend a theme that is emphasized in *Beyond Good and Evil* (especially in its preface and its first chapter, "On the Prejudices of the Philosophers"): namely, that the quest for knowledge (and a life dedicated to it) will appear discreditable if it is not accompanied by self-knowledge. Thus, at the outset of both the *Genealogy of Morality* and *Beyond Good and Evil*, the reader is presented with the possibility that philosophy is basically pretentious: a sophisticated gloss distracting from the philosopher's fundamental state of self-confusion.[5]

But at the conclusion of section 1 of the preface of the *Genealogy*, Nietzsche indicates that he holds a key to this problem: "We remain strange to ourselves out of necessity, we do not understand ourselves, we must mistake ourselves, for us the maxim reads for all eternity, 'everyone is furthest from himself'—with respect to ourselves we are not 'knowers.'" This stress on "necessity"—on the fact that "we" (that is, all would-be knowers) *must*, now and forever, begin by failing to know what is closest to us, namely, ourselves—suggests that there is a structure or logic inherent to the lack of self-knowledge that can be observed in so many would-be knowers. In that case, a would-be knower's self-misunderstanding might not reflect the futility and vanity of the quest for knowledge, but could, instead, represent a stage within that quest, which Nietzsche will help the reader to comprehend, and thereby to move beyond.

The phrasing of the first sentence of the preface supports that thought: "We are unknown to ourselves, we knowers, we ourselves to ourselves: and with good ground [or "good reason," *guten Grund*]." By proclaiming that would-be knowers lack self-knowledge, but adding that this is a matter of "necessity," of "eternity," of mistakes that we "must" make, and for which there exists "good ground" or "good reason," Nietzsche entices the reader with the prospect of learning what those grounds are—the *reasons* why would-be knowers *necessarily* fail to know themselves.

In this way, the opening of the *Genealogy* directs the reader to consider what the permanent, unavoidable, natural obstacles to philosophy are, particularly with regard to the challenge of acquiring self-knowledge.

THE *GENEALOGY*'S SECOND BEGINNING: THE PROBLEM OF MORALITY

Having opened his preface to the *Genealogy* with a strong statement on the problem of self-knowledge, Nietzsche abruptly, and without any explanation, shifts course in section 2 of the preface, which begins this way:

> My thoughts on the *origins* of our moral prejudices—for that is what this polemic is about—found their first, economical, and preliminary expression in the collection of aphorisms that bears the title *Human, All Too Human: A Book for Free Spirits*.

The remainder of the preface elaborates on this remark, explaining how Nietzsche's thoughts on morality were developed in the earlier tome.[6]

Nietzsche's "genealogy of the *Genealogy*"[7] runs through many details: he dates the composition of the *Genealogy*'s predecessor (*Human All Too Human*) to "the winter of 1876–7" (that is, ten years before the present volume, as Nietzsche makes plain for the reader by dating the end of the preface "July, 1887"); he lists a series of passages from that earlier text for the reader to compare with the present volume; he notes that the earlier text was developed in response to a book by his friend Paul Rée (which he notes had been published in 1877); he gives a brief account of his first essay on morality written "as a thirteen-year-old boy"; and he stresses a major turning point of his adult years, when he "confronted" his "great teacher" Schopenhauer with regard to the morality of compassion. With each anecdote Nietzsche adds a few self-critical remarks about these earlier stages in the development of his thought.

At first glance, then, the opening section of the preface could easily seem to be disconnected from everything that follows, with section 2 serving as a proper introduction, outlining the question of morality as the subject of the text without any further reference to the problem of self-knowledge.[8] But section 2 of the preface implicitly bears on the problem of self-knowledge, because it maps out the path of Nietzsche's own evolving self-awareness—pinpointing names, dates, texts, and epiphanies that stand out as landmarks along that path. Nietzsche thereby leaves one to wonder if the problem of why "we *must* mistake ourselves" and the question of "the *origins* of our moral prejudices" are somehow meant to be connected. Although Nietzsche will not explicitly connect the problems of self-knowledge and moral knowledge, I believe that a nexus between them lies at the heart of the preface.[9] Let us see how that works.

THE GENEALOGY OF THE *GENEALOGY*: ITS ORIGINS IN *HUMAN, ALL TOO HUMAN*

Although the preface to the *Genealogy* does not explicitly connect the problem of self-knowledge to the problem of moral knowledge, Nietzsche does embed within the preface clues about the nature of the connection.

I have already quoted the first of those clues: namely, Nietzsche's statement that with the *Genealogy* he is returning to thoughts that were initially expressed a decade prior, in *Human, All Too Human*. But in the context Nietzsche makes clear that this is not only a return, but also a reconsideration: first, by characterizing his earlier effort as "preliminary," and then by adding the "hope" that his thoughts will have improved in the meantime ("let us hope that the long period in between has done them good, that they have become more mature, brighter, stronger, more perfect!"). Next he indicates that his thoughts on morality *have* improved, and in a specific respect.

Regarding the evolution of his thoughts on morality between *Human, All Too Human* and the *Genealogy*, Nietzsche has this to say: "in the meantime" (that is, in the decade between the two publications) he has acquired a "cheerful confidence" that his thoughts "came about not singly, not arbitrarily, not sporadically, but rather from the beginning arose from a common root, out of a *basic will* of knowledge from deep within, speaking ever more precisely, demanding something ever more precise." Nietzsche's language here is revealing. He does not say that the basic content of his thoughts on morality has changed (he possesses the same "data," so to speak). Rather, he suggests that he has come to understand the ground of those thoughts more clearly—their *necessary*, and necessarily *interconnected*, nature (how "from the beginning" they arose "not singly, not arbitrarily," but "from a common root"). And it was this feature of his thought that at first was not so clear to him. In this way, Nietzsche indicates that his initial investigation of morality was lacking in some measure of self-knowledge.[10]

Section 3 of the preface drives home the point that Nietzsche's thought has evolved in crucial ways. Here Nietzsche states what "I almost have the right to call my *a priori*": namely, a characteristic skepticism directed at morality, and which inspired his first philosophic exercise, an essay about the origin of good and evil written as a young boy. But he stresses that his youthful essay made a basic mistake: it "sought the origin of evil *behind* the world." Nietzsche says that he now knows better. But when did he learn better, exactly? The argument of the *Genealogy* as a whole will suggest that the answer is much later than one might think: it was not until after *Human, All Too Human* that his thought fully matured in this respect. In other words, it took him until well into his adult career to fully understand the desires that could lead one to look beyond the world (since Free Spirits will turn out to be subject to a kind of crypto-otherworldly asceticism born of a lack of self-knowledge).

Nietzsche extends his self-criticism in section 4 of the preface, where he observes that his early efforts at treating morality in *Human, All Too Human* (efforts that he here describes as "clumsy") were accompanied by "backsliding and wavering"—a characterization that contrasts with the "ever more precise" standard that he says (in section 2) he has arrived at more recently.

To tie all these points together: Nietzsche's thoughts on morality have gone from "backsliding and wavering" (around the period of *Human, All Too*

Human) to "ever more precision" (culminating in the *Genealogy*), and that precision has involved discovering their "common root" (their grounds, their necessity, their interrelationship), and thereby enhancing his self-knowledge.

That said, in section 4 of the preface Nietzsche makes his self-criticism in a manner simultaneously emphatic and elliptical: after declaring his efforts in *Human, All Too Human* to have been "clumsy" and full of "backsliding and wavering," rather than elaborate the point any further, he suddenly presents a series of references to the earlier writing, which the reader is invited to compare with the present treatise.

The sequence of references that Nietzsche presents runs as follows: *HH* 45, 136, 96, 99; *AOM* 89; *HH* 92; *WS* 26; *D* 112; *WS* 22, 33 (as Nietzsche lists these references, he adds brief statements on the subject of the various passages). A reader who looks up the references in the order that they are listed will be conveniently equipped by Nietzsche with a rough but serviceable summary of Nietzsche's approach to morality in *Human, All Too Human* (a lengthy work that could not easily be skimmed otherwise). And, consequently, the reader will also have a reference point for comparing that work with the *Genealogy*. In what follows, I propose to walk through Nietzsche's series of references to *Human, All Too Human*, in order to gauge which aspects of the earlier work Nietzsche is highlighting here. We will then be in a position to recognize how the argument of that work is corrected by the *Genealogy*—and also why Nietzsche came to see his earlier misunderstanding (that is, his earlier lack of self-knowledge) as unavoidable, and also as archetypal.[11]

THE PURSUIT OF THE GOOD: PHILOSOPHY AND COMMUNITY IN *HUMAN, ALL TOO HUMAN*

Nietzsche does not explain the order in which his references to *Human, All Too Human* are listed. But that order is certainly not accidental.[12] By inviting the reader to consider his earlier remarks in this order, he helps to make certain themes more visible, and makes plainer how those themes are connected. The list of references even tells a story and implies an argument. In order to follow that story, we need to work through the references that Nietzsche lists, one by one.

First, a note about my procedure in what follows: in the main text I will focus exclusively on walking through the sequence of passages that Nietzsche lists. In notes to the text, I will mention related passages that Nietzsche does not list, but which confirm or clarify arguments suggested by the passages he does reference (and which, I think, can thereby help to demonstrate that

Nietzsche's list of references does, in fact, highlight central features of his thought and consequently warrants close attention).

The first six references to *Human, All Too Human* outline three interrelated stages in the establishment of morality as we now know it. These stages are related because at each point morality is defined by community: morality is part of what binds and preserves "a *community*, a people" (*HH* 96).[13] But each stage must be carefully understood, because each carries within it (to ever greater degrees) forces that have the effect of obscuring morality's essentially communal character.

Nietzsche's list of references begins with a passage explaining that the first stage of morality is "requital": "he who has the power to requite, good with good, evil with evil, and also actually practices requital—is, that is to say, grateful and revengeful—is called good" (*HH* 45). As this suggests, morality is an extension of self-interest: someone who cannot serve my good cannot be within my circle of moral concern. This stress on self-interest does not preclude the establishment of community, however—just the opposite. As Nietzsche points out at the end of this discussion, among individuals who are unable to requite one another, "a community can hardly arise, at best the most rudimentary form of community." Sophisticated forms of community (such as our own) only develop where individuals can rely on one another to reciprocate. At first, then, a "moral" being need be no more than this: one who can be "entwined" (*verflochten*) with others through the capacity for requital. To this extent, we might say that community creates morality, rather than vice versa (in other words, our nature as needy beings leads us into communities that use morality as a binding force, rather than independent, preexisting moral principles drawing us into communal relationships).[14] But, crucially, both community and morality share a natural root in the good they serve: namely, the fulfillment of the individual's needs or desires. Requital establishes this link: it ties the individual's good to the community, and thereby to morality.

This establishes an essential premise for Nietzsche's view of morality: it is rooted, along with all other human phenomena, in human beings' orientation toward their own good. But how people pursue their good will vary dramatically (depending on their particular capacities, or the extent of their knowledge).[15] Community is one form that pursuit can take, and morality is what holds together that particular form of pursuit of the good.[16]

However, if community needs support in the form of morality, morality itself is in some need of support. For, as Nietzsche indicates, tensions within the dominant morality (in this case, the morality of requital) can be papered over by appealing to supernatural forces, such as religious beliefs: "If one of the good should do something unworthy of the good, one looks for excuses; one ascribed the guilt to a god, for example" (*HH* 45). If, as this suggests, religious beliefs support morality, which in turn supports community, then we can understand why Nietzsche stresses, in the next passage that he cites, that the few "individual thinkers" who have dared to question morality have also found themselves questioning religion (*HH* 136). This reference drives home that, in Nietzsche's scheme, "morality," "religion," and "community" cluster in one camp, while the "individual" stands apart from and opposed to them.

Later, Nietzsche will address more systematically how skeptically minded individuals can set themselves off from their communities through a critique of morality. First, however, he provides a fuller account of morality, and the challenge that it presents.

Nietzsche's discussion of the first stage of morality (the morality of requital) introduces the notion of morality as essentially an instrument of community. But this becomes true in a new and more complex way as morality evolves. For it is not simply one "who has the power to requite" who counts as a member of the community, and therefore as moral; it is one who "also actually practices requital" (*HH* 45). The need for this qualification is obvious: if I join a community of those who *can* do what I recognize as good, then I must have confidence that they *will* do so (and others must have the same confidence in me). A mechanism is required for establishing such confidence. That mechanism is "custom" (*Sitte*; *HH* 96). By acting in accordance with custom, the individual shows himself to be a reliable member of the community. Morality thereby comes to be reflected in something besides requital: it is reflected in obedience, that is, in unthinking acceptance of the customs of the community (*HH* 96).[17]

Although this "morality of custom" (*Sittlichkeit der Sitte*) appears alien and off-putting to modern sensibilities (due to the apparently arbitrary and often brutal forms it often assumes), Nietzsche sees it as the form of morality that has characterized by far the longest period of human history (extending over many millennia), gradually molding an ever broader swath of humanity into beings capable of acting as ever more effective and sophisticated members of their communities.[18]

In his discussion of this second stage of morality, the morality of custom, Nietzsche is explicit about the role that religion plays in buttressing the morality that binds together community: "Every tradition now continually grows more venerable the farther away its origin lies and the more this origin is forgotten; the respect paid to it increases from generation to generation, the tradition at last becomes holy and evokes awe and reverence" (*HH* 96).

Because custom has played such a large role in cultivating humanity, it dramatically changes how morality is maintained and how it is experienced. Custom makes it possible to uphold morality without brute force or direct compulsion. Custom thereby sets in motion a process through which morality becomes more and more "internalized," or self-motivated, becoming "voluntary obedience, finally almost instinct; then, like all that has for a long time been habitual and natural, it is associated with pleasure—and is now called *virtue*" (*HH* 99).[19]

With custom, then, the link between the good and one's place in the community becomes somewhat occluded, because outward actions are no longer based on simply requiting "good with good, evil with evil," but instead depend on obedience to traditions that one has not established oneself, adherence to which demonstrate one's reliability. As the good becomes internalized in this manner, and as one even begins to take pleasure in the more "civilized" iterations of custom, one becomes more and more thoroughly oriented toward the community, and less and less aware of the demarcation between its interests and one's own.

As this all suggests, the truly fundamental principle of custom is that "the community is worth more than the individual" (*AOM* 89). But although no one would *deliberately* choose that principle for *themselves*, being raised by custom can lead one to *believe* that one is worth less than the community, and then to act as if its fundamental principle were in fact true: "through his morality the individual *outvotes* [*majorisirt*] himself" (*AOM* 89).[20] Morality then begins to take on an "altruistic" cast, but only due to the crucial feature of "forgetting," that is, forgetting the true roots of our morality (*HH* 92).[21] Nietzsche indicates in this context that such "forgetting" involves especially identifying the source of morality in divinity, rather than in the individual's precommunal, premoral good: "How little moral would the world appear without forgetfulness! A poet could say that God has placed forgetfulness as a doorkeeper on the threshold of the temple of human dignity" (*HH* 92).

In this way, Nietzsche's discussion of the history of morality consistently refers the reader to the same major phenomenon: community requires the support of morality, which in turn requires the support of religion. And at the root of these developments in the history of morality lies confusion over the extent to which the good of the community truly serves the good of the individual.

The history of morality that is outlined through this first series of references might intrigue the reader, and it might even seem plausible in parts, but it is not an empirical account, and so a reader might well find Nietzsche's suggestions too speculative to accept. However, in the series of references that follows, Nietzsche shows the reader how they might test the claims that he has just advanced.

In these last five references Nietzsche discusses politics. He focuses on phenomena that are often thought of as giving politics its distinctively moral character: justice, law, rights, duty. These qualities give us our sense that politics is the focus of human beings' concern with the common good, and is an ennobling expression of our highest moral aspirations. But Nietzsche suggests that it is precisely in these political phenomena that we can discern the hidden dimensions of morality that he has outlined, for they all have a self-serving, not an altruistic or self-sacrificial, character.

Thus, Nietzsche maintains that justice and law do not represent intrinsic, absolute moral standards; they are instrumental and therefore changeable (*HH* 92; *WS* 26). We can see this reflected in the way that our notions of rights and duties fluctuate, because these reflect assessments of relative power standing, rather than categorical moral imperatives (*D* 112; *WS* 22). As this suggests, an important clue concerning the realities of the moral universe is embedded in the way that we *talk* about politics. Nietzsche makes this point more explicit in a discussion of punishment, where he suggests that our ordinary language is studded with tensions and contradictions that we do not normally face up to: thus, we use a single term (Nietzsche uses "revenge" as an example) to refer to a range of very different motives, ranging from those that articulate a simple desire for self-preservation, to those that express a more extended, and moralistic, view of the matter (*WS* 33). Seeing the world clearly therefore requires seeing the way in which language is used to make the world appear more "moral" than it really is.[22]

At this point it may be helpful to summarize the preceding discussion. Through his references to *Human, All Too Human* Nietzsche shows the reader that his major insights in that work included the following:

- First, the good of the individual is what underlies and drives all human activity (although a process of historical conditioning has led it to do so at ever more subconscious levels).
- Second, morality is the essential yoke and instrument of one particular vehicle for the pursuit of the good: namely, society, or human community more generally.
- Third, and as a consequence of the first two points, morality can be evaluated according to the extent to which it does, in fact, serve the good of the

individual. Our good is the standard from which we can, in principle, judge (and accept or reject) any given morality.

- Fourth, and finally, in order to assess whether (or the extent to which) morality serves our good, we must determine whether (or the extent to which) we are genuinely communal beings. This means, in particular, examining whether the moral objects at the center of politics (justice, law, rights, duties) reflect genuine "altruism" and self-sacrifice.

These four points imply one further consequence: namely, that with his exposé of the hidden truth about morality, justice, and the like, Nietzsche is encouraging the reader to set out to debunk these phenomena. At the least, we can safely say that *Human, All Too Human* was written for readers who are *inclined* to do just that. But did the work *succeed* in showing them how to accomplish that objective? Or do the criticisms of the work included in the preface to the *Genealogy* suggest that *Human, All Too Human* came up short in just this respect?

SCIENCE VERSUS RELIGION: THE ARGUMENT OVER ASCETIC MORALITY

The two questions posed at the end of the preceding section raise concerns that Nietzsche himself points toward, through one of the references that he lists in section 4 of the preface to the *Genealogy*. The reference in question is the one that seems to be almost out of place on his list: aphorism 136 of *Human, All Too Human*. This aphorism discusses a particular kind of morality: the morality "[o]f Christian asceticism and holiness." And it outlines (roughly speaking) the difficulty that "science" has encountered in attempting to explain "religion." For ascetic morality, Nietzsche writes in this aphorism, has generally *not* been explained, to "the great satisfaction" of those who hold that

> [t]he unexplained should be thoroughly inexplicable, the inexplicable thoroughly unnatural, supernatural, miraculous—so goes the demand in the soul of all religious people and metaphysicians (and artists, too, should they be thinkers as well).

Against this outlook Nietzsche posits the view of the "scientific person": those "individual thinkers" who have experienced, as "a powerful drive of *nature*," an irresistible temptation to explain the morality of asceticism and holiness (that is, to explain them as natural, all too human phenomena, and thereby to discredit their claim to be products of the supernatural, miraculous, or divine). But Nietzsche concludes the aphorism by remarking that science has failed to offer such an explanation (despite its success in explaining many other phenomena), and that an adequate critique of ascetic morality therefore requires a more adequate understanding of human psychology.

Among the references to *Human, All Too Human* that are listed in the preface to the *Genealogy*, the reference to aphorism 136 stands apart. All of the other references point the reader to passages that outline Nietzsche's approach to exposing and explaining the roots of morality in the earlier work. But aphorism 136 is the one instance where Nietzsche directs the reader to a passage that stresses that a particular form of morality has *not* yet been adequately explained (despite the best efforts of the scientifically inclined). Evidently, then, Nietzsche wants the reader of the *Genealogy* to keep in mind, from the outset of the work, the difficulty that science has encountered when attempting to explain ascetic morality (a theme that will return in the work's third essay).

To be sure, in aphorism 136 Nietzsche clearly places himself on the side of "science" (that is, of those who demand an explanation, because they hold that the world is a natural phenomenon, and therefore must be explicable in principle), rather than of "religion" (that is, of those who denounce even the attempt to offer an explanation, because they hold that the world is a supernatural phenomenon, and therefore can only be properly understood as essentially mysterious). And, to that end, if one reads beyond aphorism 136, one will find six aphorisms that attempt to explain more adequately the ascetic morality that science has been unable to explain to date. But those passages are not cited anywhere in the *Genealogy*. In fact, the *only* aphorism from the entire chapter on religion in *Human, All Too Human* that is cited *anywhere* in the *Genealogy* is aphorism 136—that is to say, the *one* aphorism in which Nietzsche highlights the failure of "science" to explain "religion." By contrast, the *Genealogy* will later cite, very prominently and at length, an aphorism from *The Joyful Wissenschaft*, titled "How We, Too, Are Still Pious," which argues that modern science has a crypto-religious character.[23]

In view of these observations, a provisional contrast can be made: whereas *Human, All Too Human* suggested that "science" had not yet succeeded in explaining "religion," the *Genealogy* pushes the criticism of science even further by suggesting that modern science actually contains essential features of religion.

In order to get a fuller picture of this contrast, and to understand its connection to the problem of ascetic morality, we can start by looking at the aphorism on "How We, Too, Are Still Pious." This aphorism appears in book 5 of *The Joyful Wissenschaft*. The work was originally published with four books in 1882, but in 1886 Nietzsche reissued it with a fifth book, written only a few months before the *Genealogy*. In the first aphorism of book 5 Nietzsche describes the "gratitude, amazement, foreboding, [and] expectation" that "we philosophers and 'free spirits'" have lately experienced in response to the news that "the old god is dead." Yet in the very next aphorism, "How We, Too, Are Still Pious," Nietzsche explains how the old god's fire continues to burn even for "we knowers of today, we godless anti-metaphysicians." Nietzsche's argument here turns on the claim that modern science rests on a "faith" of its own—a faith in truth as something absolutely and always good, and which therefore cannot consider that, as Nietzsche here puts it, "the great sweep of life has, in fact, always shown itself to be on the side of the most unscrupulous *polytropi*" (a reference to Homer's Odysseus, who thrived through his capacity for deceit, rather than his commitment to truth).[24] Nietzsche's remarks here are not inspired by his own indifference toward truth. Rather, they are meant to indict a certain reflexive posture toward truth characteristic of modern science—a posture that assumes, and overestimates, the compatibility of truth with the demands and desires of human life, rather than recognizing a tension between them.[25] Thus, as Nietzsche says, "faith in science presupposes" an ideal of "the truthful man" (as opposed to, say, a polytropic Odysseus), and so it must deny "*our* world," and instead "*affirms another world* than that of life, nature, and history."[26] This form of faith makes modern science crypto-religious—and also, as we can now see, makes it attached to a kind of ascetic morality, because it turns away from the world as it is, and affirms an ideal that could only exist apart from that world.

This last point is stressed and elaborated when Nietzsche quotes from the aphorism toward the end of the third essay of the *Genealogy* (titled "What Do Ascetic Ideals Mean?"). In section 23 of that essay, Nietzsche pauses in the midst of a polemic against ascetic ideals to observe that although he has been *told* that they have been battled and mastered today—especially by modern science (which is said to have "gotten along well enough so far without God, Beyond, and the virtues that negate")—he cannot agree with that claim. He cannot agree, in the first place, because most of science is lacking any powerful ideal.[27] But his greater concern is with "rare, noble, and select" cases in the realm of modern science where a strong passion, and a powerful ideal, is, in fact, at work. He turns to these cases in section 24, where he labels them "the last idealists among philosophers and scholars"—and, shortly after, adds to that, "free, very free spirits." These devotees of modern science, Nietzsche suggests, are so far from being opponents of the ascetic ideal that they are better understood as unwitting artifacts of it, because of their unexamined faith in truth. By way of explanation, he quotes from the aphorism "How We, Too, Are Still Pious." He concludes by advising readers who require further elaboration to consult, not only the full text of that aphorism, but also (and, he says, "even better") the entirety of book 5 of *The Joyful Wissenschaft*, and the preface to *Daybreak*.

Paul Franco, in a helpful discussion of these two passages (*GS* 344 and *GM* III.24), notes that Nietzsche makes a "somewhat confusing" use of the first person in each instance. This leads Franco to ask: "Does [Nietzsche] include himself among those who are still pious and who take their inspiration from the moral and metaphysical faith upon which science ultimately rests? . . . Another way of putting the question is whether Nietzsche sees the free spirit as ultimately bound by the ascetic ideal of science."[28] Franco's question cuts at the core of the problem raised by these passages, and it is a question that has to be considered by anyone trying to understand the relationship between *Human, All Too Human* and the *Genealogy*. Franco addresses this issue by pointing out that in several texts Nietzsche indicates that there are multiple stages to free spirithood (moving from more to less ascetic), but here I want to take a somewhat different tack, and address the question of the potential self-criticism at issue in these passages by tying them back to the *Genealogy*'s autobiographical framing.

The importance of Nietzsche's autobiography to the issue at hand is evident in the first place from the extent to which he makes the argument in *Genealogy* III.24 rely on references to other texts that he composed at the same time, but which were written for the purpose of being appended to works from earlier in his career (the preface to *Daybreak* and book 5 of *The Joyful Wissenschaft*). In the case of the preface to *Daybreak*, that took the form of a directly autobiographical statement and critical self-commentary. Book 5 of *The Joyful Wissenschaft* is not a self-commentary in a direct sense, but (as my brief remarks on it above suggested) it has implications for understanding Nietzsche's development insofar as it is a commentary on the status of the Free Spirit. So by referring the reader to these two writings so emphatically in *Genealogy* III.24, Nietzsche suggests that the argument of that passage needs to be understood within the context of the broader project of self-reflection and self-criticism that he undertook in 1886. Moreover, we have already seen that in the preface to the *Genealogy* Nietzsche stresses to the reader that the work reflects an evolution of his thought from the period of *Human, All Too Human*, when he had first adopted the outlook of a Free Spirit (and recall that when Nietzsche gives the title of the work in section 2 of the preface, he also gives its subtitle, "A Book for Free Spirits"). In all these ways, Nietzsche invites the reader to consider whether the criticism of the Free Spirits expressed in *Genealogy* III.24 ultimately ought to be taken as a *self*-criticism on his part.

The preface to the *Genealogy* provides a crucial clue about what the character of Nietzsche's self-criticism here would be. For the preface opened by stressing that would-be knowers *always* begin by misunderstanding themselves—and that this is something they *must* do, of *necessity*, now and for *eternity*. So if that point is kept in mind, then when one comes to the criticism of the Free Spirits in *Genealogy* III.24 (where their scientific outlook is said to have more in common with religion, and especially with the ascetic ideal, than they realize), one will be able to ask whether the criticism amounts, not to an outright dismissal of the Free Spirits, so much as the recognition of a necessary stage in their thought. (Notwithstanding Nietzsche's polemic against the Free Spirits in section 24, he is at the same time including them among the "rare, noble, select" cases mentioned toward the end of section 23). Let us, therefore, look at what the *Genealogy* suggests about the source of the necessity that compels Free Spirits to misunderstand themselves (especially with regard to their degree of independence from ascetic morality).

THE PURSUIT OF THE GOOD: PHILOSOPHY AND COMMUNITY IN THE *GENEALOGY*

The third essay of the *Genealogy* discusses the challenge that ascetic morality poses to philosophy. In the early sections of this essay, Nietzsche explains how ascetic ideals attract thoughtful artists (Wagner), metaphysicians (Schopenhauer), and priests. And in section 7 of the essay, he gives a lengthy explanation of why the ascetic ideal is particularly, and pervasively, appealing to the whole class of *philosophers*:

> It is indisputable that for as long as there have been philosophers on earth and wherever there have been philosophers (from India to England, to take polar opposites in talent for philosophy) there has existed a characteristic philosophers' irritability and rancor against sensuality.

Moreover,

> There has likewise existed a characteristic philosophers' prepossession and cordiality regarding the whole ascetic ideal; one ought not to entertain

> any illusions about this or against this. Both belong, as noted, to the type; if both are absent in a philosopher then he is always—of this one may be certain—only a "so-called" philosopher.

With this statement Nietzsche makes the striking claim that sympathy for the ascetic ideal is practically a *prerequisite* for philosophy. Despite all his polemics against ascetic ideals, Nietzsche will never retract this claim. The *Genealogy* cannot be understood without grasping how these two aspects of Nietzsche's position fit together.

An explanation begins to appear toward the end of section 7 of the essay. Here Nietzsche states plainly that the ascetic ideal attracts philosophers because it appears to be a means toward their most desired end: *independence.*[29] And in sections 9 and 10, he lays out what philosophy had to become *independent of*, including morality, custom, and community. As the presumed (and real) opponent of these universal features of human life, philosophers had to justify themselves—and not only to their communities, but also and above all to themselves, their consciences having been weighed down so heavily by the evaluations of the broader collectives in which they found themselves. And so (as Nietzsche writes in section 10 of the essay), "the philosophical spirit always had to slip into the disguise and chrysalis of the *previously established* types of contemplative human beings." The ascetic ideal served that purpose.

On Nietzsche's account, then, the ascetic ideal appeals to philosophers on two distinct grounds: first, as a *mask* for their true inclinations; second, as a *justification* of their activity to their own consciences. Nietzsche would not object to the first use of the ascetic ideal taken on its own; but the second presents a problem, because with it philosophers begin to moralize, and thus misunderstand, their own activity. And this means, in part, that philosophers come to *overestimate their independence*, because they come to believe, like the religious ascetic, that they can free themselves from self-interest.

This last point initially appears in section 6 of the essay, where Nietzsche refers to Schopenhauer's preference for Kant's definition of beauty as "pleasure *without interest*" (which he contrasts unfavorably with Stendhal's definition of beauty as "the promise of happiness"). What precisely this "without interest" entails will vary from one individual case to the next, but Nietzsche contends that in Schopenhauer's case it was specifically part of an attempt to "counteract *sexual* 'interestedness.'"[30] On the basis of this claim, Nietzsche is able to generalize that the desire to escape interest is part of a broader desire to escape from the experience of worldly human existence as being a form of torture. Thus, Nietzsche concludes section 6 by restating his question "what does it mean if a philosopher pays homage to ascetic ideals?" and answers that "here at least we get a first hint: he wants to *escape from torture*!" In other words, the ascetic ideal tempts philosophers with the promise of "independence" not only in the narrow sense of independence from others, but also in the sense of independence from those aspects of oneself that are tied to a life experienced as unpleasant, as torture.[31]

This failure to affirm life as it truly is connects the asceticism of philosophers from earlier ages to the asceticism of the modern Free Spirits. We have already seen Nietzsche's explanation of what the asceticism of the Free Spirits involves. The remaining puzzle is why the modern adherents of ascetic ideals fail to recognize themselves as such. The answer, I believe, is consistent with Nietzsche's explanation of why philosophers have *historically* been attracted to ascetic ideals—but includes a unique variation on that theme, one suggested by the self-account that Nietzsche provides in the preface to the work.

Let me sketch what is at issue in this way: as we have seen, in the preface to the *Genealogy* Nietzsche presents the reader a series of references to *Human, All Too Human*, showing how in that work he was concerned with exposing morality as a communal phenomenon, and drawing attention to the individual good as a standard for evaluating and debunking morality. That project is entirely consistent with the goal that, in the *Genealogy*'s third essay, Nietzsche stresses is pursued by the whole class of philosophers: achieving *independence*. But we also saw that providing an adequate explanation of *ascetic* morality was a major stumbling block for the project of *Human, All Too Human*. And the explanation for that difficulty may be that in *Human, All Too Human* Nietzsche did not acknowledge, because he did not fully recognize, what he stresses in the *Genealogy*: namely, the extent to which the ascetic ideal naturally serves the interests of philosophy. It naturally serves those interests precisely because philosophers are *not* entirely independent of community (and certainly not so at first), and therefore have required the ascetic ideal as a means for engineering a greater degree of independence for themselves. Today's Free Spirits, therefore, come to overestimate their independence, as did the philosophers of old, but in a unique way: not by deliberately becoming advocates of ascetic ideals (like the philosophers of old), but by failing to recognize their own need for those ideals, and the extent to which those (false) ideals have served the interests of philosophy (which has seen itself, then and now, as dedicated entirely to truth). An adequate understanding of ascetic ideals would therefore require Free Spirits to appreciate the aspects of their nature and the conditions of human life that have made the ascetic ideal so valuable to philosophy. And that would, in turn, require an exercise in self-knowledge that philosophers will at first resist, because it would require acknowledging the full extent of their own dependence. Because Nietzsche (like all philosophers) acquired that self-knowledge only *after* setting out on the path to independence in *Human, All Too Human*, it was only by the time of the *Genealogy* that he was able to recognize what genuine independence must consist of.

CONCLUDING REMARKS

Let me now offer an overview of what has been said so far. To begin with, I noted that the *Genealogy* illuminates philosophy's attempt to ground its own activity. The preface suggests that a central problem for any such attempt is that would-be knowers necessarily begin by failing to adequately know themselves; and it also suggests that if we want to know ourselves better, we will have to look above all at our moral prejudices. Nietzsche then offers the reader a short tour of his own earlier attempts to do exactly that, by showing how, in *Human, All Too Human*, he had diagnosed morality as essentially an aspect and an instrument of community, and discovered the individual good as that which stands apart from community, and thus can be used to critically evaluate morality. But he also suggests that his early efforts came up short in a specific respect—namely, fully comprehending and explaining the phenomena of ascetic morality—and the *Genealogy* suggests the reason why: because Nietzsche, like any other philosopher, at first overestimated his own independence, and, as a consequence, he did not fully comprehend and master ascetic morality's continuing hold on himself.

I take this last thought to be at issue when Nietzsche suggests, in the preface to the *Genealogy*, that his thoughts on morality have acquired "ever more precision" in that text, in contrast to the period of "backsliding and wavering" characteristic of *Human, All Too Human*. The latter work was accompanied by "backsliding and wavering" because in that work Nietzsche was determined to separate himself from community and morality without immediately understanding all that would be involved in doing so. The *Genealogy* is characterized by "ever more precision" because Nietzsche has in the meantime come to appreciate the necessary tensions involved in attempting to set oneself off from community, and although he has recognized that any attempt to do so can only be temporary or imperfect, he has also found a way to revel in that productive tension, and thus affirm life as it truly is.[32]

But with this last statement I am getting ahead of myself, because what I have said up until this point does not sufficiently demonstrate that in *Human,*

All Too Human Nietzsche was determined to separate himself from morality without immediately understanding all that would be involved in doing so. To demonstrate the point, we will need to look more carefully at *Human, All Too Human*, and map out the path to independence that Nietzsche traveled with this work. For the work ultimately came to consist of three separate installments, and Nietzsche refined the Free Spirit ideal, and made it more demanding, as he worked through them—above all in the final installment, *The Wanderer and His Shadow*.

Before proceeding, however, let me suggest a provisional conclusion, based on what we have seen so far: in the *Genealogy* Nietzsche is inviting us reread his oeuvre in a specific light. He wants us to see how his own career illustrates a perennial problem, a problem to be faced by anyone traveling along the path to philosophy: namely, that the natural desire for independence leads one to underestimate the extent to which one is still naturally tied to one's community. To put this point a bit more broadly: human beings are constructed so as to be confused about their constitution. They differ not in the fact of being confused, but in the manner of their confusion: most people are inclined to overestimate the degree to which their interests are genuinely covalent with the interests of their communities; the class of people from which philosophers emerge overestimate the degree to which they are genuinely independent of their communities.

As this suggests, Nietzsche sees human nature as naturally divided, torn between individual and community, and although Nietzsche focuses on the implications of "natural dividedness" for would-be philosophers, that division is actually something that philosophers share with other human beings. To that extent, Nietzsche's focus on the case of the philosopher is meant to provide a window onto our common humanity, rather than an escape from it.

This conclusion can be confirmed and elaborated by turning to the one work in which Nietzsche focuses his attention most directly on the fate that philosophers share with other human beings: *The Wanderer and His Shadow*.

CHAPTER TWO

The Program of Self-Discipline in *The Wanderer and His Shadow*

When Nietzsche suggests that *On the Genealogy of Morality* represents the culmination of a train of thought that began with *Human, All Too Human*, he points to a central fact about his development: namely, that the latter work marked a dramatic change of course in his career. It was, in effect, a new beginning. Nietzsche's first two books—*The Birth of Tragedy* and the *Untimely Meditations*—were the product of a period when he was dominated by the influence of the philosopher Arthur Schopenhauer and the composer Richard Wagner. *Human, All Too Human* amounted to a declaration of independence.

This fact is well known, and stressed by Nietzsche himself. What is less commonly recognized is that a change in Nietzsche's career occurs not only *with* the publication of *Human, All Too Human*—a change also occurs *within* the work. This fact is difficult to appreciate, in part because the text is divided into installments that were initially published separately, but which scholars today generally refer to as a single entity. But, as I will argue, the third and final installment—*The Wanderer and His Shadow*—reflects a position that is related to its predecessors, but also distinct from them in crucial respects. *The Wanderer* reflects a substantial development in Nietzsche's understanding of the Free Spirits, and of the ideal that they represent in this work. The task of this chapter will be to trace out the evolution of Nietzsche's thought in this respect. But in order to set the stage for those developments, I need to begin with a few words about the larger project of *Human, All Too Human*, and then unpack the relationship between its component parts.

THE MONUMENT TO A CRISIS: NIETZSCHE'S *ALL TOO HUMAN* TRILOGY

Human, All Too Human is generally recognized as the first entry in the "Free Spirit trilogy" that constitutes Nietzsche's "middle period."[1] Nietzsche's own statements authorize this classification in the following manner. On the back cover of the first edition of *The Gay Science*, he announced: "This book marks the conclusion of a series of writings by Friedrich Nietzsche whose common goal is to erect *a new image and ideal of the free spirit*." He then listed that "series of writings" as follows: *The Gay Science* itself (in its initial form, comprising only four books), its predecessor *Daybreak*, and three publications before that. Those last-mentioned three were *Human, All Too Human: A Book for Free Spirits* (published in 1878), *Assorted Opinions and Maxims* (1879), and *The Wanderer and His Shadow* (1880). Although these three works were originally written and published separately, in 1886 Nietzsche reissued them as a single unit. For the reissue, the text from 1878 appeared as a first volume, and the texts from 1879 and 1880 appeared as a second volume. Each volume was outfitted with an autobiographical preface discussing the composition of the material. These composite texts were produced by taking unsold copies of the previous publications, stitching them together with the new prefaces attached, and then placing a new cover page on each volume, with the title for both volumes reading: *Human, All Too Human: A Book for Free Spirits*. Two years later, in *Ecce Homo*, Nietzsche delivered a retrospective evaluation of all of his publications, devoting a single chapter to "*Human, All Too Human*, with Two Continuations." In this way, Nietzsche indicated that *Human, All Too Human*, *Assorted Opinions and Maxims*, and *The Wanderer and His Shadow* form a trilogy-within-a-trilogy, a sort of tripartite first entry within the broader Free Spirit trilogy of the middle period.

Nietzsche did not just draw these three works together when evaluating them retrospectively, however. Close connections between the three existed from the time of their composition. Most notably, the three writings are designed to follow a nearly identical thematic structure: although only the first installment is divided into discrete chapters (each with a title indicating its major subject), the aphorisms in the next two installments turn out to treat the same subjects in the same order (a sequence of aphorisms on relations between men and women, followed by a sequence on modern politics, and so forth).[2] *Human, All Too Human*, *Assorted Opinions and Maxims*, and *The Wanderer and His Shadow* were therefore designed, from the outset, as a series of variations on a consistent set of themes.[3]

These facts have led many readers to conclude that *The Wanderer* amounts to a subordinate, and largely repetitive, addendum to *Human, All Too Human*. But Nietzsche's remarks on *The Wanderer* actually suggest that he accorded the text a more important, and more independent, status.[4] Thus, I believe that *The Wanderer* has to be understood as occupying a twofold status: it extends the project of *Human, All Too Human*; at the same time, *The Wanderer* arrives at an original set of insights, which deepen and emend the position of its predecessor in several ways. More particularly: *Human, All Too Human* shows Nietzsche setting out the project of the "Free Spirit," while *The Wanderer* shows him coming to terms with implications of that project that had not initially been so clear to him. This is why I have suggested that *The Wanderer* can best be thought of as "variations on a theme" first set down in *Human, All Too Human*.

Although a single, overarching theme runs throughout all three installments of *Human, All Too Human*, that theme is not easy to grasp at first glance, because Nietzsche does not make it explicit. However, he made the crucial issue easier to recognize in the retrospective assessment of *Ecce Homo*, where he characterizes the trilogy as "the monument to a crisis" (*EH* HH 1). The crisis in question was his break with the great composer Richard Wagner—and, moreover, his disenchantment with the whole ideal that Wagnerian opera had once represented to him.[5] When viewed in light of that crisis, the most important connection among the three installments of the *All Too Human* trilogy becomes visible: they document the process through which Nietzsche gradually came to terms with his break with Wagner. And, in particular, they reflect a process through which Nietzsche first established—and then gradually refined or came to terms with—the new image of the Free Spirit that he devised as an alternative to the Wagnerian ideal.

This pivotal turn in Nietzsche's career—away from Wagner, and toward the Free Spirit—required an extended process of reflection on his part because of how thoroughly it challenged every aspect of his life and thought. It drove him to reassess virtually every question that he had formerly taken for granted: from his understanding of philosophy to his view of religion to his political stance. And it was bound up with changes in every aspect of his life: from his occupation, to his place of residence, to his preferences in music. To understand why the break with Wagner had such wide-ranging implications for Nietzsche, we need to begin with some background information about his relationship to the composer.

THE EARLY NIETZSCHE: THE FOLLOWER OF WAGNER AND SCHOPENHAUER

Nietzsche's first book, *The Birth of Tragedy Out of the Spirit of Music*, was published in 1871. The work was dedicated to Wagner, "whose sublime lead I follow" (as Nietzsche put it in his original foreword to the text). Just how Nietzsche aimed to follow Wagner can be grasped by briefly outlining the work's main argument.

The Birth of Tragedy is, in large part, an interpretation of Wagner's artwork. But the discussion of Wagner follows a lengthy analysis of Greek tragedy and Socratic philosophy, in which Nietzsche establishes an important contrast between "tragic" and "Socratic" worldviews. The "tragic" worldview is one that recognizes the deeply mysterious status of the universe, and thus the unstable status of all products of the human mind, which cannot be a reliable tool for self-understanding and world improvement. The tragic worldview is redeemed, however, by its ability to face these harsh facts, and then to craft a form of art through which individuals are able to escape their ordinary existence and commune, in quasi-mystical fashion, with the subrational roots of reality: thus, Nietzsche's famous declaration that "only as an *aesthetic phenomenon* is existence and the world eternally *justified*" (*BT* 5). The tragic worldview was, however, debunked and overtaken by a Socratic worldview that was "rationalist" and "optimistic," meaning that it saw the individual mind as capable of comprehending the universe, and thereby of correcting and progressively improving human existence (*BT* 12–15). Modern science is the contemporary legacy of this "Socratic" worldview—but recently the premises of modern science have been debunked by the philosophy of Arthur Schopenhauer (building on Immanuel Kant's critique of pure reason) (*BT* 16). This means that a *rebirth* of tragedy has become possible. And this is what Wagner is helping to bring about. As described by Nietzsche, Wagner's art is nothing less than an instrument for transforming the collective consciousness of the German nation and revolutionizing the broader course of human history, ushering in a post-Christian, neoclassical Germanic civilization (*BT* 24; also see *RWB* 4).[6] Wagner is thereby helping the world to see how human existence might once again be justified in the only way that it can be justified—as an aesthetic phenomenon, that is to say, through works of art that make life worthwhile.

As this summary suggests, Nietzsche's position in *The Birth of Tragedy* was shaped by his sympathetic interest in the philosophy of Arthur Schopenhauer. Nietzsche's interest in Schopenhauer was matched by Wagner's—indeed, that shared interest was the foundation for the friendship between

Wagner and the young Nietzsche. The two spent many hours together discussing Schopenhauer's philosophy.[7] The philosophy of Schopenhauer was a direct response to Kant's famous distinction between the "phenomenal world" (the world that we perceive through sense perception, and which we can manipulate with the assistance of the intellect, creating objects that represent certain aspects of reality) and the "noumenal world" (the world in which our reality is rooted, but which we can never perceive directly, and therefore cannot claim to have any knowledge of). Schopenhauer accepted Kant's distinction between a phenomenal and noumenal world, but he claimed, *contra* Kant, that it is possible to know the noumenal world. Indeed, Schopenhauer contended that we all perceive something of the noumenal world ordinarily, because our experience of the world is dualistic: divided between our physical existence and an existence of desiring or willing that stands apart from (but helps to shape our experience of) our physical existence. But although Schopenhauer identified the "will" with the noumenal world, he also held that the world *as we ordinarily experience it* is a miserable one: for what we see all around us is *frustrated* desire—the will in a distorted, deficient form. There is one great exception, one medium that gives us direct access to the world of "will," and that is music. For Schopenhauer, music stands apart from all other forms of art, because music alone does not communicate itself through images of the human world; it speaks to us from beyond that world, and thereby gives us our best access to the real, noumenal world in which all other things are rooted. This claim impressed Wagner, giving his late operas a kind of existential significance: they were designed to transform human consciousness, and thereby transform human life.[8]

As a consequence, although Nietzsche's early writings summarily dismiss any concern with the German politics of his time (*SE* 4), their tributes to Wagner still imply a deep concern with the condition of the contemporary world—for it was Wagner's operas that he hoped might transform that condition more thoroughly than any ordinary process of political reform could.[9] Thus, Wagner was ultimately no mere composer of music: not by his own account, and not by Nietzsche's. "Wagner has a legislative nature," Nietzsche observed in two separate fragmentary reflections written toward the end of their friendship.[10] By this Nietzsche meant that Wagner had an unusual ability to draw on, shape, and synthesize diverse elements of music, theater, philosophy, and politics, in order to produce a unified dramatic effect on his audiences.[11] It was in this light that the early Nietzsche was able to judge that Wagner's operas had the potential to create a new kind of political community, and even to found a state (*RWB* 5). Wagner never expressed his ambitions in exactly these terms (although he was very pleased by the early Nietzsche's characterizations of his project), but he did famously decree that his works (or, rather, those that he completed after his discovery of Schopenhauer) ought to be understood, not as "operas," but as something that he called *Gesamtkunstwerk*, or "total work of art," which aimed to distill and synthesize multiple art forms. Thus, at the moment when Nietzsche encountered Wagner, the composer understood himself to be the successor of (and superior to) not only Beethoven, but also Aeschylus and Shakespeare—that is, not merely a great musician, but a sort of honorary poet laureate of a whole culture, as well as a vehicle for the philosophy of Schopenhauer, and, on that basis, someone who would present to the public a new, quasi-religious mythology that would give meaning to, and help to shape, human existence.[12]

In order to realize all these ambitions, Wagner had established the Bayreuth Festival, with a theater built specifically for the performance of his operas, as the new centerpiece of a town to which his acolytes would make pilgrimages. And so they did: in 1876 Wagner inaugurated the Bayreuth Festival with the premiere of his titanic cycle of four operas, *Der Ring des Nibelungen*. Leading lights from across Europe attended the event. Also in attendance was a fairly obscure young professor: Friedrich Nietzsche. Although he was not yet famous, Nietzsche was very much part of Wagner's inner circle: he had been a frequent guest at the Wagners' home, he had been privy to the composition of the *Ring* while it was still a work in progress, and in advance of the festival he wrote a celebratory essay to commemorate the event (*Richard Wagner in Bayreuth*). And yet, when the event finally arrived, Nietzsche turned passionately against the whole Wagnerian project, fleeing from the festival into the forests, where he worked on the notebooks that became *Human, All Too Human*.

The confluence of factors that turned Nietzsche against the Wagnerian project at Bayreuth is complex. Nietzsche found a great deal there to criticize (everything from the design of the sets for the operas to the character of the audience). However, behind all of this lay a rejection of the Wagnerian enterprise of revivifying cultural-political life on a self-consciously mythological basis. By the time of Bayreuth, Nietzsche's private sympathies had already begun to shift in the direction of science and Enlightenment; being confronted with the full spectacle of Wagner's attempt to construct a new Romantic mythology repulsed him. Nietzsche's commitment was now to pursuing the truth (even harsh and unpalatable truths), not to constructing myths (no matter how comforting they might be).[13] *Human, All Too Human* thereby amounts to Nietzsche's attempt to work through the "crisis" that he experienced at Bayreuth, giving a full account (both to himself and to the world at large) of what led him to reject Wagner's project for cultural-political reform.

DISCOVERING THE FREE SPIRIT IN *HUMAN, ALL TOO HUMAN*

As I noted earlier, *Human, All Too Human* is the first in a series of writings through which Nietzsche claims to establish the Free Spirits as "a new image and ideal." However, it should be added that the Free Spirits amount to an "ideal" in rather a qualified sense, because the purpose they served for Nietzsche was, at least initially, not so much constructive as destructive. This is consistent with the larger purpose of *Human, All Too Human* (disentangling Nietzsche, and the popular imagination more generally, from Wagnerian and Schopenhauerian enthusiasms). The task for the Free Spirits is, accordingly, a negative one, and it might therefore be most accurate to describe them as Nietzsche's *model* for how to criticize *existing* ideals, without aiming to refurbish or replace them. To be sure, throughout *Human, All Too Human* Nietzsche takes up the question of what forces *ought* to be responsible for shaping and sustaining a healthy culture—in particular, whether that task is the proper work of art, science, or religion. And he approaches that question with a newfound sympathy for modern principles of Enlightenment, science, and liberal democracy.[14] But his reflections no longer aim at transforming politics and philosophy *through* culture.[15] To the contrary: what Nietzsche stresses here is the need to securely *separate* the realm of culture from the realm of politics (*HH* 235, 438).[16]

At a practical level, this concern comes out most clearly in the (roughly speaking) "libertarian" political posture that Nietzsche adopts in the work: defending individual freedom against both socialistic and theocratic schemes for resuscitating state power (*HH* 235, 472–75), and endorsing the ability of democratic government to place brakes on potentially tyrannical individual ambition and arbitrary power (*WS* 275, 281, 289, 292).[17] This defense of limited government is made in the interests of philosophy. Its objective is to secure a domain in which Free Spirits can test out different aspects of the modern world, without being compelled to take part in any great collective project on its behalf.[18] In other words, Nietzsche's aim is to cultivate a class of Free Spirits who have a broad range of opportunities for engaging the modern world experimentally (in the realm of culture), without having to commit themselves too strongly to any given aspect of it (as tends to be demanded in the realm of politics).[19]

This is not to say that Nietzsche is counseling the Free Spirits to be "apolitical." It is not so much that the Free Spirits are meant to be indifferent or hostile to politics, as that Nietzsche thinks that because the modern world is a relatively *new* creation, and therefore still very much a *work in progress* (see *WS* 275, 350), that the Free Spirits—if they are to retain the ability to explore and experiment with the modern world most freely and fully—will have to remain unaffiliated with respect to any particular conglomeration of social forces (such as a political party or ideology) (see *HH* 229–30; *AOM* 211, 301, 305, 318; *WS* 293).

That being said, as Nietzsche's understanding of the modern world evolved, his notion of the Free Spirits adjusted itself accordingly. They remained the leading image or ideal of his writings, but his understanding of the challenges that their project would face deepened—especially with regard to the difficulties entailed in retaining a critical distance from any project of cultural or political reform. As a result, Nietzsche's view of the Free Spirits' task in the world, and their particular characteristics, evolved over the three installments of the *All Too Human* trilogy. And the catalyst for that evolution is to be found in the biographic context in which they were composed.

The key biographic detail at issue is this: when Nietzsche published the first installment, he knew that it would alienate him from Wagner, but he also sought to minimize that fact—initially by attempting to publish it under a pseudonym (a plan scuttled by his publisher), and ultimately by toning down language that indicted Wagner too directly.[20] Thus, although Nietzsche composed *Human, All Too Human* knowing that its content would alienate him from Wagner, he did not exactly embrace that aspect of the work, and he attempted to minimize its practical consequences.[21] That strategy failed entirely. A few months after the publication of *Human, All Too Human*, Wagner decried the work in the leading journal of the Wagnerian circle. And not long after having been cut off from the Wagnerian world in Bayreuth, Nietzsche resigned from his position as a professor at Basel, where long-standing struggles with his health had made it difficult for him to continue his work (and where he had in any case become increasingly restless working within the confines of the field of classical philology—having tried, unsuccessfully, to transfer into philosophy). During this time Nietzsche wrote the *Assorted Opinions and Maxims*. He also adopted an itinerant lifestyle that would characterize the rest of his career, moving throughout each year among different cities in Italy (Turin being his favorite), with summers spent largely in Switzerland, and winters sometimes in Nice, France.[22] His longer term residences were selected primarily for the effect of the local climate on his health, which at its worst brought him close to death—and which brought his thoughts close to death even more, including the possibility of death by his own hand.[23] In spite of this condition, he spent most of his days hiking, and the remainder of his time working on books that would struggle to find their way into publication. It was only once Nietzsche had established this way of life that *The Wanderer and His Shadow* was completed.

In sum: *Human, All Too Human* was written at a time when Nietzsche still hoped to minimize the consequences of his break with Wagner, but *The Wanderer and His Shadow* was written at a time when Nietzsche had been forced to live with those consequences, which involved a process of ever deepening professional and personal isolation, compounded by the suffering brought on by his bad health.

Nietzsche placed great stress on this biographic context for *The Wanderer* in his retrospective assessment of his career, where he notes that the work was written during the year of his life when he "lived through the summer like a shadow at St. Moritz and the following winter, the least sunny of my life, *as* a shadow in Naumburg" (*EH* Wise 1; also see *EH* HH 4). Thus, what began for Nietzsche in *Human, All Too Human* as a somewhat experimental turn toward the ideal of the Free Spirit had become a gravely serious matter by the time of *The Wanderer and His Shadow*—and the book is, accordingly, Nietzsche's fullest digest of, and most thorough reflection on, what living according to the Free Spirit ideal would entail. With this background having been established, in what follows we will be able to identify more precisely exactly how Nietzsche's ideal of the Free Spirit evolved between *Human, All Too Human* and *The Wanderer and His Shadow*.

THE PHILOSOPHY OF THE "CLOSEST THINGS" IN *THE WANDERER AND HIS SHADOW*

Human, All Too Human is, as its subtitle says, *A Book for Free Spirits*. Nietzsche had never mentioned the Free Spirits before writing the book, but they were to become a permanent fixture of his writings.[24] He outlined their character clearly at the outset:

> We call someone a free spirit who thinks differently from what we expect of him on the basis of his origin, environment, his social rank and position, or on the basis of the prevailing views of the time. He is the exception. (*HH* 225)

In other words: the Free Spirit is one of a kind, not one of society. Nietzsche held to this basic definition of a Free Spirit for the rest of his career.[25] This is not to say, however, that Nietzsche is exhorting would-be Free Spirits to "relax," "let go," or engage in any other sort of self-indulgence.[26] To the contrary: throughout his career Nietzsche stresses that free-spiritedness constitutes an *achievement*, which is to say, an overcoming of obstacles that demands at least as much discipline (and even self-denial) as would be required of any competitive athlete or skilled dancer (indeed, Horst Hutter contends that dance is of special significance in Nietzsche's thought precisely because dance uniquely fuses modes of self-expression and self-discipline).[27] To that end, the *All Too Human* trilogy is centrally concerned with the problem of just how difficult it is for a would-be Free Spirit to truly separate themselves from the spirit of their age—and, as we shall see, it is only with *The Wanderer and His Shadow* that it becomes clear to Nietzsche what would be required for a Free Spirit to attain and maintain their exceptional perspective.

Nietzsche had opened the first installment of the *All Too Human* trilogy with a chapter titled "Of First and Last Things," offering a debunking treatment of "metaphysical philosophy" (which purported to investigate realms of knowledge that transcend the all too human temporal world), along with an endorsement of "historical philosophy" in its place (*HH* 1–2, 26–27). From that starting point, Nietzsche goes on to show how "historical philosophy" could function as the crucial tool required to craft oneself into a Free Spirit—enabling those who possess it to separate themselves from "the dominant views of the age" by uncovering the extent to which modern objects of admiration have been infected by the residue of discreditable ideals inherited from metaphysical philosophy and theology. Nietzsche exemplifies just such a critical perspective by engaging in an extended exposé of the popular phenomenon of Wagnerian opera, dissecting its appeal as the decayed vestige of bygone Christian grandeur, offering a form of escapist entertainment to an undiscerning public (*HH* 150, 212, 215, 217, 219, 221; *AOM* 134, 171, 172; *WS* 149, 156, 165, 170). Indeed, the *All Too Human* trilogy as a whole shows Nietzsche constantly debunking the potentially intoxicating ideals of modern culture, seeking to inspire in their place an appreciation of seemingly ordinary or prosaic "little unpretentious truths" that have been overlooked or despised for a great many ages (*HH* 3, also 6, 609; *AOM* 25; *WS* 16).[28]

Yet in *The Wanderer and His Shadow* this becomes true in a new and more rigorous manner: it makes the all-too-human thematic to a degree that surpasses its predecessors. It does so by clarifying that the difficulty of consistently appreciating the all-too-human is not merely a *historical* problem (the obstacle of an accumulated tradition whose residual power the diligent scholar must deconstruct via "historical philosophy"). Even more, it is a psychological difficulty—something intrinsic to the Free Spirit, rather than created by the society in which the Free Spirit happens to live. *The Wanderer and His Shadow* thereby completes and enlarges the mission that Nietzsche first set out on in *Human, All Too Human*. We can get a sense of how the two works dovetail and differ by comparing the opening sequence of aphorisms in each volume.[29]

The Wanderer and His Shadow mirrors its predecessor by opening with a series of aphorisms directed against the traditional notion that the subject of philosophy is something called "metaphysics," and that, moreover, it responds to some "metaphysical need" that human beings have—a desire to know "first and last things" beyond the human sensory world (*WS* 16). Philosophy in this sense is typically viewed as either laying the groundwork for a properly religious teaching (as Nietzsche understood Plato to have done), or acting as a latter-day substitute for a decaying religion (as Nietzsche had encountered it in Schopenhauer). In view of that tendency, Nietzsche hammers away that as religious belief continues to decline, its aspirations and exalted status must not be projected back onto philosophy. In particular, he emphasizes that philosophy must not be thought of as a means for justifying or satisfying many of the most pervasive human longings, but instead can only be a tool for showing why those longings are unjustifiable and insatiable. Philosophy so understood does not show human beings that they are "the goal and purpose of the existence of the whole universe," but instead shows them how little of the universe it is even possible for them to know (*WS* 1, 2, 14, 16).[30]

In these respects, *The Wanderer* echoes its predecessor volume. But, on closer examination, *The Wanderer* also pushes the argument into new territory, by highlighting permanently problematic facts about human psychology, which are connected to a basic tension in the relationship between individuals and their communities. For, as Nietzsche now stresses, the delusions that have lent philosophy (and, through it, human self-understanding more generally) a grandiose but unwarranted sense of self-importance have their source in demands emerging out of sociopolitical life, which manipulates and distorts individuals' distinctive and personal understandings for its own, larger ends (*WS* 5–6, 9–13). It is easy to become preoccupied with the mysteries of the universe when social authorities claim to have special insight into them, but, Nietzsche suggests, if we reject those authorities, we will be content to leave the mysteries of the universe alone, and turn our attention toward the needs and nature of our individual selves (*WS* 2, 5–6). This point, however, is not primarily to be discovered through the academic task of historical research laid out in *Human, All Too Human*. In fact, historical philosophy is scarcely even mentioned here. In the opening sequence of aphorisms in *The Wanderer*, the need for "a *history* of the ethical and religious sensations" is only broached at the very end (*WS* 16)—and there it is presented as in the service of a deeper concern, one that preoccupies Nietzsche throughout the work, and which is original to this work.

The primary subject of philosophy as *The Wanderer* conceives of it turns out to be, not history, but "the closest things": for instance, "eating, housing, clothing, social intercourse" are proposed as "the object of constant impartial and general reflection and reform" (*WS* 5–6; also see the second half of aphorism 16). This basic insight would remain one of Nietzsche's central concerns until the end of his career (see *EH* Clever 1–2).[31] *The Wanderer and His Shadow* therefore constitutes a decisive turning point in Nietzsche's thought, for it is specifically in this work that his turn to "the closest things" occurs—and, in this way, the Free Spirit's concern with historical philosophy is supplemented, and to some degree overshadowed, by a deeper emphasis on psychology (that is, the way in which our minds divert and delude themselves, becoming occupied with everything apart from those concerns that are naturally closest).

To elaborate on this last point: the concern for "the closest things" in *The Wanderer* is distinct from the commendation of "little unpretentious truths" in *Human, All Too Human*, because in the latter case Nietzsche is referring mainly to discoveries made with the aid of modern scientific method (including historical philosophy) that might seem unimpressive when placed next to the grander claims advanced by traditional religion and metaphysics.[32] Consequently, in *Human, All Too Human* the primary point of contrast is between science and metaphysics, but in *The Wanderer* the key contrast is between individual and civic concerns ("metaphysics" acting as a tool of the latter). The latter conflict is the more essential one, as is indicated by the fact that in *The Wanderer* Nietzsche focuses on Socrates and Epicurus as models for philosophy: they were not concerned with modern science, but they were concerned with "the closest things," and so their respective responses to the perennial conflict between philosophy and the city remains relevant for readers in the modern world (this point will be elaborated in the discussion that follows).

The evolution of Nietzsche's thought, toward greater concern for "the closest things," is flagged for readers by the title of the work, *The Wanderer and His Shadow*. That title refers readers to two characters who appear in short dialogues presented at the work's opening and closing. These characters are not identified until the closing dialogue, which indicates that the

Wanderer is the author of the book, Nietzsche himself, in conversation with his Shadow. A central theme of both dialogues is to reveal that the Shadow represents what the Wanderer (standing in for Nietzsche here) typically neglects about himself, and even what he simply fails to understand about himself. Accordingly, the dialogue between the two at the outset of the book reveals that although the Wanderer's Shadow is ever-present, the two hardly ever speak. This is so much the case that the Wanderer initially does not recognize the Shadow's voice as his own; that is to say, he does not initially understand that the Shadow's existence is a part of his own. But despite the Wanderer's initial surprise at encountering the Shadow, the two proceed to affirm that they do not exist in opposition to one another; in fact, they presuppose one another. And the Wanderer concludes their first exchange by declaring that their conversation will be a quest to find what they can agree on. That point of agreement is revealed in the exchange between the Wanderer and his Shadow at the end of the work, which the Shadow opens by observing: "of all that you have said [that is, of all the things that Nietzsche has written in the book's 350 aphorisms] nothing has pleased me *more* than one promise: you wish once again to become a good neighbor of the things closest at hand. This will benefit us poor shadows too." In this way, Nietzsche shows the reader that his turn to "the closest things" is unique to this book—and to this moment in his life.

Having recognized that *The Wanderer and His Shadow* supplements *Human, All Too Human* in this way, we may pause to caution against a potential misunderstanding of this point. It would be tempting to take Nietzsche's turn to the "the closest things" in a roughly "Rousseauian" vein, as if he were suggesting that once "historical philosophy" has succeeded in unshackling us from the various pathologies introduced into human nature over the course of many ages, we will then be free to tend to those closest things that constitute our most elemental and enduring needs, and that can be enjoyed most securely in a tranquil retreat away from society via immersion in an uncorrupted natural environment (*à la* Émile or the Solitary Walker, Rousseau's exemplars of the healthiest ways of life possible in the corrupt modern world). And, indeed, at several places in *The Wanderer* Nietzsche seems to come close to such a prototypically Rousseauian vision (*WS* 192, 200, 295, 338). Nevertheless, Nietzsche's renewed appreciation of the goods of ordinary life does not lead him down the Rousseauian path.[33] Very much the opposite: the turn to the "closest things" leads Nietzsche to call for a more direct *confrontation* between the Free Spirits and social-political authority. In order to see how this works, we need to consider the two classical models that Nietzsche introduces as models for the free spirits: Socrates and Epicurus (each of whom *The Wanderer* presents as exemplifying, in different ways, the proper orientation toward the "closest things").

THE FREE SPIRIT'S SOCRATIC PREDECESSOR

Nietzsche's sympathetic interest in Epicurus is well known, and it was expressed consistently over the course of his career (*AOM* 408; *D* 72; *GS* 45; *A* 58). Nietzsche's interest in Socrates is even better known, and somewhat notorious for his sharp, and occasionally vituperative, criticism of the ancient Athenian.[34] *The Wanderer and His Shadow* takes a very different approach to the subject. Nietzsche's first book, *The Birth of Tragedy*, had advanced the thesis that Socrates was an opponent of all that was great and good in Athens, and had blamed Socrates for setting in motion the destruction of classical Greek civilization. *The Wanderer and His Shadow* presents a surprising variation of that charge: Socrates is once again presented as an opponent of Greek civilization—only now in a manner that redounds very much to his credit, inspiring Nietzsche's praise rather than blame.

Nietzsche's praise of Socrates first appears early on in *The Wanderer*'s discussion of "the closest things." The immediate context is Nietzsche's condemnation of social authorities who "hammer even into children that what matters" is not "the requirements of the individual" but instead "the salvation of the soul, the service of the state, the advancement of science, or the accumulation of reputation and possessions, all as the means of doing service to mankind as a whole." In response, Nietzsche insists that all such claims (whether derived from politics, religion, or science) are illegitimate because they distract our attention from those things that are closest to us, which ought to matter most. On that basis, *The Wanderer* advises Free Spirits to refrain from involvement in any larger social project, any greater good that does not serve their individual good (*WS* 6).

The great difficulty with following this injunction, Nietzsche stresses, is that the various mechanisms of society have been constructed to confuse us about what in fact serves our individual interests:

> Already in ancient Greece Socrates was defending himself with all his might against this arrogant neglect of the human for the benefit of the human race, and loved to indicate the true compass and content of all reflection and concern with an expression of Homer's: it comprises, he said, nothing other than "that which I encounter of good and ill in my own house."[35] (*WS* 6)

With this remark *The Wanderer* introduces Socrates in a sharp light: as a representative of the individual and individual interests against attempts to sacrifice those interests to a greater communal project, especially by confusing the individual about what their interests actually are. Socrates's example serves as a reminder that we must struggle to keep our attention continually focused on those things that are naturally closest to us (but from which we are easily distracted), in order for our individual interests and self-concern to retain primacy throughout our lives, and not become subsumed within the interests and demands of the larger communities in which we find ourselves.[36] Subsequently, Nietzsche will indicate (through a discussion of Epicurus) that this means we ought to limit ourselves, as far as possible, to pursuing goods that can be attained and enjoyed without falling into dependence on others.

For present purposes, however, we can observe that, as the text proceeds, Nietzsche sharpens his depiction of Socrates as representing one pole in a larger struggle between the individual and the community.

Aphorisms 72–86 of *The Wanderer and His Shadow* constitute a subsection dealing with religion.[37] The first and last aphorisms in this sequence happen to be about Socrates. In a way, this should not be surprising. After all, in Platonic dialogues, such as the *Republic*, *Phaedo*, and *Gorgias*, Socrates promulgates quasi-theological teachings that Nietzsche famously blamed for spawning Christianity (*BGE* Preface 191). However, we have just noted that *The Wanderer*'s presentation of Socrates is unique in Nietzsche's corpus—and, accordingly, Socrates's religious significance in this text differs from how he presents it elsewhere. Here Nietzsche has Socrates bookend his discussion of religion in order to stress that Socrates was not *and could not have been* the founder of any dogma, and was in fact a consistent critic of popular belief.[38] Moreover, through these two aphorisms Nietzsche proposes that Socrates furnishes a model of how such criticism ought to be undertaken: not via a peaceful retreat from society, but, rather, through a combative contest with it.[39]

Nietzsche illustrates the Socratic spirit through an interpretation of Socrates's famous "divine mission." The divine mission is mentioned in Plato's *Apology of Socrates*, where Socrates defends himself against the charge of impiety by insisting that the dialectical interrogations to which he habitually subjected his fellow Athenians were part of a quest to determine whether the Delphic oracle had been correct to claim that he was the wisest man alive; on this basis, Socrates characterizes his dialectical cross-examinations as part of a "divine mission." Nietzsche, however, suggests that this story hardly proves that Socrates was genuinely devoted to the Greek god; on Nietzsche's view, the divine mission is better understood as Socrates's playful or ironic manner of accommodating himself to popular piety—that is to say, a disingenuous way of claiming a divine imprimatur for his rather upsetting practice of interrogating popular beliefs.[40]

For Nietzsche, then, Socrates's "divine mission" was the means through which he "put the god to the test in a hundred ways"—that is, critically scrutinized its claims rather than accepting or rejecting them outright. Nietzsche concludes by calling this "one of the subtlest compromises between piety and freedom of spirit ever devised," and thereby suggests that Socrates is the proper model for a certain sort of Free Spirit—a prudential Free Spirit who maintains an intellectual and spiritual independence from society without feeling compelled to launch a direct assault against it.[41]

This notion of Socrates as a model of free-spiritedness is underscored by Nietzsche's final reference to him, at the end of the subsection on religion, in aphorism 86, which declares, "If all goes well, the time will come when one will take up the Memorabilia of Socrates rather than the Bible as a guide to morals and reason," and concludes, "The pathways of the most various philosophical modes of life lead back to him." Nietzsche's own return to and reconsideration of the problem of Socrates in *The Wanderer and His Shadow* indicates that the Athenian philosopher persuaded him that the essential task of a Free Spirit could not be simply that of correcting the problems bequeathed to the contemporary world by a decaying (Platonic-Christian) tradition; instead, the primary task had to be one of recovering and reaffirming the inherent disjunction between individual and communal interests—a tension exposed by Socrates in terms that hold true for the modern world. In this way, Nietzsche's reading of the Delphic Oracle story works to suggest that Socrates's example can still serve to inspire and guide Free Spirits today, furnishing them with a model of how to critically engage and interrogate the broader society in which they happen to be situated, seeking out and contesting its most authoritative claims in order to enrich their own self-understanding (consider Plato, *Apology of Socrates* 37e–38a)—all without thereby seeking to lead a movement to overthrow those authorities or transform popular opinion.

The Socratic turn that Nietzsche recommends to the Free Spirits is then a political turn, insofar as it entails a new recognition of the importance of political questions for structuring the life and thought of even the freest spirit—but the turn is made in the service of understanding and protecting those things that remain closest to the Free Spirit, not for the purpose of remaking politics in accord with the Free Spirit's own ideas or ideology.

THE SELF-DISCIPLINED HEART OF THE FREE SPIRIT PROJECT

Nietzsche's Socratic exemplar provides only one-half of his model for Free Spirits. For in the context of introducing the closest things as the new focus of the Free Spirits' concerns, Nietzsche introduces his second classical model of how best to pursue those things: Epicurus (*WS* 7). The Epicurean model turns out to supplement the Socratic one in a crucial way, because it shows that the division between individual and communal interests results not only from social engineering and propaganda (which the Socratic model, as outlined above, is designed to combat), but also from a division in the Free Spirit's own soul. Nietzsche's turn to Epicurus is meant to address this latter difficulty, and thereby reveals a key part of what is most distinctive about the Free Spirits' way of life: the exceptional self-discipline required to maintain it.

Nietzsche places the theme of self-discipline at the core of his discussion of Epicurus, by reminding us that Epicurus's philosophy of pleasure (his hedonism) was directed not at sources of pleasure indiscriminately (as contemporary usage of the term "hedonist" tends to imply), but, rather, specifically at those that lay closest to him and, to the maximum extent possible, *those things only*. Epicurus's great insight, therefore, was to appreciate that a consistent and truly satisfying hedonism must limit itself to those pleasures that are closest at hand (that is to say, those that can be acquired and enjoyed using one's own, individual powers, rather than relying on others), because only they provide a reliable and secure source of pleasure.

This disposition fits well with a major concern of *The Wanderer* as a whole: freeing oneself from dependence on others. We have already seen this to be a central feature of *The Wanderer*'s treatment of Socrates. Toward the end of the work, Nietzsche puts the point this way:

> To satisfy one's requirements as completely as possible oneself, even if imperfectly, is the road to *freedom of spirit and person*. To let others satisfy many of one's requirements, even superfluous ones, and as perfectly as possible—is a training in *unfreedom*. (*WS* 318)

Thus, in *The Wanderer* the freedom particular to the Free Spirits consists above all in freedom from dependence on others, or maximal self-sufficiency.

In the pursuit of such freedom, Nietzsche explains, Epicurus had to restrain himself from indulging many of the pleasures (or prospective pleasures) that so ubiquitously attract human beings: pleasures that draw one out of one's individual self and thereby into a potential dependence on other people, or that rely on our capacity for hopefulness and thereby lead us into painful disappointments. Any sort of ambition (including political ambition, or hopes for fame or influence more generally) would have to count prominently among the pleasures to be resisted. Thus, Nietzsche stresses that the Epicurean way of life allows for little more than a retired, anonymous, and simple existence (*WS* 192, 227, 295).[42]

These remarks on the Epicurean way of life help to illuminate what Nietzsche has in mind when he refers to "the closest things." When Nietzsche first introduces that notion, he lists "eating, housing, clothing, social intercourse" as examples of such things (*WS* 6). Later we see these examples brought to life in his description of "the pleasures of Epicurus": "a little garden, figs, cheeses, and in addition three or four good friends" (*WS* 192). Moreover, this description shows that while Epicurus enjoyed "social intercourse," he did so only in a relatively limited sense of enjoying the private company of "three or four good friends," rather than in the sense of seeking fame or influence.[43] Sociability in the former sense can be consistent with the conception of freedom quoted above ("satisfy[ing] one's requirements as completely as possible oneself"), insofar as it plausibly lies within one's own powers to carefully select and tend to a small number of productive friendships (and this would be particularly true of friendships centered upon the simple good of shared conversations in Epicurean gardens);[44] sociability in the latter sense would be a path to unfreedom (since the conditions of fame and influence are not reliably within one's own control). As this suggests, proper care for the things that are closest to oneself brings with it attentiveness to the transitory nature of the all-too-human.

This last point is brought out in a striking way by an aphorism that gives a particularly lyrical description of a pastoral scene that evokes a feeling of awe and love of nature in Nietzsche, who associates that scene and the response it evokes with Epicurus (*WS* 295). The scene that Nietzsche describes here is inspired by a painting by Nicolas Poussin. Nietzsche uses the title of Poussin's painting as the title for his aphorism: *Et in Arcadia ego* (I, too, in Arcadia). In Poussin's painting, three shepherds are shown discovering this Latin motto inscribed on a tomb lying in the Arcadian paradise.[45] This scene—the awareness of death as a part of nature even in the midst of rapt wonder at the beauty of nature—very much encapsulates the state that Nietzsche would have found himself in at the time the aphorism was written, when he continued to regularly venture on long hikes in idyllic regions of Italy and Switzerland, notwithstanding his interminable struggles with his health.[46]

At any rate, the illusory pleasures that Nietzsche's Epicurean model warns against are not limited to the desire to stretch out one's individual influence in the world. They also include a warning against the desires associated with the quest for knowledge—the hope to know more than one's modest powers naturally make possible. To that end, Nietzsche stresses that the Epicurean model demands that one "quiet the heart," that is to say, refrain from concerning oneself with matters that one cannot satisfactorily resolve, such as the existence of a supernatural realm, or its possible concern for the natural world (*WS* 7). Now, to speak of quieting the heart in this context implies that the heart has a natural inclination to reach out beyond what it can naturally know, or that we have natural longings that we cannot naturally satisfy. And this, I would like to suggest, is how Nietzsche is encouraging us to understand traditional philosophic metaphysics: as a desire, which can be indulged or resisted just as we might indulge or resist a desire for any other sort of sensuous or erotic pleasure.[47]

If this last suggestion seems fanciful, it is worth recalling that Nietzsche's turn away from metaphysics in the *All Too Human* trilogy is of a piece with his turn away from Wagnerian music. This is no coincidence. In Wagner's operas (particularly *Tristan und Isolde*) love and music are the twin intoxications that are meant to lead to the metaphysical world. Both love and music provide an escape from tortured, this-worldly individuality, into a tranquil, other-worldly unity—and therefore also hold out the possibility of revolutionizing or redeeming the world.[48] This thought is also articulated by Nietzsche. Throughout his corpus he views music as providing the listener with the illusion of access to some sort of "primordial oneness," a transcendent realm of unity and harmony.[49] The transfiguring or revolutionary potential that seems to be contained within music is a theme that runs from Nietzsche's earliest writings through to his latest, because music is at all stages what for Nietzsche makes the feeling (and thereby the reality) of human community possible.[50] Against that tendency, in the period of the *All Too Human* trilogy Nietzsche puts aside his musical enthusiasms, and focuses on those "closest things" that are most personal and idiosyncratic, such that they cannot be held in common.[51]

As these remarks suggest, Nietzsche's turn away from the world of music and metaphysics in his *Book for Free Spirits* brings along with it a program of rigorous self-discipline, because that turn amounts to a determined effort to invest himself in satisfying only a certain, narrowly circumscribed set of desires, and conducting his whole life so as to dampen down or quarantine more expansive inclinations. Nietzsche formulates what is at issue with great eloquence, as follows:

> How strong the metaphysical need is, and how hard nature makes it to bid it a final farewell, can be seen from the fact that when the free spirit has divested himself of everything metaphysical, the highest effects of art can easily set the metaphysical strings, which have long been silent or indeed snapped apart, vibrating in sympathy; so it can happen, for example, that a passage in Beethoven's Ninth Symphony will make him feel he is hovering above the earth in a dome of stars with the dream of *immortality* in his heart: all the stars seem to glitter around him and the earth seems to sink farther and farther away.—If he becomes aware of being in this condition he feels a profound stab in the heart and sighs for the man who will lead him back to his lost love, whether she be called religion or metaphysics. It is in such moments that his intellectual probity is put to the test. (*HH* 153)

If we read this passage in light of the Epicurean exhortation to "quiet the heart," we can conclude that the free-spirited model of philosophy which Nietzsche endorses here, does not so much involve a straightforward return to blissful nature (in the manner of the "Rousseauian" ideal)[52] as require a self-disciplined attempt to counteract naturally wayward human nature.[53]

Nietzsche stressed just this point when, several years after his "middle period," he issued a newly detailed analysis of the character of the Free Spirits, and highlighted the rigorous program of self-discipline characteristic of their way of life:

> *Tethered heart, free spirit.*—If one tethers one's heart severely and imprisons it, one can give one's spirit many liberties: I have said that once before. But one does not believe me, unless one already knows it. (*BGE* 87)

An aphorism toward the end of *The Wanderer and His Shadow* makes the same point:

> *The most needful gymnastic.*—A lack of self-mastery in small things brings about a crumbling of the capacity for it in great ones. Every day is ill employed, and a danger for the next day, in which one has not denied oneself one small thing at least once: this gymnastic is indispensable if one wants to preserve in oneself the joy of being one's own master. (*WS* 305, see also 318)

In sum: the return to "the closest things" to which Nietzsche exhorts philosophy requires an intense self-discipline because Nietzsche sees the philosophic "metaphysics" that leads away from them as the product of natural human inclinations (we might think of this as the heart's natural inclination to draw the mind outside of nature).[54]

As this suggests, Nietzsche's turn away from the promise that Schopenhauer and Wagner had once held out to him might be best understood, not as result of his having become simply or thoroughly "disenchanted" with them, but, rather, as part of a broader attempt to conscientiously counteract a persistently simmering set of desires woven into his nature. From this observation we can also gather why the turn toward "historical philosophy" alone would not have been sufficient to sustain the critical perspective of the Free Spirit: for debunking a popular or intoxicating phenomenon (such as Wagnerian opera) simply on the grounds that its origins were more "human, all too human" than previously supposed could not, by itself, extinguish the desires that made one susceptible to such a delusion in the first place.[55] Thus, *The Wanderer and His Shadow* shows that when Nietzsche exhorts philosophy away from "metaphysical" concerns and toward "the closest things," it will not be enough to limit oneself to clearing away the cobwebs of tradition and the machinations of social authority. It is also a matter of maintaining an appropriate internal disposition—placing a restraint on the heart that liberates the spirit and frees the mind.

THE CHALLENGE FOR THE FREE SPIRITS

We can conclude that, taken together, Nietzsche's Socratic and Epicurean models recommend the following way of life to prospective Free Spirits: on the one hand, a continual process of engaging and challenging the world around them; on the other hand, a constant refraining from any attempt to guide or transform that same world. Given the persistence of the Free Spirit's natural attachments to the broader world, this posture can only be sustained with the aid of a rigorous regimen of self-restraint. Nietzsche's own project during this period exemplifies the proper outlook: throughout *Human, All Too Human* he goes about attacking and critically scrutinizing the phenomenon of Wagnerian opera, without thereby seeking out (or attempting to create) any alternative to it, even though the attraction to all that it represented continued to run within him.

But if this was the objective of *Human, All Too Human*, it is not so clear that it remained Nietzsche's aim for the duration of his career. Indeed, his later works have often been taken as attempts to succeed where his early infatuation with Wagner failed. In particular, *Thus Spoke Zarathustra* has been seen as a poetic and quasi-musical attempt to transform European culture, and, through it, global politics.[56] To that extent, it might seem as if Nietzsche ultimately rejected the model of philosophy outlined in *The Wanderer and His Shadow*—or perhaps that he did not take it very seriously in the first place.[57] In what follows, I argue to the contrary, and show that Nietzsche's turn away from the posture outlined in *The Wanderer* might be better understood as the result of serious and sympathetic (yet still critical) reflection on that ideal.

The Free Spirit as Nietzsche came to understand that figure in *The Wanderer and His Shadow* is, then, in many ways an attractive and necessary ideal, but also a limited and limiting one. This point can only be fully substantiated by looking at Nietzsche's writings that followed *Human, All Too Human* (including his retrospective assessments of the work), where possible criticisms of the Free Spirit come into view more clearly. We will look at some of those writings in the chapters that follow. First, however, it is worth observing that the basic claim I am making here is implicit in an aspect of *The Wanderer* that I have already touched on, but that still needs a fuller explanation: the uniqueness of the "Socratic" posture that Nietzsche commends in the work.

THE SOURCES OF *THE WANDERER*'S SOCRATISM

When Nietzsche recommends the example of Socrates as a model for the Free Spirit in *The Wanderer and His Shadow*, he does so in a somewhat unorthodox way: namely, by referring the reader specifically to *Xenophon*'s Socrates, rather than to Plato's more famous portrait of the Athenian philosopher. This reference constitutes the culmination of a reevaluation of the old Athenian that Nietzsche began around the same time that he broke with Wagner.

A few scholars have noted that Nietzsche's estimation of Socrates changes dramatically in *Human, All Too Human* (although one major study remarks that this change is "strange and difficult to explain").[58] But in *The Wanderer* Nietzsche provides an essential clue to explaining that change. For, as we saw above, when he holds up Socrates as a model of the philosophic life in this work, he singles out "the Memorabilia of Socrates" as *the* authoritative source for that claim. This is an endorsement of Xenophon's *Memorabilia*, as opposed to Plato's more famous Socratic dialogues. This detail is not accidental, and it is not trivial. The significance of Nietzsche's privileging of Xenophon is confirmed and clarified by several remarks found in his notebooks and letters from the second half of the 1870s (that is, during the period when he broke with Wagner and wrote the *All Too Human* trilogy).[59]

When, as a young philology professor, Nietzsche issued his first assessment of Socrates in *The Birth of Tragedy*, he shared the common judgment of his profession, according to which Xenophon's portrait of Socrates amounted to prosaic history, not bearing on the heart of Socratic philosophy.[60] Around 1875, however, Nietzsche developed an intense interest in Xenophon's *Memorabilia*, as evidenced by a number of unpublished remarks.[61] These remarks all have the same gist: other classical scholars have wrongly judged the work to be "boring"; to the contrary, Nietzsche judges it to be a more accurate and compelling representation of Socrates than that found in Plato, and, moreover, he takes the Xenophontic Socrates as a "model" to be imitated in the modern world. This last suggestion is given a special resonance by the fact that, in one instance, Nietzsche describes himself as "haunted" by the Xenophontic Socrates's judgment that those who teach for pay forfeit their independence in the process;[62] Nietzsche left the academic profession in 1879. In view of this, we can conclude that when Nietzsche expressed in print his hope that the Socrates of the *Memorabilia* would replace the Bible as a guide to the proper conduct of life, he was actually in the process of following that injunction himself.

These details add weight to *The Wanderer*'s various exhortations to a simple way of life, unencumbered by external needs or personal dependencies. Those exhortations, we can now conclude, appeal (at least in part) to a way of life whose "model" Nietzsche found in Xenophon's Socrates, who took great pride in the independence that he acquired through his bare-bones existence.[63] And, as I have already suggested, the full significance of this model of Socratic independence comes from the fact that it differs in important ways from the Platonic portrait: for while the Xenophontic Socrates places great emphasis on his freedom from material needs, he also stresses that it is a freedom acquired not through his fixation on a superior supersensible world or through a perfect harmony of his soul's desires (as Plato's portrait of Socrates sometimes suggests), but instead through a rigorous program of self-discipline, imposed even in the teeth of his natural desires.[64] Xenophon's Socrates thereby offers an outstanding example of the self-sufficiency that characterizes a philosophic life[65]—while also making readily apparent the formidable challenge (emanating from one's more ornery inclinations) involved in acquiring and maintaining such an austere independence. In other words: the Xenophontic Socrates offers a more human, all too human model of philosophic life than the Platonic Socrates, and the former could, therefore, serve as an inspiration for Nietzsche's Free Spirit project in a way that the latter could not. Let me try to flesh out this last thought by elaborating on the comparison between the Platonic and Xenophontic Socrates.

Plato and Xenophon both present Socrates's self-mastery, or self-control, as one of his most outstanding characteristics (Plato, *Symposium* 216c–221d; Xenophon, *Apology* 16–18; Xenophon, *Memorabilia* 1.2.1, 1.5, 1.6). However, in book 4 of the *Republic* Plato has Socrates suggest that a genuine harmony can be achieved between the competing elements of an individual soul, analogous to the harmony of competing elements in a political community. This analogy is perplexing in many respects, but Plato gives readers the impression that Socrates attained very much such a state of soul. For instance, in the *Symposium* he shows us that Socrates's ambitious young follower, the future tyrant Alcibiades, was both impressed and confounded by Socrates's capacity for self-control (exhibited by his apparent imperviousness to the effects of either extreme weather or sexual desire). Alcibiades is so frustrated by Socrates's unique facility in this regard that he likens Socrates to a Silenus, as if Socrates possessed some sort of divine power.[66] And throughout his *Symposium* Plato offers circumstantial evidence for this assessment of Socrates (depicting him as both uninterested in alcohol and uniquely untouched by its effects, all while proclaiming rare insight into the divine nature of eros)—to say nothing of Plato's *Phaedo*, where Socrates appears to be preternaturally serene in the face of death. As a result, Plato's Socrates can come across as something of a quasi-mystical ascetic.[67] It is Xenophon who shows that this sort of seemingly mystical asceticism is exactly what Nietzsche suggests in the *Genealogy* that philosophic asceticism was originally: not the true core of Socratic philosophy, but a mask for that core. Thus, Xenophon acknowledges many of the features of Socrates's unusual character that are highlighted by Plato (such as Socrates's self-control, his semi-mystical self-presentation, the intoxicating impact he had on some of his followers), only Xenophon gives readers a more critical (though still admiring) way of understanding those traits.[68] Early in the *Memorabilia* Xenophon addresses the impact Socrates had on future political criminals like Alcibiades. And, in asking why Socrates failed to moderate the ambition of those associates, Xenophon quickly admits that certain individuals' inclinations might be organized so as to resist any attempt to harmonize them;[69] "the drives want to play the tyrant," as Nietzsche would have said (*TI* Problem 9). If, then, a perfect harmony of soul is ruled out from the outset, perhaps a rigorous regimen of self-discipline might have done the job? Xenophon indicates that such a solution is imperfect, by pointing out that Socrates employed just such a program of moralistic exhortation with his young companions, who, "while they kept company with Socrates, were able to overpower their desires by using him as an ally," only to lose their way after they lost contact with him (*Memorabilia* 1.2.24). Perhaps, then, their zeal could have been kept in check through the constant presence of Socrates's schoolmarmish moderating influence?[70] Xenophon gives us reason to doubt that even that much would have been possible, because he presents us with the noteworthy example of a student of Socrates who remained close to him, and yet still did not entirely adhere to his stern counsel: the student being Xenophon himself. This point is made by the only two exchanges that Xenophon depicts between himself and Socrates. The first of these occurs shortly after the aforementioned discussion of Alcibiades, and involves Socrates upbraiding Xenophon for indulging his attraction to a beautiful young man. Socrates does not deny the delightful charm of the young man's beauty; to the contrary, he characterizes its power as so tremendous that it threatens to overwhelm all other concerns. On that basis, Socrates concludes: "I counsel you, Xenophon, whenever you see someone beautiful, to flee without looking back!" (*Memorabilia* 1.3.9–13). Now, Xenophon often enthusiastically commends the effectiveness of Socrates's exhortations, but this is one case where he is not moved to do so.[71] Moreover, if the second of his exchanges with Socrates is any indication, Xenophon cannot be presumed to have felt obligated by Socrates's counsel in any case: for, as he shows us, he embarked on the major escapade of his adult life—joining a military campaign, and eventually assuming control of it as the de facto ruler of a band of mercenaries—against the advice of Socrates (*Anabasis* 3.1.4–7). Xenophon gives no indication that he regretted that decision (to the contrary, he recounts his military-political exploits in engaging detail in the *Anabasis*), nor does he suggest that he held Socrates in any lower esteem as a result (to the contrary, he accords Socrates the most elevated status among all of his acquaintances: *Memorabilia* 4.8.11). To this extent, the case of Xenophon is a piece of evidence for a maxim of Zarathustra's: "One repays a teacher poorly if one always remains only a student" (*TSZ*, On the Bestowing Virtue 3; *EH* Foreword 4). More to the point, in Xenophon's portrait, Socrates's relationship to various students is one more respect in which philosophy appears in a distinctly human, all too human light: that is to say, very much mediated (shaped and limited) by individual natures. And, as a result, in Xenophon's portrait Socrates and his austere independence appear as a deeply admirable paragon of philosophy, but not as an awe-inspiring idol. I therefore conclude (albeit, unavoidably, somewhat speculatively) that in discovering Xenophon's Socrates around the time of *The Wanderer*, Nietzsche landed upon a model of philosophy that could serve as a genuine inspiration for his Free Spirit project, though not one that would (or could) be the subject of precise imitation.[72]

CONCLUDING REMARKS

In chapter 1 we saw the late Nietzsche's suggestion that with his early landmark work *Human, All Too Human*, he had set out on the path to independence without immediately understanding all that would be involved in doing so. We now have an important piece of evidence for that self-assessment. For, as we have seen in this chapter, Nietzsche was led to supplement *Human, All Too Human* with *The Wanderer and His Shadow*—where the conflict between individual and community comes to concern him in a new way (and in a way that he now recognizes as transcending any particular historical context), constituting a sharper challenge to the Free Spirit project than he had initially recognized. At the same time, however, precisely in turning toward the individual (or toward the all-too-human in a more thorough sense), *The Wanderer* becomes the work through which Nietzsche comes to recognize what the Free Spirit shares with fellow human beings, rather than what sets him apart from them (thus, the new philosophy of "the closest things"). This is not to say, however, that with *The Wanderer* the Free Spirit becomes a figure any less concerned with standing apart from society: what the Free Spirit learns here is the rigorous self-discipline required to maintain that stance. This is why, in *The Wanderer*, the Free Spirits are instructed to "quiet the heart," that is, to counteract natural attachments or desires that are at odds with their determinedly critical, independent activity. In later writings Nietzsche will stress even more emphatically the degree of self-denial and solitude characteristic of a Free Spirit.

By bringing tensions within the Free Spirit project into view with *The Wanderer*, Nietzsche leaves us to wonder whether what is most valuable in the Free Spirits' example is less the way of life they represent (which may remain inadequate or unsatisfactory in various respects), and more their ability to face up to challenges that are an essential (though all too often overlooked or evaded) aspect of the human condition.

At least, it seems to me that these possibilities are suggested by a striking reflection that Nietzsche included toward the end of *The Wanderer and His Shadow*:

> *At Midday.*—For anyone whose life has been allotted an active and stormy morning, his soul overflows in the midday of life with a strange desire for peace that can last for months and years. It grows still around him, voices sound farther and farther away; the sun shines steeply down around him. In a hidden forest meadow, he sees the great Pan sleeping; all things in

> nature have fallen asleep with him, an expression of eternity upon their faces—so it seems to him. He wants nothing, he worries about nothing, his heart stands still, only his eyes are alive—it is like death with eyes wide open. This human being sees many things that he never saw before, and as far as he sees, everything is entangled in a net of light, as if buried therein. He feels himself to be happy, but it is a heavy, heavy happiness.—Then finally the wind rises up in the trees, noon is over, *life* draws him in, life with blinded eyes, behind which its retinue come storming in: desire, deceit, forgetfulness, pleasure, destruction, transience. And so evening arrives, stormier and more active than even the morning was. (*WS* 308)

If the argument of this chapter has been sound, I believe that we can take Nietzsche's Wagnerian beginnings as the "active and stormy morning" of his life, and *Human, All Too Human* as the noon in which voices begin to recede into the distance for Nietzsche, leading to *The Wanderer and His Shadow* as the moment of isolated rediscovery, granting him a new clarity near death, along with the "heavy happiness" (*schweres Glück*) that attends such a hard-won awareness. At the same time, the aphorism suggests that this moment—the moment of *The Wanderer and His Shadow*—is only midday, that is, it only represents one moment in time, and points to an existence beyond itself (even and especially one characterized by "desire, deceit, forgetfulness, pleasure, destruction, transience").

Nietzsche later made that allegory almost literal by including in part 4 of *Thus Spoke Zarathustra* a chapter titled "Midday" (which happens to follow a chapter in which Zarathustra is addressed by his shadow—whom Zarathustra addresses, at the end of that chapter, as "you free spirit and wanderer"). This observation compels one to wonder: just how is the project of *The Wanderer* to be squared with the project of *Zarathustra*? Did some inadequacy with the Free Spirit project move Nietzsche to abandon the self-restraint of the former work in favor of the seemingly revolutionary posture of the latter? In particular, did Nietzsche find that *The Wanderer*'s austere model of independence was ultimately unsatisfying and untenable? And could *Zarathustra* have been an attempt to engage in a more thorough and fulfilling way with human needs and longings that *The Wanderer* had insisted on remaining independent of?

I will begin to address these questions in part 2. And the point of departure for my discussion will be that Zarathustra clearly does surpass the Free Spirit with regard to at least one crucial point, a point that is central to the evolution of Nietzsche's thought as a whole: the understanding of love.[73]

* 2 *

Love

CHAPTER THREE

The Promise of Self-Transformation in *The Case of Wagner*

Few subjects are as central to Nietzsche's oeuvre as love.

Nietzsche employs some of his richest and most famous imagery in order to draw the reader's attention to the theme of love. For instance, as Robert Pippin has suggested, the opening metaphor of *Beyond Good and Evil*—where philosophers are likened to "awkward lovers"—makes it possible to understand Nietzsche's writings as nothing less than an attempt to teach philosophers a new way of pursuing and embracing wisdom, a new way of loving the truth.[1]

The concern with love—as a motive of human life and as material for philosophic reflection—overarches Nietzsche's whole career. Yet at first sight it also seems to divide his writings more than it unites them, since Nietzsche's statements on love appear to shift markedly over time.

Early in Nietzsche's career, while he was still captivated by the alliance of Schopenhauerian philosophy and Wagnerian art, he set down some of his most eloquent statements on the subject:

> There are moments and as it were bright sparks of the fire of love in whose light we cease to understand the word "I," there lies something beyond our being which at these moments moves across it, and we are thus possessed for a heartfelt longing for bridges between here and there.

Thus,

> It is love alone that can bestow on the soul, not only a clear, discriminating and self-contemptuous view of itself, but also the desire to look beyond

> itself and to seek with all its might for a higher self as yet still concealed from it.[2]

Here love appears to be the power that, like none other, is capable of lifting us beyond ourselves, of inspiring self-forgetting and self-transcendence. Experienced in this light, love seems to carry with it a promise of what Nietzsche sometimes calls transfiguration: a wholesale transformation of oneself and of the world.

Yet this view of love is exactly what Nietzsche set out to dismantle in the writings of his Free Spirit trilogy, where he relentlessly insists (in a deliberate indictment of the whole Schopenhauerian-Wagnerian worldview) that human psychology is fundamentally and ineradicably "egoistic," so that even love must be understood in "selfish" terms—that is to say, as an extension of self-concern, not as an instrument of self-transcendence.[3] Moreover, when Nietzsche first sketched the character of the Free Spirits in *Human, All Too Human*, he remarked that they would maintain a wary distance from others, which could very well make them appear "poor in love."[4]

Nevertheless, love appears in a new light in the landmark work that succeeded the Free Spirit trilogy, *Thus Spoke Zarathustra*, whose title character is practically defined by his great capacity for love. The work begins with Zarathustra descending from his solitary mountain home in order to engage with the great swath of life, a descent that he explains in these terms: "I love human beings." In the remainder of the text, Zarathustra speaks at length about the nature of his love, observes the need for love in others, and, at the end of book 3, sings of his love for life (personified as a woman) and the eternity within which he lives.[5] Zarathustra's statements are too complex and variegated to admit any simple summary. But it is certainly fair to say that the self-transcending and intoxicating aspects of love articulated in Nietzsche's early writings are given powerful voice once more through his Zarathustra (and in a manner that is certainly capable of intoxicating the reader as well).

Even so, in the writings of his final year, Nietzsche offers some of his most explicitly "egoistic" and "debunking" statements concerning the power of love: "Love is the state in which man sees things most of all as they are *not*. The illusion-creating force is there at its height, likewise the sweetening and *transfiguring* force."[6]

Any assessment of Nietzsche's thought must, then, come to terms with his understanding of love: how exactly should his final position on the subject be characterized? And to what extent did his position change over the course of his career? Did Nietzsche definitively reject the self-transcending, intoxicating view of love from *Human, All Too Human* onward? Or did he find new reasons to appreciate that point of view (as *Thus Spoke Zarathustra* may reflect)? These are the questions that I examine in this chapter.

One major difficulty should be acknowledged at the outset: any attempt to address Nietzsche's view of love must ultimately deal with *Thus Spoke Zarathustra*—which, as I have already indicated, contains Nietzsche's most extensive statements on the subject, but also by far his most opaque. The opacity derives partly from *Zarathustra*'s dense and poetical literary style, but also from the simple fact that in this work Nietzsche never speaks in his own name. As a result, any attempt to deal with *Zarathustra* is liable to get bogged down in questions about the extent to which the title character can be fairly associated with Nietzsche. In view of this difficulty, I suggest that we may approach *Zarathustra* most profitably if we approach it only secondarily—as a point of comparison, after having examined the mature Nietzsche's thoughts on love, as they are delivered in his own name. As it happens, the best place to undertake that examination is the one place that has been least frequently considered: *The Case of Wagner*.

The Case of Wagner is an especially valuable text for several reasons. In this essay, Nietzsche gives his own definition of love, and contrasts it with a whole series of competing understandings. Nietzsche is led to this reflection naturally, since the subject of the essay is Wagner, and love was a leading theme of Wagner's operas. Moreover, a major task of the essay is to explain Wagner's contribution to Nietzsche's own development as a thinker. Indeed, in *The Case of Wagner*, the great composer proves to be a perfect foil for Nietzsche: Wagner's development as an artist contrasts with Nietzsche's evolution as a philosopher in an especially revealing way, as we will now see.

THE CHALLENGE OF WAGNER

No single figure is such a pervasive and prominent presence in Nietzsche's oeuvre as Richard Wagner (with the possible exception, at least in later writings, of Zarathustra and the "character" of Nietzsche himself).

This point is not difficult to demonstrate. In the first place, Wagner's name appears in the title of three of Nietzsche's works: *Richard Wagner in Bayreuth* (a celebration of the composer written in 1875 and published the next year as the fourth of the *Untimely Meditations*);[7] *The Case of Wagner* (written between April and August 1888); *Nietzsche contra Wagner* (a compilation of modified excerpts from earlier writings that Nietzsche put together in December 1888). Moreover, Nietzsche's first book, *The Birth of Tragedy Out of the Spirit of Music*, was an extended tribute to Wagner. And even after the break with Wagner, the composer's name appears in every work that Nietzsche wrote (with the exception of *Thus Spoke Zarathustra*).[8]

In one respect, Wagner's significance for Nietzsche is easy to explain: as we have already seen, the break with Wagner precipitated the major "crisis" of Nietzsche's career, setting him on the path to independence that began with *Human, All Too Human*. To that extent, Wagner (and all that he represented) was what Nietzsche defined himself *against*. But it would be a mistake to take Nietzsche's assessment of Wagner as altogether negative, or merely debunking.

It is true that in his later writings Nietzsche's remarks on Wagner are highly polemical, but they are also interspersed with notes of appreciation. Thus, in the preface to *The Case of Wagner* Nietzsche remarks, "Wagner is merely one of my sicknesses"—but then he adds, "Not that I wish to be ungrateful to this sickness." He explains himself as follows:

> When in this work I assert the proposition that Wagner is *harmful*, I wish no less to assert for whom he is nevertheless indispensable—the philosopher. Others may be able to get along without Wagner: but a philosopher is not free to do without Wagner. He has to be the bad conscience of his age,—for that he needs to understand it best. But for the labyrinth of the modern soul, where would he find a leader more initiated, a more eloquent herald of the soul, than in Wagner?

In other words: a philosopher always has to overcome his time—which, for a modern philosopher, will have to entail overcoming Wagner, a figure in whom modernity is encountered in an especially revealing and challenging form.

As this suggests, for Nietzsche the value of Wagner cannot be assessed in an entirely straightforward way. Wagner is an ambiguous phenomenon, of a piece with the ambiguity of modernity as a whole. Nietzsche points to this ambiguity with a playful remark: "I understand perfectly when a contemporary musician says, 'I hate Wagner, but I cannot stand any other type of music.'" The suggestion here seems to be something like this: Wagner's music has readily identifiable failings that mark its inferiority to other forms of music, but, at the same time, it possesses distinctive virtues that give it an unusual sort of hold over the listener—and those virtues somehow make music that is undoubtedly superior to Wagner in many respects nevertheless seem obsolete or unsatisfying by comparison. At the least, we can say that, in Nietzsche's estimation, Wagner is abhorrent and admirable all at once.[9]

This is the curious character of Wagner's artwork for Nietzsche: it is, in some sense, definitely bad, yet it remains, in some way, deeply compelling. In this regard, Wagner's achievement is not only of a piece with modernity as a whole, it also reflects, in particular, the cultural impact of Christianity. Wagner's greatest significance for Nietzsche may be the way in which the composer re-presented and revivified, for a late-modern audience, central features of Christianity.[10] Nietzsche found that Wagner and Christianity both warp modern people's ability to accurately view the human soul, while simultaneously revealing new and intriguing depths of that same soul. This is the challenge that Nietzsche brings out in *The Case of Wagner*, and it bears especially on the question of how to understand love—for Christianity is, as Nietzsche notes in several places, the "religion of love."[11]

In *The Case of Wagner*, the challenge that the German composer represents is treated in an especially instructive way by the first four sections of the essay, where Nietzsche opposes Wagner to the French composer Georges Bizet. Comparing the two artists provides Nietzsche with a platform for addressing (albeit in a very compressed and somewhat elliptical way) the nature of love.

THE DEFINITION OF LOVE

In section 1 of the essay Wagner is only mentioned briefly, and then only in contrast to the main focus of the section: Bizet—and, in particular, Bizet's opera *Carmen*, which Nietzsche describes listening to in somewhat rhapsodic terms.[12] The contrast that is established here clearly elevates the French composer above Wagner.[13] Only in section 2 does Nietzsche explain his preference for Bizet more concretely, by emphasizing Bizet's superiority to Wagner in a specific respect: Bizet's understanding of *love*. The relevant passage reads as follows:[14]

> Finally, love, love that has been translated back into *nature*! Not the love of a "higher virgin"! No Senta-sentimentality! But love as fatum, as *fatality*, cynical, innocent, cruel—and precisely in this it is *nature*! Love, whose means is war, whose basis is the *deadly hatred* between the sexes!

This may be one of the most important statements in Nietzsche's entire oeuvre.

Indeed, Nietzsche draws this statement to the attention of his readers by quoting it in his autobiography, *Ecce Homo*: "Did anyone have ears for my definition of love? it is the only one worthy of a philosopher—war in its means, its basis in deadly hatred between the sexes" (*EH* book 5). The suggestion that the definition of love at issue here is "the only one worthy of a philosopher" also appears in *The Case of Wagner*, just a few lines after the definition of love. We will come to that suggestion in due course, but for present purposes we can simply note that by insistently framing his understanding of love in these terms ("the only" understanding "worthy of a philosopher"), Nietzsche raises the stakes of the discussion: he suggests that to understand philosophy as he understands it, one must understand love as he does. If that is what is at issue here, then no attempt to grasp Nietzsche's thought as a whole can afford to overlook his definition of love.

Although Nietzsche makes his definition of love difficult to overlook, some readers will still prefer to overlook it. The difficulty for many readers will be that Nietzsche's statements on love are bound up with one of the most jarring aspects of his writings: his remarks on relations between the sexes, and on women more generally.[15] In this area Nietzsche's remarks frequently seem as crude as they are deliberately obnoxious (particularly in his later writings). As a result, Nietzsche has sometimes been taken for a simple misogynist (in the literal sense of a "hater of women").[16] At the least, it is difficult not to take him for a chauvinist (a partisan of men, over and against women), since he often sharply differentiates between male and female traits, and ostensibly sides with the former while denigrating the latter. Nietzsche's rhetoric in this regard presents real difficulties, and I think that it is in many ways ill-judged (and at times indefensible). Nevertheless, it is important to grasp that there is a *rhetoric* at play here: when examined closely, Nietzsche's chauvinism turns out to be somewhat more apparent than real (he initially seems to be more on the "side" of men than he actually is, as we will have an occasion to observe in the discussion that follows).[17] At the same time, Nietzsche is convinced that relations between men and women are a natural source of struggle and conflict—and he wants to force readers to face up to that conflict, as facts of love and of life. Nietzsche's intentionally offensive rhetoric is meant to serve that end, but a (somewhat) less obnoxious position lies beneath that rhetoric. Moreover, one does not have to choose between accepting Nietzsche's remarks uncritically or dismissing them altogether. One can, instead, approach them in the spirit he once recommended to a correspondent:

> It is absolutely unnecessary, and not even desirable, for you to argue in my favor: on the contrary, a dose of curiosity as if you were looking at an alien plant, with an ironic resistance, would strike me as an incomparably more intelligent attitude towards me. (Letter to Carl Fuchs, July 29, 1888)

All of which is to say that although there is an understandable impulse to overlook these passages in Nietzsche's writings, I do not think that one should overlook them on the basis of a belief that dwelling on them can only serve to lend credence to expressions of simple prejudice: to the contrary, paying careful attention to these passages undermines much of their seemingly simple prejudice. Here, as elsewhere in Nietzsche's writings, his position is more nuanced than it seems at first.

The degree of nuance at play is indicated by the fact that, with just a few artful strokes in sections 2 and 3 of *The Case of Wagner*, Nietzsche offers the reader a whole series of different understandings of love that can be compared with his own. I will work through each of those understandings in turn. But first we should consider one of the most striking features of his definition of love: its relationship to nature.

LOVE AS NATURE

Nietzsche's definition of love is, at the same time, a definition of nature: "love as fatum, as *fatality*, cynical, innocent, cruel—and precisely in this it is *nature*!" The theme of nature needs to be emphasized here, in the first place because Nietzsche himself emphasizes the term. In fact, in the passage where Nietzsche gives his definition of love, he places *nature* in emphasis each time that he employs the term.[18]

Nietzsche had given a closely related definition of love two years earlier, in a passage that states the equation of love with nature even more directly. That passage appears in book 5 of *The Joyful Wissenschaft*. The central aphorism of that book (aphorism 363) is titled "How Each Sex Has Its Own Prejudice about Love." It contrasts a female understanding of love as devotion or faithfulness with a male understanding of love as "possession." With that contrast established, Nietzsche turns to observe:

> I do not believe one can get around this natural opposition through any social contracts or with the best will to justice, desirable as it may be not to remind oneself constantly how harsh, terrible, enigmatic, and immoral this antagonism is. For love, when one considers it in its perfect, wholly developed state, is nature, and nature is eternally "immoral."

"Love is nature": but nature understood as "immoral." This understanding of nature is echoed and elaborated throughout Nietzsche's writings, but perhaps most prominently in aphorism 9 of *Beyond Good and Evil*:

> Think of a being such as nature, wasteful without measure, indifferent without measure, without purposes and considerations, without mercy or justice, fertile and barren and uncertain at the same time; think of indifference itself as a power—how *could* you live according to this indifference? Living—is that not precisely wanting to be different than this nature?

Since Nietzsche says here that nature is "indifferent" in the sense of acting "without purposes and considerations," we can infer why (in the passage quoted previously), when he referred to nature as "immoral," he placed that word in scare quotes—because the immorality is how nature appears from a human point of view (it is something that we can experience as "harsh," "cruel," and so forth), rather than being something intrinsic to nature itself (it is in itself amoral, or beyond good and evil).

When Nietzsche refers to love/nature, then, he has in mind a power capable of shaping human desires and ends, but which does not *serve* them. The world has necessities, but it does not have purposes, aims, or intentions (see *GS* 109). And it is in this sense that love/nature can be a *fatum*, or fatality—it is something that happens to us, for good or for ill, rather than something we can control or make demands of.

What Nietzsche has in mind here may seem more clearly applicable to our experience of the natural, physical world (with its earthquakes, droughts, and diseases) than to our experience of love. After all, love is in many respects the opposite of indifference: it is, among other things, a form of human caring (and to that extent very much part of "living"). And Nietzsche is well aware of this aspect of love. Here we can recall again the words with which Zarathustra explains his engagement with the world: "I love human beings." But this aspect of love, which begins the journey of Zarathustra, is precisely *not* what Nietzsche begins with in *The Case of Wagner*. Instead, his initial emphasis is on love as an aspect of nature, rather than of human concerns, and as an aspect of nature love is "fatum, *fatality*, cynical, innocent, cruel"—beyond good and evil.[19] To put this point another way: Nietzsche speaks of "love that has been translated back into nature" (into nature's amorality and indifference), not of nature that has been translated into love (into love's human caring and moral purpose).[20]

That being said, it should also be noted that since Nietzsche refers to "love translated back into nature," he implies that nature is not what is most immediately accessible to us, as if there is work that needs to be done (the work of "translation") if we are going to be able to recognize love for what it is. If that is the case, then understanding love as a piece of nature is a *task* for the reader.[21] And it may be for this reason that Nietzsche follows his definition of love by discussing (or alluding to) a series of competing understandings, which Nietzsche knows that readers are likely to find more intuitive (and more worthy of approval or sympathy), even if those understandings are less "natural" in his sense.

It should be clear by this point that Nietzsche's understanding of what is natural is not prototypically classical, because he does not view nature in teleological terms, as an ordered whole that gives human life a special place and sense of meaning; but neither does he view nature in prototypically modern terms, as something mechanistic, predictable, and subject to human control. His account of love, as an aspect of nature, is at odds with either picture, as we will see.

For Nietzsche, then, our access to nature is obstructed, but nature is not simply inaccessible: we have an insight into nature through our experience of love (that is, through our human nature). Yet that experience needs to be properly reflected on and interpreted—and, to that end, Nietzsche offers Bizet's *Carmen* as a valuable tool, which can assist the reader in the task of recovering love in the natural sense that he has proposed ("as fatum, as *fatality*, cynical, innocent, cruel," or beyond good and evil).

We can add that the procedure Nietzsche suggests here (looking to works of art that powerfully portray, evoke, and compel reflection upon, the basic human passions, for the window they provide onto nature) is fitting for the conception of philosophy that he calls for quite prominently in another text, namely, a philosophy that makes the "demand" that

> [p]sychology again be recognized as the queen of the sciences, for whose service and preparation the other sciences exist. For psychology is now once again the path to the fundamental problems. (*BGE* 23)

And for Nietzsche, love is an essential subject for any philosophic psychology, since love (or, more broadly, eros) opens up a basic fault line in human experience: on the one hand, erotic attachments are not something that individuals deliberately *choose* (we cannot simply decide whom or what to love, or when to fall in or out of love, and we can be surprised or even commandeered or "led around" by the force of our erotic attachments);[22] yet those attachments do express or reflect something fundamental about what we take to be *choiceworthy* (what it is that we find lovable, what we value and care for, what we associate ourselves with, what we are willing to sacrifice for).[23] In other words, the power of eros is experienced in a way that is intensely personal, but not in a way that is susceptible to being determined (or even necessarily deliberated over) by the individuals who are subject to it.[24] Because the experience of love has this self-transcendent aspect, it can lead us to question how we are (or ought to be) oriented toward whatever lies beyond our individual selves. Nietzsche raises that issue by associating love with both "fate" and "nature," and by directing us to *Carmen* he helps us to recognize different ways in which the issue can be addressed.

LOVE AS FATALITY

Love "as fatum, as *fatality*, cynical, innocent, cruel" has hardly ever been articulated and brought to life in a more striking way than by Bizet's *Carmen*. This is especially true of the famous song that introduces the heroine, her "Habanera." In his copy of the opera score, Nietzsche wrote next to the "Habanera": "*Eros* as the ancients sensed him" (*Eros, wie die Alten ihn empfanden*).[25] Thus, *Carmen* as a whole, and the "Habanera" in particular, can be considered as an inlet to the somewhat foreign view of love that Nietzsche wants to make modern readers familiar with. Reflecting on the opera can help us to think through what is at issue in Nietzsche's definition of love.

We can begin by noting that, for Nietzsche and for *Carmen* alike, love is a "fatality" in a specific sense: it is an aspect of the power of nature that cannot be mastered or even fully comprehended, and it operates without concern for the interests and intentions of individuals. In other words, our experience of love reminds us of all that lies outside our control, and thereby of the limits set to human powers.[26]

The "Habanera" introduces the view of love that is dramatized by the opera as a whole. Love, Carmen sings, is beyond the power of any person, it cannot bend to their will, or simply serve their interests, it is not to be reasoned with, it is not rational, it is not subject to any law, it retains its hold on us even while being indifferent to our intentions.[27] Throughout the opera, Carmen embraces this understanding of love, claiming that by living in accord with it she is free—which for her does not mean being wholly unencumbered, but, rather, being subject only to fate.[28]

Carmen's freedom is reflected by her life as a Gypsy, where she lives without many social conventions or other ordinary attachments (such as family).[29] In act 1 of the opera, she takes an interest in Don José, a young soldier who is very much attached to his family and his home. His view of love is quite different form hers. From the outset, he sees their love as a promise, as involving loyalty and reciprocity[30]—precisely the attributes that her "Habanera" had denied that love was capable of. José had heard her song, but he persists in his understanding of love to the end, insisting that he and Carmen are bound together until death.[31] José abandons his duties and neglects his family in order to follow Carmen, but she quickly grows bored with him, turning her attention to the bullfighter Escamillo. In the opera's final scene, José finds Carmen and attempts to convince her that their love can be rekindled; when she denies it, he kills her.

Since Don José's conception of love is linked to an expectation of loyalty and reciprocity, when it is not satisfied, it becomes an angry desire for punishment.[32] Insofar as José asserts these criteria of loyalty and reciprocity, and insists on punishment when those criteria are not met, his language of love shades into a language of justice (of a particular, and particularly punitive, sort). José is too confused to articulate or understand his own motives clearly,[33] but his confusion is made clear enough to the audience, and his declarations, although in some respects conflicted, nevertheless evince a consistent desire to find some way to control his love with Carmen, by making her affections bend to his will (whether through persuasion or through threats).

For her part, Carmen may appear foolhardy, but she is certainly more clear-sighted than José, and she does not arrive at her end blindly. In act 3 she plays a fortune-telling game, where she learns that her fortune is death, linked to José's. This discovery is marked by a famous chord, next to which Nietzsche noted on his score: "Bizet's fatalistic music."[34] Carmen does indeed face her discovery in a fatalistic spirit, viewing death, like love, as a power outside human control, a challenge to be faced up to, but which cannot be avoided or manipulated.[35] As a result, although Carmen is disturbed to hear of her death, she is not exactly daunted by it. In her final confrontation with José, she seems to accept the possibility of death as a necessary consequence of her commitments: "Jamais Carmen ne cédera! / Libre elle est née et libre elle mourra!" (Carmen will never give in! / Free she was born and free she will die!), and, then, declaring to José about her affair with Escamillo, "Je l'aime, et devant la mort même, / je répéterai que je l'aime!" (I love him, and before death itself / I will repeat that I love him!]).

Notwithstanding Carmen's rebuke to Don José, there is little reason to conclude that she has found a "true love" with Escamillo that will prove to be more enduring than her affair with José. We can easily believe that Carmen will ultimately tire of Escamillo, just as she has tired of José. Escamillo seems to be well aware of this. In act 3 he remarks: "Les amours de Carmen ne durent pas six mois" (The loves of Carmen don't last past six months). That thought is entirely consistent with the sentiment of the "Habanera" that had introduced Carmen.[36] Accordingly, when facing death, Carmen not only refers to her love for Escamillo but, even more, she affirms her commitment to her sense of her freedom, that is, her determination to be subject to nothing more than fate—which means, in part, following the desires of her heart, but also being subject to death.

For Carmen, then, love is one part of a broader fate allotted to her—a piece of nature, as it were, along with death, beyond human control. Don José, by contrast, approaches love as something to be controlled, and hopes that he can reason with it, threaten it, or otherwise make it conform to his will, and he is ready to take revenge on it when it does not. In the end, however, he has vengeance without true control: in the opera's last moments, a crowd envelops José as he stands over Carmen's lifeless and loveless body, and we recall the fortune that predicted not only her death, but his along with it. By showing us the futility of José's quest for control, Bizet suggests that to see love as José does leads one to become destructive both to others and to oneself. Love, as Carmen says, follows no law, and to demand that what is fundamentally irrational make itself conform to reason is the very height of irrationality.[37]

To this extent, at least, Bizet's masterpiece vindicates the understanding of love that Carmen had first expressed in her "Habanera"—while also illustrating that, as Nietzsche would have it, love so understood ("as fatum, as *fatality*") is indeed "cruel," "harsh," "terrible," and "immoral."

LOVE AS POSSESSION

Bizet's *Carmen*, then, illuminates Nietzsche's definition of love not least of all through the figure of Carmen herself. To begin with, Carmen articulates a view of love as a power indifferent to human purposes and "beyond good and evil," and as a result she adopts a certain kind of "fatalism," which recognizes (without finding any cause for comfort in) the limits set to human life and human powers, including the ultimate limit represented by death.[38]

I do not think that Nietzsche's interest in *Carmen* can be understood without taking these features of the work into account (and his notes on the score—highlighting the depiction of eros in the "Habanera" and the "fatalistic music" of the fortune-telling scene—testify to this point). Nevertheless, in *The Case of Wagner* his discussion does not deal with the figure of Carmen herself. Instead, he focuses on the figure of Don José, whom we therefore need to consider at greater length.

Immediately after his statement regarding the "deadly hatred between the sexes," Nietzsche writes as follows:

> I do not know any case where the tragic joke that constitutes the essence of love is expressed so strictly, is formulated with so much terribleness [*schrecklich*], as in Don José's last cry, which brings the work to an end.

Then he presents Don José's final words in the following way:

> Ja! *Ich* habe sie getödtet, / *ich*—meine angebetete Carmen!
> (Yes! *I* have killed her, / *I*—my beloved Carmen!)

This is a paraphrase of Don José's lyrics, which read as follows in the libretto:

> Vous pouvez m'arrêter. / C'est moi qui l'ai tuée! / Ah! Carmen! ma Carmen adorée!
> (You can arrest me. / I was the one who killed her! / Ah! Carmen! My beloved Carmen!)

The significance of the change that Nietzsche makes here is indicated by the word that he has Don José utter twice, and places in emphasis each time: "*ich.*"[39] Don José's love for Carmen is an expression of self-assertion, of an "I" over another.

Having reframed Don José's words in this way, Nietzsche adds a comment: "Such a conception of love (the only one worthy of a philosopher) is rare: it raises a work of art above thousands." The great puzzle of this section of the text is to determine what exactly Nietzsche means by this remark. Can it be that a philosopher loves in a manner akin to Don José? Or if not, why would it be so important for a philosopher to understand love as represented by José? Nietzsche does not explain himself. Instead, what he does next is explain why those who are *not* philosophers ("all the world," he says) "misunderstand love":

> They believe one becomes selfless in love because one desires the advantage of another human being, often against one's own advantage. But in return, they want to *possess* that other person.

Here, then, we have a direct contrast: on the one hand, Don José, who represents love as an expression of self-assertion; on the other hand, "all the world," who understand love as selflessness. Insofar as a philosopher is to be associated with the position of José, philosophy seems to be associated with an assertion of the self (the importance of the "I") and a denial of selflessness.

But presumably this point could be made without appealing to the murderous passion of Don José. Assuming, then, that Nietzsche's choice of example is dictated by something more than a taste for the macabre, why would the passion of José be especially instructive for one who wants to understand love in what Nietzsche has suggested is a properly philosophic manner (as "selfish" rather than selfless)?

An answer to this question may be suggested if we focus for a minute on how Nietzsche characterizes the widespread misunderstanding of love as "selfless." This position has two striking features. First, Nietzsche describes that position as universal: it is characteristic of "all the world" to misunderstand love in this way. Second, this misunderstanding of love is a form of self-deception (those who love in this spirit "believe" that they are selfless, although they are mistaken). If these are both basic features of human psychology (the feeling of selflessness, and the self-deception that it involves), then it must follow that a philosopher could not be one who had never *experienced* love-as-selfless—rather, a philosopher would have to be one who had disentangled themselves from the self-deception entailed in that experience.

To see how this sort of disentangling might occur, consider that the experience of love is naturally divided or conflicted in the following way: on the one hand, it is common for lovers to become somewhat self-forgetful, and enraptured, when beholding the object of their love, and that self-forgetting is intensified when their love is returned. On the other hand, when an expression of love is rejected or ignored, the lover will be shocked back to a stronger sense of self (whether by being moved to question their own worth, or by demanding that it be recognized and rewarded by the beloved). So in love we seem to be capable of vacillating between a kind of ecstatic self-forgetting (when our desires are kindled or reciprocated), and a frustrated sense of self (when our desires are thwarted). This, I believe, explains why Nietzsche makes the paradigmatic case of love the *unrequited* lover—because it is specifically in the case of an unrequited lover that the self-forgetting intrinsic to love gives way to a heightened sense of self.

Because *Carmen* shows us so vividly what desire looks like when it is frustrated (because it focuses our attention on the psychology of the unrequited lover, through the character of Don José), Nietzsche was able to judge that the opera brings to light the true motives and concerns of love—above all in José's last words, which (especially in Nietzsche's rephrasing) expose the passionate sense of self, and the impulse to self-assertion, that are present even in love. I take it, then, that what Nietzsche admires in the final scene of *Carmen* is not the angry passion of Don José himself, but, rather, the way in which the character's example exposes crucial features of human psychology that we otherwise might be inclined to hide from ourselves, but which Nietzsche thinks are essential for a philosopher to come to terms with.[40]

We can add that Don José is an especially revealing case because his love for Carmen is never wholly requited at all—his expectations from her are frustrated almost from the start (although their relationship disintegrates more and more as the opera proceeds). Thus, as we have seen, for Don José love is articulated to an unusual degree as a matter of self-concern (of reciprocity and loyalty, with a concomitant threat of punishment), or almost as a matter of justice, rather than a matter of self-sacrifice. And because José believes that he has justice on his side, he believes that he is entitled to punish Carmen when she does not reciprocate his love.[41]

Nietzsche makes clear that the righteous demand for reciprocity and the concomitant threat of punishment are both at issue in the conception of love represented by Don José, by adding the following remark:

> Even God does not constitute an exception at this point. He is far from thinking "what is it to you if I love you?"—he becomes terrible [*schrecklich*] when one does not love him in return.

So the love of God, like the love of Don José, is a demand placed onto a beloved by a lover—and in each case the lover becomes *terrible* when the demands of his love are not met. This image certainly calls to mind the punitive gods of the Greeks—but also the God of the Old Testament, who loves and promises to become terrible if not loved in return (Ezekiel 16:38; see also *GS* 141). In either case, however, the love of God is understood on the model of the human passions—and, to that extent, it represents a "pagan" affirmation of life, rather than a Christian transcendence of it.[42]

As this last observation implies, Nietzsche's remark regarding the "terrible" love of God does more than just emphasize the passionate, punitive nature of love-as-possession. The remark also subtly suggests why this conception of love is especially "worthy of a philosopher," by contrasting it with a very different conception. Let me explain.

LOVE AS DISINTEREST

With the same stroke that Nietzsche points to divine love as passionate, possessive, and punitive, he also points to a rival understanding. Here again is the relevant remark:

> Even God does not constitute an exception at this point. He is far from thinking "what is it to you if I love you?"—he becomes terrible when one does not love him in return.

The phrase that Nietzsche quotes here ("What is it to you if I love you?") is taken from the autobiography of Goethe.[43] In the original context, Goethe describes being inspired by a remark from Spinoza's *Ethics* (part V, proposition XIX), where the philosopher asserts that to truly love God one must not expect to be loved in return. Goethe comments that what struck him about this (and every other) sentence that he encountered in Spinoza was the "boundless disinterestedness" it reflected. As a consequence, Goethe writes, "[t]o be disinterested in everything, and most of all in love and friendship, was my highest desire, my maxim, my constant practice"—and so he coined the motto that is quoted by Nietzsche ("what is it to you if I love you?") in order to express the ideal of a love that asks for nothing in return.

Here, then, we have a view of love associated with a philosopher—and not just any philosopher, but Spinoza, who is sometimes taken as the paradigmatic modern philosopher. And it is a view of love that Nietzsche has just stressed is absolutely incompatible with his own: to imagine oneself disinterested, or unselfish, in love is to fundamentally misunderstand the phenomenon. But although the "Spinozist" view of love is a delusion, we know from the *Genealogy* that Nietzsche recognized it as a delusion common among philosophers, who often strive to see the world "without interest" (*GM* III.6). And in that context Nietzsche had stressed that philosophers who speak of being free of interest are vulnerable to being made use of as quasi-mystical sources of support for artists and theologians (as Spinoza was indeed used by the Romantic movement in the eighteenth century).

To be sure, Nietzsche himself compares the love of Don José to the love of God. But, as I suggested earlier, Nietzsche's comparison is most intelligible as referring to a (roughly speaking) "pagan" God—that is to say, a divinity whose love reflects all too human desires and passions (one who is possessive and punitive, demanding and jealous)—rather than the Christian God, whose love is supposed to transcend human passions. Thus, where Spinoza points toward the ideal of a God who, like the Christian God, is free from the desire for requital,[44] Nietzsche would rather have philosophy model itself on precisely the unrequited lover, that is, the lover who is admittedly and even demandingly concerned with his own good.

To that end, Nietzsche concludes section 2 of *The Case of Wagner* by offering the reader a maxim from Benjamin Constant: "Love is of all the sentiments the most egoistic, and, as a consequence, when it is wounded, the least generous." "This saying," Nietzsche comments, "remains true among gods and men." In this way, Nietzsche concludes by stressing that the experience of the unrequited lover (an experience that is essentially universal) remains the most accessible and compelling piece of evidence regarding the self-interested or egoistic core of love.

To summarize: Nietzsche's point is that "the only conception of love worthy of a philosopher" is one that forces us to recognize and accept the reality of the all too human passions. Since philosophy has so often been misunderstood or misrepresented as involving the transcendence of the passions, Nietzsche stresses their value as the indispensable raw material for philosophy.

CHALLENGES FOR UNREQUITED LOVERS

For Nietzsche, then, Bizet's image of the unrequited lover is worthy of a philosopher because the human passions are worthy of philosophy. To draw out the full significance of this point, we may digress for a moment by reflecting on the role the unrequited lover plays in Nietzsche's larger body of work.

The image of the unrequited lover appears prominently in *Daybreak*, and I think that it is key to understanding what is distinctive about Nietzsche's position in that work and its successor, *The Joyful Wissenschaft*. Two of the most instructive scholarly commentaries on these writings—by Marco Brusotti and Paul Franco, respectively—conclude that *Daybreak* and *The Joyful Wissenschaft* represent a new stage in Nietzsche's Free Spirit project. But Brusotti and Franco understand that evolution somewhat differently: Brusotti emphasizes that these writings move beyond *Human, All Too Human* because they incorporate passion into philosophy, and specifically a "passion for knowledge" that is modeled on Stendhal's analysis of the passion of love;[45] Franco, while granting the broad outlines of Brusotti's argument, contends that Brusotti nevertheless understates the degree of moderate detachment and self-control that is carried over into these writings from *Human, All Too Human*.[46] In my judgment, both of these interpretations identify authentic elements of Nietzsche's position, and they can be considered complementary, if one takes into account that the model of passion that Nietzsche brings to philosophy in these works is that of the *deliberately* unrequited lover—a posture that requires passion and restraint to work in tandem. Let me spell out this thought further.

In a crucial passage of *Daybreak* titled "The New Passion," Nietzsche reflects on the consuming power the *"drive for knowledge"* has for "us" today:

> Restless discovering and divining has such an attraction for us, and has grown as indispensable to us as is to the lover his unrequited love, which he would at no price relinquish for a state of indifference—perhaps, indeed, we too are *unhappy* lovers! Knowledge has in us been transformed into a passion which shrinks at no sacrifice and at bottom fears nothing but its own extinction. (*D* 429)

This impassioned spirit certainly moves beyond the cold-eyed debunking of *Human, All Too Human*—but it still stands in need of some moderating detachment, because the power of the passion that Nietzsche describes derives in part from the fact that it is *unrequited.*[47] It comes as no surprise that the defining passion of *Daybreak* is an unrequited one, since only a few aphorisms earlier Nietzsche had plainly declared, "The cure for love is in most cases still that ancient radical medicine: requited love" (*D* 415). This last thought is made most vividly in an aphorism that presents a "fable" about the "Don Juan of Knowledge," who is driven inexorably forward in the pursuit of knowledge but is unable to love what he learns, and so is eventually compelled to enter into a self-lacerating embrace with pain and disillusionment (*D* 327). Nietzsche's fable echoes a passage from Stendhal, who contends that the successful seducer Don Juan is ultimately in a worse position than Goethe's passionate but perennially frustrated Werther, because Don Juan's conquests leave him miserably jaded instead of genuinely satisfied.[48] So Stendhal and Nietzsche agree that being lovelorn is preferable to being love*less* (and, to that extent, they are both capable of writing in an impassioned spirit).[49] But neither author's position is a conventionally "romantic" one: Nietzsche follows—and intensifies—Stendhal's analysis of how the passion of love falsifies reality, generating deceit and self-deception.[50] Each author is therefore compelled to stake out a delicate (and perhaps rather awkward) position: less naive than Werther, more hopeful than Don Juan. In Nietzsche's case, this means presenting a philosophy that is driven by an invigorating passion for knowledge (see *GS* 123), while retaining an unsentimental awareness of the deluding and frustrating character of the passions (see *D* 543), and therefore resisting their full consummation (thus my suggestion that Nietzsche here adopts the somewhat eccentric position of a *deliberately* unrequited lover).[51]

This situation changes in Nietzsche's next work, *Thus Spoke Zarathustra*, whose title character sets out to bestow his love, and who claims to find a genuinely fulfilling (and not disillusioning) manner of doing so through the teachings of the will to power and the eternal return. But although those teachings are occasionally intimated in *Daybreak* and *The Joyful Wissenschaft*, they are not directly presented or named, and to that extent the passions that are stoked here remain more restrained than they will be in *Zarathustra*.[52] This is to say that, on the one hand, *Daybreak* and *The Joyful Wissenschaft* differ from *Human, All Too Human* in that they bring passion into philosophy, but, on the other hand, they differ from *Thus Spoke Zarathustra* in that they leave ambiguous how (and even whether) that passion can be fulfilled.[53] In that context—suspended between the "no-saying" of *Human, All Too Human* and the would-be world-transformative teaching of *Thus Spoke Zarathustra*—the appeal of a deliberately unrequited love is that such a love is able to be passionate without falling prey to the delusions and disillusionment that it identifies in so many love affairs.

On the basis of these somewhat digressive remarks, we can understand why the image of the unrequited lover was such an important one for Nietzsche: it suggests how philosophers might relate to their passions. But we are also now in a position to conclude (returning to the main thread of our discussion) that while the passion of Don José might be instructive *for* a philosopher, it cannot be the passion *of* a philosopher. That is because Don José, in all his righteous and punitive fury, cannot even attempt to reconcile himself to being an unrequited lover (let alone find any reason to celebrate that predicament, as Nietzsche and Stendhal both recommend). By contrast, the philosopher as unrequited lover is passionate but not possessive, self-concerned but not controlling (consider *D* 552). To be sure, given Nietzsche's preference for the notion of love as possession over that of love as disinterest, a philosopher might well understand the passion of José as a truer and, *to that extent*, a healthier, image than one that denies the primacy of self-concern in love. But this is only a beginning for philosophy, not an ending: a philosopher's manner of loving is ultimately closer to (although not identical with) that of Don José's victim, Carmen.[54]

I will return to this last claim in due course. For present purposes, however, let me acknowledge that Nietzsche's treatment of Don José in *The Case of Wagner* presents the reader (at least initially) with a rather less nuanced picture of the unrequited lover than the one I have just sketched out. But that treatment is, to reiterate, a beginning and not an ending. Let me, therefore, turn back to *The Case of Wagner*, in order to follow Nietzsche's argument through to its end.

LOVE AS PARASITISM

Nietzsche's whole treatment of love as possession has a certain polemical one-sidedness (it makes that conception of love seem more self-evidently accurate than it is). One indication of this is Nietzsche's declaration that the maxim of Benjamin Constant (to the effect that love is the most egoistic of the sentiments) "remains true among gods and men." Nietzsche must have known that he was overstating the case here, since in innumerable other places he stresses that the reigning God is one who denies (or claims to transcend) the human passions, rather than reflecting them[55]—and so long as that is the case, Nietzsche's egoistic premises, and the understanding of philosophy that he advocates on that basis, will remain open to challenge.

At this point in *The Case of Wagner*, then, Nietzsche has made plain enough to the reader what conception of love he *prefers*, but he has not adequately addressed the alternative understanding. But this is just the purpose that is served by the discussion of Wagner that follows the encomium to Bizet—for Wagner represents what "remains" of the (self-transcending, self-sacrificial) ideal that is most opposed to Nietzsche's own. Understanding Wagner, and all that he represents, therefore proves to be essential to any true understanding of the world, in general, and of the human capacity for love, in particular.

Nietzsche alludes to the importance of this contrast when he gives his definition of love in section 2 of the essay. In the midst of giving that definition, he admonishes readers, "No Senta-sentimentality!" This refers to the heroine of Wagner's *Der fliegende Holländer*, who sacrifices her life for her beloved. Nietzsche wants us to see that, although "Senta-sentimentality" (sacrificial love) is an illusion, it is an illusion that artists (above all Wagner) have been tempted by, and have in turn made alluring to others. Nietzsche makes a derisive comment about such artists:

> Man is a coward, confronted with the Eternal-Feminine—and the females know it.—In many cases of feminine love, perhaps including the most famous ones above all, love is merely a more refined form of *parasitism*, a form of nestling down in another soul, sometimes even in the flesh of another—alas, always decidedly at the expense of "the host"!

Love as parasitism is ultimately not fundamentally different from love as possession: both are means through which one partner makes use of the other for their own ends.

Both of these "egoistic" aspects of love are portrayed vividly by Bizet. As we have seen, in *Carmen* Don José represents love as possession; Carmen, we can now add, to some degree reflects the notion of love as parasitism (she initially seduces Don José partly in order avoid being taken to jail—where he winds up after helping her to escape). This may explain why Nietzsche says that the opera represents love as a "war," fueled by "deadly hatred between the sexes": because it presents us with a conflict between the passions of self-seeking lovers that culminates only in death.

This last thought leads us to another level of the contrast between Bizet and Wagner: nothing in *Carmen* encourages the audience to hope that the passions and conflicts that love engenders, or their fatal result, can be transcended—they are facts of life to be confronted, not something to be eliminated or escaped. To that extent, we can say that Nietzsche offers Bizet as a kind of tonic to brace us against precisely the sort of hopes that Wagner made it virtually his entire mission to inspire: namely, the thought that life's passions or conflicts can in some way be eliminated or escaped—and that this is made possible, above all, by the self-forgetting or self-sacrificial power of love.

It would not be unfair to say that Wagner's operas are in large measure a reflection on "the power of love": a reflection on what the force of love is capable of accomplishing, its effect on individuals and on the world. As a result, Wagner represents and articulates a whole constellation of possibilities, of human hopes and longings, that are not dramatized by Bizet. Nietzsche's discussion will help to bring out just how much Wagner's operas are consumed by concerns that are practically absent from Bizet.[56]

I have already suggested that Nietzsche uses his discussion of Bizet partly in order to indicate the superiority of a "pagan" to a "Christian" worldview for a philosopher. The discussion of Wagner elaborates on this point, by using Wagner as a representative of Christianity. But the discussion of Wagner does something more than this as well, since it carries its own, distinct lessons for a philosopher (as Nietzsche had promised in the preface). These lessons are twofold: first, the case of Wagner shows how the "Christian" outlook develops within, and becomes attractive to, the human soul, including a philosophically inclined soul; second, Nietzsche uses his own example to show the proper philosophic response to that predicament.

To that end, we should note that Nietzsche's discussion of Bizet actually concludes by alluding to a difficulty with the French composer, while acknowledging the relative attraction of Wagner. Here is the relevant statement, which Nietzsche uses to mark the transition between his discussion of Bizet and his treatment of Wagner:

> But you do not hear me? You prefer even Wagner's *problem* to Bizet's? I, too, do not underestimate it, it has its magic. The problem of redemption is certainly a venerable problem. There is nothing about which Wagner has thought more deeply than redemption: his opera is the opera of redemption.

With these words, Nietzsche admits (albeit in a muted way) that there is a *problem* present in Bizet just as there is in Wagner—and that Nietzsche is himself capable of sharing some common ground with the reader who "prefers" Wagener's problem to Bizet's. Now, Nietzsche never makes explicit exactly what Bizet's problem *is*. However, he does plainly state Wagner's problem—it is the problem of redemption—and that problem turns out to be Nietzsche's major concern for the remainder of the essay. Perhaps, then, reflecting on that problem (and the reasons why it should not be "underestimated") will offer some insight into what Bizet's problem might be, by way of contrast.

LOVE AS REDEMPTION

Redemption may well be Wagner's fundamental problem, as Nietzsche says. We should immediately add, however, that it is not a problem that can stand on its own, to be understood independent of other concerns: redemption must be redemption *from* something. Nietzsche makes a remark that bears on this point when he explains Wagner's effect on his acolytes (including on the young Nietzsche): "What a clever rattlesnake! It has filled our whole life with its rattling about 'devotion,' about 'fidelity,' about 'purity,' and with its praise of chastity it withdrew from the *corrupted* world!" We might therefore characterize Wagner's outlook in this way: it reflects a desire to be redeemed from the "*corrupted* world."[57]

Nietzsche makes clear that for Wagner the mechanism of redemption is, in one way or another, love. We have already seen him make this point by identifying the prospect of redemption via the "eternal feminine" as a temptation or danger threatening "artists" and "geniuses." But he makes the point even more incisively by offering short, sardonic summaries of Wagner's mature operas, showing how each dramatizes an aspect of the problem of redemption—and that this involves, in a variety of ways, redemption through love.[58]

Nietzsche's summaries of Wagner's operas in section 3 of *The Case of Wagner* echo a similar set of summaries that he had given twelve years earlier, in the last section of *Richard Wagner in Bayreuth*. There he had introduced the summaries in a particularly revealing way:

> Only nature can enjoy genuine satisfactions and redemptions: unnature and false feeling cannot do so. If it should become aware of itself, unnature can only long for nothingness, while nature desires transformation through love: the former wants *not* to be, the latter wants to be *different*.

The summaries of the operas that follow this statement are meant to show how they each provide examples of just such "transformation through love" (although of course in this case Nietzsche offers the summaries with earnest admiration, as opposed to sarcastic contempt).

So from early on until the end of his career, Nietzsche identified redemption through love as Wagner's leading theme. This judgment of Wagner is entirely plausible at a general level.[59] At the same time, however, it is clear that exactly how Wagner understood the prospects for redemption through love changed considerably over the course of his career. *The Case of Wagner* shows how Nietzsche understood Wagner's evolution in this respect.

Nietzsche gestures toward Wagner's evolution at the end of section 3 of the essay, when he explains how Goethe characterized the threat facing all romantics—namely (in the phrase that Nietzsche attributes to Goethe), as "suffocating of the rumination of moral and religious absurdities," or, Nietzsche adds, "In brief: *Parsifal.*" Indeed, in his published writings Nietzsche consistently singles out *Parsifal* for special scorn, denouncing it time and again as Wagner's capitulation to Christianity ("Rome's faith without the text" is Nietzsche's often quoted comment on *Parsifal*).[60] But *The Case of Wagner* clarifies, as no other text of Nietzsche's does, that the "Christianity" of *Parsifal* was no aberration within the context of Wagner's career (it was not some late misstep or an unnecessary error on Wagner's part). It was (so to speak) the last gasp in a long-term process of asphyxiation brought on by the composer's "romantic" premises. More simply stated: *Parsifal* is the culmination of a crypto-religious tendency running throughout Wagner's entire life and thought.[61] And, in particular: the late Wagner's "religiosity" fulfills the fundamental goal of redemption through love that had animated Wagner from the start.

Nietzsche supplies the key to understanding Wagner's evolution in section 4 of the essay, which deals with the composer's *Ring* cycle. Section 4 begins this way: "I shall still relate the story [or "history": *Geschichte*] of the *Ring.*" To understand the significance of this "history," one needs to know that Wagner's *Der Ring des Nibelungen* is a series of four operas, a mammoth epic that the composer worked on for twenty-six years, spanning the lion's share of his mature career. So although Nietzsche comments exclusively on the *Ring* in section 4 of his essay, by focusing on that work, he in effect comments on Wagner's entire evolution.[62]

Nietzsche places the *Ring* in the context of Wagner's biography with this remark: "Half his life, Wagner believed in the Revolution as much as ever a

Frenchman believed in it." This is a weighted observation. The first half of Wagner's life is marked by the year 1848—the year when the wave of revolutionary enthusiasms that had first caught fire in France came to Germany. At that time Wagner was a deeply committed revolutionary:[63] a close reader of Ludwig Feuerbach (whose debunking treatment of Christianity had exerted a strong influence on Marx and Engels) and Pierre-Joseph Proudhon (the first self-described anarchist political thinker), and a friendly acquaintance of the continent-wide rabble-rouser Mikhail Bakunin. As a result, Wagner had been an enthusiastic supporter of the revolutions of 1848—and even a participant in the uprisings that occurred in Dresden in May 1849.

Wagner's first sketches for the *Ring* were made in the year before the Dresden uprising. Wagner's creation contains many layers, but the *Ring* saga has been fairly summarized as "a story of the 'twilight of the gods,' the end of the old regime that has ruled the world until now, so that it might be replaced by something better."[64] The engine for that transformation is the character of Siegfried, who Nietzsche notes represented "the typical revolutionary" for Wagner. Nietzsche elaborates on the significance of Siegfried this way:

> "Whence comes all misfortune in the world?" Wagner asked himself. From "old contracts," he answered, like all revolutionary ideologists. In plain: from customs, laws, moralities, institutions, from everything on which the old world, the old society rests. "How can one rid the world of misfortune? How can one abolish the old society?" Only by declaring war against "contracts" (tradition, morality). *That is what Siegfried does.*

The *Ring* is based on pieces of German mythology, but Nietzsche notes that in order to make Siegfried fit his revolutionary purposes, Wagner altered his sources in a number of ways.

In Wagner's hands, Nietzsche declares, Siegfried's "main enterprise" is to "redeem Brünnhilde." This remark refers to Siegfried's rescue of Brünnhilde, a Valkyrie goddess made human and imprisoned as part of a punishment by her father, Wotan, the king of the gods. Wotan's power derives from agreements that he records on his spear; Brünnhilde's crime is to violate those contracts due to her recognition of the superior claims of love.[65] Siegfried, meanwhile, is raised beneath the earth (so although he is human, he is not exactly of the world), and he holds its conventions in contempt. When Siegfried rescues Brünnhilde from her punishment, the two are united in their shared recognition of love as the only power worth respecting.[66]

While Siegfried and Brünnhilde are united in their rejection of the old order of the gods and their embrace of love, the question remains what the result of their love will be. That question is taken up by the last opera of the *Ring* cycle, *Götterdämmerung*. Nietzsche makes a schematic remark on the conclusion to the saga: "Siegfried and Brünnhilde; the sacrament of free love; the rise of the gold age; the twilight of the gods for the old morality—*all ill has been abolished*." But, a few lines later, he amends this remark: "Brünnhilde was initially supposed to take her farewell with a song in honor of free love, putting off the world with the hope for a socialist utopia in which 'all turns out well.'" But this is not actually how the *Ring* wound up concluding—as Nietzsche says, with laconic understatement, "now she gets something else to do."

Nietzsche's reference here is to the final scene of the *Ring*—the portion of the work that Wagner revised more than any other. It occurs shortly after Siegfried's death, in which he falls victim to the treachery of the world's power-mad schemes. In the final scene, Brünnhilde denounces Siegfried's traitors and proclaims her loyalty to him. In Wagner's earliest plans, Brünnhilde is then reunited with Siegfried in the home of the gods, and a more enlightened rule over the earth by Wotan is established. In later versions, Brünnhilde sets the world aflame, and jumps into the flames to be united with Siegfried in death. But Wagner had Brünnhilde explain her actions in several different ways. In an early version, Brünnhilde gives what Nietzsche calls her "song in honor of free love" (or what is more commonly referred to as the "Feuerbach ending"), in which she declares, "I leave behind me / a world without rulers"—a world to be ruled by love.

As Nietzsche indicates, however, Wagner ultimately rejected all of his more "optimistic" endings for the *Ring*. The world was not to be reformed, whether through the power of more enlightened rulers, or through the power of love. Nietzsche identifies Wagner's change of mind with his discovery of Schopenhauer's philosophy. This is true enough, but a word should be added about the biographical context for that discovery (a context that Nietzsche alludes to by his reference to the two halves of Wagner's life).

After the Dresden uprisings were put down, Wagner was forced into exile, where he would remain for over a decade. Thus, Wagner's political commitments led to expulsion from his country just as his operas had begun to find success, and during his exile he would struggle mightily with debts, as well as with his inability to consummate a passionate relationship with Mathilde Wesendonck (due to their respective marriages). During this painful period of exile Wagner would come to feel transformed by his discovery of Schopenhauer's philosophy, which explained to him how to make sense of the frustrations he had encountered.[67] Schopenhauer explained to Wagner that human beings are incapable of satisfying their natural desires and passions, so that life is *inherently* frustrating and human striving *inevitably* futile. This argument is what led Wagner to conclude that his revolutionary enthusiasms had been misplaced.[68] Wagner stated the implications of this realization in bracing terms:

> [Schopenhauer's] principal idea, the denial of the will to live, is of terrible seriousness, but it is uniquely redeeming. Of course, it did not strike me as anything new, and nobody can think such a thought if he has not already lived it. But it was this philosopher who first awakened the idea in me with such clarity. When I think back on the storms that have buffeted my heart and on its convulsive efforts to cling to some hope in life—against my own better judgment—, indeed, now that these storms have swelled so often to the fury of a tempest,—I have yet found a sedative which has finally helped me to sleep at night; it is the sincere and heartfelt yearning for death: total unconsciousness, complete annihilation, the end of all dreams—the only ultimate redemption![69]

In sum: Schopenhauer convinced Wagner that his hopes for reforming the world were futile, and that only escape from the world could bring redemption.

As a consequence, Wagner revisited Brünnhilde's final statement. He deleted the "Feuerbach ending" to the *Ring*, with its hope of a world renewed through the power of love, and wrote instead what is generally called the "Schopenhauer ending." In this version, Brünnhilde declares that "grieving love's profoundest suffering opened my eyes for me" [*Trauernder Liebe / tiefstes Leiden / schlosz die Augen mir auf*], so that, in setting the world aflame, "I depart from the home of desire / I flee forever the home of delusion," and by escaping that world she is delivered to another world "free from desire and delusion."[70] As this suggests, in Wagner's revised ending for the *Ring*, the experience of love can no longer redeem the corrupted world—but it still has an essential role to play in helping to direct us beyond the world.[71]

The importance of this point for Wagner is evident from the fact that, although he revised his position on redemption in light of Schopenhauer, at the same time he aimed to correct Schopenhauer on the issue of love. Schopenhauer viewed love as a basically negative force,[72] whereas Wagner was convinced that it was precisely in love, and the heartfelt devotion to another that it inspires, that we get a rare and precious glimpse of what it would be like to live free of our burdensome "individuality," and the frustrations of the will that come with it (this means that, for Wagner, love gives us access to the "noumenal" world that Schopenhauer believed to lie beyond our "phenomenal" world). For Wagner, then, erotic love can be fully consummated only in death, because death alone can preserve the state of deindividualized bliss that envelops two lovers in the heat of passion.[73] This is dramatized most fully in *Tristan und Isolde*, Wagner's most clearly Schopenhauerian work (which he wrote in the midst of completing the *Ring*). In this work the lovers long for, and are finally united in, death—Wagner's idea of a "happy ending."[74] *Tristan* is a crucial work because it dramatizes most fully the longing to resolve the problems of this world by escaping to *another* world—indeed, the opera's lovers sometimes invoke an afterlife in which they will be reunited (language that appears at times in the *Ring* as well).[75] *Parsifal* pushes this quasi-religiosity (or other-worldliness) a step further, by having redemption come from a "pure fool," that is to say, from a character (Parsifal) who is raised apart from and ignorant of the world, but who is enlightened by his compassion for the suffering of others, and whose love has a redemptive power because it is not contaminated by corporeal desires.[76] These operas simply tease out (albeit in extraordinarily rich ways) possibilities implied by the "Schopenhauer ending" to the *Ring*: namely, the thought that redemption *of* the world must be rethought as redemption *from* the world, and that the experience of love is the mechanism that inspires a longing for a world beyond our own (and even gives us a foretaste of that world, by giving us a temporary escape from our "individuality").

Nietzsche remarks on Wagner's revised ending for the *Ring*: "Everything goes wrong, everything perishes, the new world is as bad as the old." But Nietzsche stresses that this does *not* mean that Wagner had given up on redemption: "in all seriousness," he adds at the end of the section, "this [the Schopenhauerian ending to the *Ring*] *was* a redemption."[77]

Nietzsche elaborates this thought in a revealing way. He summarizes Wagner's evolution using the following terms: the discovery of Schopenhauer was, at first, Wagner's "shipwreck," that is, it seemed to discredit the revolutionary optimism of the *Ring*. But Wagner was able to rewrite the *Ring* in a way that made sense of that very impasse—by making the discovery of Schopenhauerian wisdom into "the *goal*, the secret intent, the true significance of his voyage."[78] To conclude this summary, Nietzsche adds a motto: *Bene navigavi, cum naufragium feci* ("When I suffer shipwreck, I have navigated well"). This Latin motto, which Nietzsche presents without translation or explanation, has a complicated provenance.[79] It is reported by Diogenes Laertius as the words of Zeno the Stoic, who coined the motto in order to characterize his good fortune at having suffered a shipwreck that left him stranded in

Athens, since it was in Athens that he discovered Socratic philosophy (upon which he would base the remainder of his life). This same motto is quoted by Schopenhauer, in a passage describing the universal appeal of notions of personal Providence, even among thinkers who are ostensibly "averse to all superstition," but who require a source of consoling meaning in the face of the frustration or misery they experience.[80]

Nietzsche's judgment is clear: Wagner was driven by a longing for redemption in the second half of his life no less than in the first half—but the later Wagner had discovered that the desire would have to be brought to fruition in a manner different from what he had originally anticipated. As a result, the experiences of the first half of Wagner's life are not disregarded, so much as they are reinterpreted—reinterpreted in Schopenhauer's terms, which showed Wagner that his earlier frustrations were not in vain, but that precisely in the disappointments and anguish they entailed, they revealed a different, and truer, source of redemption. To that extent, the words that Wagner wrote for Brünnhilde as part of the "Schopenhauer ending" to the *Ring* ("grieving love's profoundest suffering opened my eyes for me") could just as well have been spoken by Wagner himself. We may say, then, that Schopenhauer's gift to Wagner was to make his suffering appear *meaningful.*

Indeed, Nietzsche stresses that Wagner's artwork is driven by, responds to, and amplifies the human desire for "meaning"—and his work is "redemptive" for others precisely insofar as it appears to be *meaningful.*[81] Of course, Nietzsche indicts the whole Schopenhauerian-Wagnerian worldview for its attempt to bestow meaning on the world by embedding it (and particularly the fact of human suffering) within a transcendent order.[82] Nevertheless, Nietzsche was not insensitive to the experiences that led Wagner to look for meaning beyond the world: "Wagner is one who has suffered deeply—that is his *distinction* above other musicians. I admire Wagner wherever he puts *himself* into music" (*NCW* "Where I Admire"). The intense experience of suffering unites Nietzsche and Wagner. Nietzsche seems to comment on this in an oblique way by means of the Latin motto (derived from Zeno and commented on by Schopenhauer) that he employs to help explain Wagner. For, as we have seen, when the sources of the motto are taken into account, it suggests that in the experience of suffering all human beings are united, since it is not so obvious that even the most skeptically minded or philosophically inclined individuals can avoid being tempted by a "superstitious" response to their suffering (as in a providential interpretation of the events of one's life).[83] The inclination to make suffering "meaningful" in some cosmic or transcendent sense seems to be a pervasive temptation.

To be sure, in many (or most) individuals, these longings or tendencies will remain inchoate; Wagner is something of a unique case. But it does not follow that the case of Wagner should be taken as simply idiosyncratic or incongruous. To the contrary:

> One doesn't understand a thing about Wagner so long as one finds in him merely an arbitrary play of nature, a whim, an accident. He was no "fragmentary," "hapless," or "contradictory" genius, as people have said. Wagner was something *perfect*, a typical decadent in whom there is no trace of "free will" and in whom every feature is necessary. If anything in Wagner is interesting it is the logic with which a physiological defect makes move upon and takes step upon step as practice and procedure, as innovation in principles, as a crisis in taste.[84]

And this, I take it, explains why Nietzsche stresses so strongly that Wagner's operas all reflect his wrestling with the same fundamental problem, the problem of redemption. The case of Wagner shows how a certain orientation toward the world—one characterized by "the problem of redemption," which is at root the conviction that the *corrupted* world must be *corrected*—ultimately resolves itself in "Christian" terms (looking to *another* world to redeem this one).

THE CONTRAST BETWEEN BIZET AND WAGNER

As we have seen, Nietzsche offers us Bizet and Wagner as representatives of competing conceptions of love: love as possession versus love as redemption. At this point we can draw some broad conclusions about the comparison, beginning from the following observation: Bizet focuses our attention on the moment of unrequited love and dramatizes the passions it gives rise to; Wagner focuses us on the moment of consummated love and immerses us in the longing to extend that blissfulness infinitely. And Wagner, if made to respond to Bizet's depiction of love, might say something like this: it is true that the bliss of consummated love cannot be prolonged indefinitely, since our all too human nature always calls us back to our needy (selfish, individual) selves—but Bizet shows precisely what results from that fact, namely, the conflict, violence, and suffering that our passions generate. So for the promise of love to be redeemed, a transcendence of the world is needed, and thus in Wagner human mortality comes to appear as a new and hopeful beginning, rather than as a final ending. The contrast between Wagner and Bizet, therefore, appears most clearly from the fact that for Tristan and Isolde death is something to be longed after, whereas for Carmen the prospect of death is a source of foreboding (a harsh and unyielding fact of life to be faced up to, although not despaired over).[85] In other words, Bizet reflects and inspires an acute and invigorating awareness of the limits of human life; Wagner reflects and inspires a constant searching for and stretching toward some way beyond those limits.[86]

I have already stressed that, despite Nietzsche's elevation of Bizet above Wagner, he acknowledges that the attraction of Wagner must not be "underestimated." To see why that is, we might compare Nietzsche's argument in *The Case of Wagner* with the position that he had set out in *Human, All Too Human* (his declaration of independence from Wagner). As we saw in chapter 1, in the earlier work Nietzsche had assessed the emergence of religious belief in mainly instrumental or utilitarian terms: community cannot hold together without the support of morality, but morality needs to be fortified by religious belief in a divinity that is capable of rewarding and punishing human actions. On this view, religious belief is not something that one would arrive at freely and independently, but is, instead, largely inculcated into people as a kind of "false consciousness." By contrast, in *The Case of Wagner* we see "religiosity" emerging in a different way: not for narrowly utilitarian or instrumental reasons, and not as the result of confusion or indoctrination, but instead as the final and fully realized expression of primordial longings that emerge from the pain of suffering and the bliss of love—and, as a result, it cannot be expunged merely by debunking morality or rejecting communal authority.[87] Religion is more deeply rooted in human nature, in our natural experience of the world, than Nietzsche had suggested when first breaking with Wagner. This explains why, even though the critically minded ideal of the Free Spirit that Nietzsche constructed when breaking with Wagner may have helped to give him greater independence, nevertheless, the resolutely irreligious posture that it entailed may not have separated him as fully as he initially hoped from the challenge represented by Wagner (the quasi-religious hopes and longings that Wagner's artwork spoke to).[88] To that extent, *The Case of Wagner* proves to be something of a tribute to the authentic power of Wagner's art. Thus, in the first postscript to the essay, Nietzsche is able to make the following statement about *Parsifal*: "I admire this work; I wish I had written it myself; failing that, *I understand it*."

As we have seen, however, Nietzsche understands *Parsifal* as the final and necessary conclusion to a basic premise: namely, that the world is *corrupt*, and therefore *in need of* redemption. And it is just this premise that Nietzsche stresses must be rejected. This point is made most plainly in the first postscript to the essay, where Nietzsche proposes that the Wagnerian watchword "Redemption for the redeemer" (the last words of *Parsifal*) ought to be "corrected" to: "Redemption *from* the redeemer." Nietzsche thereby makes plain that although he "understands" the attraction of Wagner, and is able to sympathize with it, he also aims to reject Wagner root and branch, by putting an end to the search for redemption—a goal that can only be achieved through a change in orientation toward the world that one wants to be redeemed *from*. What such a change in orientation would require is suggested by Nietzsche's epilogue.

THE PHILOSOPHER SPEAKS UP

In the epilogue to his essay Nietzsche declares that he will now broaden his focus: instead of treating the narrow or personal problem of Wagner, "I will give my thoughts on what is *modern*." But the preface had made clear that the problem of Wagner was an aspect of that broader question (an aspect that would shed an especially revealing light on the broader question). So we are entitled to take Nietzsche's broader, didactic statement on "what is modern" as a framework that can be used to clarify his assessment of Wagner (and vice versa).

Nietzsche uses the epilogue as an opportunity to reintroduce a conceptual framework that he had first established in *Beyond Good and Evil*, and then elaborated in *On the Genealogy of Morality* (to which he refers the reader in a note to the epilogue). The framework involves an opposition between "*master morality*" ("Roman," "pagan," "classical," "Renaissance") and "the morality of *Christian* values and concepts" (in the earlier texts Nietzsche had referred to this as "slave morality"): "master morality *affirms* as instinctively as Christian morality *negates*." Then he makes the object of Christian morality's negation more precise: "it *negates* the world"; "'World' is a Christian term of abuse." It is obvious which side of this opposition Wagner represents.

Having outlined this opposition, Nietzsche adds a very striking remark: "These opposite forms in the optics of value are *both* necessary: they are ways of seeing, immune to reasons and refutations. One cannot refute Christianity; one cannot refute an illness of the eye." This comparison of Christianity to an eye illness might seem odd, intemperate, or simply in bad taste, until one recalls what Nietzsche had said in the preface: "Wagner is merely one of my illnesses." And this remark has a special resonance coming from Nietzsche, who makes "health" one of his primary themes, to a degree that hardly any philosopher had done before—and this as a consequence of the fact that Nietzsche's own life was defined by his struggles with his health as hardly any philosopher's had been before. And not the least of these struggles was with the illness of his eyes—a debility that had plagued him since childhood, which made reading and writing during his adult life often intolerably painful, and which he nonetheless suffered through as best he could in order to continue with his work.

Nietzsche reminds readers of these facts in his autobiographical writings of 1886 and 1888, and the argument of those writings illuminates what he has to say here, as we will see in some detail in chapter 5. For present purposes, however, let us focus on the hints that Nietzsche offers in the text at hand: since Wagner is "one of my illnesses," and since Wagner is on the side of Christianity, it follows that Christianity is akin to one of Nietzsche's illnesses (illness of the eye). If we take this suggestion in the most literal sense, then it implies a way to understand why "one cannot refute Christianity; one cannot refute an illness of the eye": Christianity cannot be "refuted," any more than illness can be, insofar as they both reflect or express some aspect of one's basic constitution (they are both "ways of seeing")—that is to say, insofar as they are both aspects of one's nature.

It might seem counterintuitive to characterize Christianity as "natural," because Nietzsche famously speaks of it as "anti-nature,"[89] but what he means by this is that Christianity desires (and teaches) something that is unnatural (negation or transcendence of the world). But the desire itself is a naturally occurring phenomenon—a particular way of processing and responding to the world, something that individuals are disposed to in varying degrees.[90] To that end, the epilogue contends that Christian dissatisfaction with the world is rooted in dissatisfaction with the self:[91] one finds oneself unable to affirm the world because one is unable to affirm one's self and one's experience of the world (the experience of an illness, for example, or one's suffering more generally).[92] The case of Wagner documents just this point: on Nietzsche's account, Wagner's evolution did not follow an arbitrary or accidental course—the "Christian" conclusion of *Parsifal* was the full realization of tendencies that characterized his entire career, the consequence of a particular experience of the world.

To characterize Christianity as a naturally occurring phenomenon, like the illnesses of one's physical constitution, by no means precludes opposing that phenomenon in a particular manner. Thus, Nietzsche's remark that "these opposite forms in the optics of value [master morality and Christian morality] are *both* necessary" is supplemented by this remark: "What alone should be resisted is that falseness, that deceitfulness of instinct which *refuses* to experience these opposites as opposites—as Wagner, for example, refused." In other words: rather than acknowledge the necessary tension between competing moralities, Wagner attempts to make such an opposition appear unnecessary; Nietzsche, by contrast, acknowledges the natural necessity of his illnesses while nevertheless opposing them.

But in what spirit did Nietzsche oppose his illnesses? In the preface, Nietzsche speaks clearly on this point:

> Wagner is merely one of my illnesses. Not that I wish to be ungrateful to this illness. When in this essay I assert the proposition that Wagner is harmful, I wish no less to assert for whom he is nevertheless indispensable—for the philosopher.

In the last lines of the epilogue (the last lines of the essay as a whole), Nietzsche echoes that sentiment: "The case of Wagner is for the philosopher a *windfall*[93]—this essay is inspired, as you hear, by gratitude." It is not enough, then, to oppose an illness such as Christianity or Wagner: if one wants to do so in a manner that affirms the world (rather than denies it), one must also be grateful to it, or affirm it, as a part of nature that can still be put into the service of one's own good (thus, Nietzsche stresses Wagner's benefit "for the philosopher," that is, the service that the encounter with his "antipode," the artist Wagner, did for himself as a philosopher).

So, precisely in order affirm the natural world, world-denying Christian morality must be understood (and affirmed) as an aspect of that world.[94] Thus, what Christianity sees (or claims to see) must be appreciated by and integrated within the vision of one who today wishes to affirm the world.[95] Nietzsche's position is, then, distinguished from *both* "master morality" and "Christian morality," because it is able to acknowledge the necessity of *both* to its own constitution.[96] Thus, at the end of the epilogue, Nietzsche stresses: "<u>all</u> of us have, unconsciously, involuntarily in our bodies values, words, formulas, moralities of *opposite* descent—we are, physiologically considered, *false*." But this fact, he adds, is one to be analyzed, not lamented—it is, as he says, "*most instructive*," before concluding with his expression of gratitude to Wagner. As this suggests, the "gratitude" that Nietzsche finds is due to his illnesses is gratitude for what they have contributed to his *understanding*.[97] It is from this vantage point (that of those who find satisfaction in coming to understand themselves and their world) that an "illness" may be judged to have performed a service, and even be indispensable, "for the philosopher."

CONCLUDING REMARKS

For the philosopher, then, the lesson of *The Case of Wagner* proves to be twofold: on the one hand, philosophy must turn against the search for redemption from the world that characterizes Christianity, and modernity as a whole, as exemplified by Wagner; on the other hand, precisely in order to accomplish this, a philosopher must not judge that the world is so corrupt as to be *in need of* redemption. This means that those who exhibit the need for redemption must be subjects of the philosopher's gratitude, and must not be judged to have so corrupted the world, or be so at odds with the way the world "ought" to be, as to render that world any less worth affirming—or, indeed, any less lovable.

It is not, then, only Wagner's conception of love as redemption that must be found wanting. The conception of love as possession (represented by Bizet's Don José) must also be judged inadequate. I have already suggested that when Nietzsche elevates that conception of love above Wagner's, he exaggerates and overstates the case. Now I think that we are in a position to grasp both the most important virtue of, and the primary problem with, love as possession: on the one hand, it is admirably focused on the natural human passions, rather than seeking to deny them; on the other hand, in its desire for possession or control, it fails to affirm the world as it is, and to that extent constitutes a denial of the world. Notwithstanding all of their differences, then, love as possession and love as redemption overlap in a crucial respect: they are both ways of trying to make the world *different*, in order to satisfy desires that cannot be satisfied. This is why I suggested earlier that a philosopher must ultimately love in a spirit closer to (though not identical with) that of Bizet's Carmen, and her articulation of love as fatality, since that spirit is closer to loving the world as it is, rather than as the lover would wish to make it.[98] The challenge that Nietzsche leaves for the reader is, then, to determine whether such love is truly *possible*: can the world be loved for what it is, just as it is?[99]

That being said, when Nietzsche directs the reader's attention to the conceptions of love as possession and love as redemption, he does so not only to indicate their shortcomings, but also for a more positive purpose, since both must be reckoned with *if* the world is to be loved as it is, for both are part of the makeup of our world and of ourselves. The first conception is a fate allotted to all human beings (as a consequence of our natural passions); the second is a fate allotted at least to all modern human beings (as a consequence of the triumph of a particular moral worldview, which has a natural source, even if its power is felt more strongly now than in other eras). Both these forms of love must be experienced and come to terms with.

It is just this sort of reckoning, or quest, that Nietzsche has depicted for us with the odyssey of the title character of *Thus Spoke Zarathustra*. Indeed, the problem of Zarathustra is related to the problem of Wagner, since both are depicted by Nietzsche as (at least would-be) "founders" or "creators"—and to that extent they both explore a problem, or perspective, which goes far beyond the (merely critical, negating or destructive) task of Free Spirits of *Human, All Too Human*.[100] Thus, *Zarathustra* proves to supplement and enrich the position staked out in *Human, All Too Human*, by showing us a character for whom love is a motive to be acted upon (through a project of creative founding), rather than something to be resisted (as it is for the Free Spirits—who therefore remain confined in *Zarathustra* to a skeptical and sterile solitude, as we shall now see).

CHAPTER FOUR

The Project of World-Transformation in *Thus Spoke Zarathustra*

No reader of Nietzsche can reasonably ignore *Thus Spoke Zarathustra*. To begin with, Nietzsche made the work impossible to ignore by referring to it in wildly extravagant terms (for example: "Among my writings my *Zarathustra* stands alone. With it I have given humanity the greatest gift it has ever been given" [*EH* Foreword 4]). The work itself contains the most explicit and extended treatments of Nietzsche's two famous doctrines (the will to power and the eternal return)[1], as well as passages of exceptional poetic brilliance. But it is also Nietzsche's most unusual, and frequently bewildering, work.

The strangeness of *Thus Spoke Zarathustra* was highlighted by the very first commentator on the work: its author himself, in a letter to his publisher of February 13, 1883. There Nietzsche described the work as "a 'poem,' or a fifth 'gospel,' or something else for which there is no name yet." Five years later he raised another possibility: "[*Zarathustra*] may perhaps be counted as music" (*EH* TSZ 1). These remarks are all somewhat playful (as Nietzsche's use of scare quotes and "perhaps" indicates). But they are not entirely misleading: *Zarathustra* really does read like a mixture of philosophy, poetry, prophecy, and a political manifesto all at once. And more recent commentators have recognized that this combination of characteristics is key to understanding the work, because although the text presents crucial elements of Nietzsche's philosophy, it does so through a fictional narrative whose protagonist takes on the role of a prophetic lawgiver (on the model of Zoraster, Moses, Saint Paul, or Muhammad).[2] The work thereby explores at length the project of a *founder* or *creator*: one who establishes the "horizon" within which a large community of human beings live from that point onward.

I say that *Thus Spoke Zarathustra* "explores" the project of a founder or creator because that project is not static: Zarathustra's self-understanding *evolves* over the course of the work. Through the unfolding of the drama, Nietzsche is able to cast the title character's founding project in both its best possible light and a more critical light, and this obviously raises serious questions about just how much Nietzsche identifies with Zarathustra.[3] However, I will defer those questions until the next chapter of this study (where I will examine Nietzsche's retrospective assessment of the work). In this chapter, I will focus on the narrower question of how Zarathustra understands his founding project—and I focus on that question in order to highlight how Zarathustra's self-understanding constitutes an advance beyond the outlook characteristic of earlier stages of Nietzsche's career (in which the leading figures were, initially, Wagner, and then the Free Spirit). To that end, there are three key points to be made:

- First, Zarathustra's project fundamentally differs from that of the Free Spirits. The Free Spirit project is in the first place one of self-cultivation; Zarathustra's project is (or begins as) one of cultivating broader human community. This difference is reflected in the fact that the Free Spirits seek solitude, whereas Zarathustra is drawn out of it.
- Second, the motivating force that draws Zarathustra out of solitude is at each stage his defining trait of *love*. Zarathustra's love is not a romantic love that finds satisfaction in a particular person, but a kind of neediness that requires others for its fulfillment (others whom it can benefit through its creative activity). The drama of Zarathustra consists of Zarathustra's attempt to fulfill this need (or determine whether it *can* be fulfilled).[4]
- Third, what causes Zarathustra to wrestle with how (or whether) his need for love can be fulfilled is that he has determined that it must be made compatible with truth. Zarathustra's understanding of what exactly that would entail evolves over the course of the drama.

This last point is key to grasping how, in *Zarathustra*, Nietzsche not only revisits the creative founding spirit that he first encountered in Wagner, but also recasts it. For, by joining the motive of love to the insistence on truth, Nietzsche is able to show how a project of creative founding can be brought around to a recognition of the insights presented in *The Case of Wagner*: namely, that such a project must move beyond the longing for redemption, and that this must be done by reconciling oneself to the world as it is (which is to say, not within one's power to reshape at will). What I offer here is, then, not a comprehensive commentary on *Thus Spoke Zarathustra*, but rather an outline of how the work goes beyond Wagner by virtue of the truth, and beyond the Free Spirit by virtue of love.

The comparison between Zarathustra and the Free Spirit is raised within the work itself, where the Free Spirits are mentioned and alluded to in a variety of ways (and in ways that bring to the fore their difference from Zarathustra with regard to solitude and love), as we shall see. However, the comparison with Wagner requires more background information, since it is not made explicitly within the work.[5] Nevertheless, its significance for the work can be understood in light of how the young Nietzsche understood the Wagnerian enterprise, and particularly the interrelation of love and illusion in that enterprise, to which I now turn.

WAGNER AND THE PROBLEM OF THE CREATOR

In discussions of Nietzsche and Wagner, attention is often focused on Nietzsche's assessment of *Parsifal*, or the *Ring*, or *Tristan und Isolde*. In a way this is understandable, because Nietzsche makes prominent (and important) references to those operas. But the work of Wagner's that he was most familiar with was actually *Die Meistersinger von Nürnberg*. Nietzsche became seriously interested in Wagner around the same time that he was appointed to the faculty at the University of Basel. During this period he described *Die Meistersinger* as "my favorite opera"; he often played the score for friends, and he attended several performances of the work (whereas he never actually saw complete performances of the *Ring* or *Parsifal*, and only a few of *Tristan*). Nietzsche's enthusiasm for the opera resulted in his being introduced to Wagner (who was curious to meet the young professor who had become such an advocate for the work).[6]

Nietzsche's interest in *Die Meistersinger* is reflected in the writings of his Wagnerian period: he quotes from the opera in his first book, *The Birth of Tragedy Out of the Spirit of Music* (where the reference appears very prominently, in paragraph 2 of section 1), and then again in *Uses and Abuses of History for Life* (the second of the *Untimely Meditations*). In each case Nietzsche cites almost the same point from the opera. The significance of these citations cannot be grasped without some knowledge of the opera (after all, at the time Nietzsche was writing in large part for fellow Wagnerians, who would have known the work well). For readers who are not familiar with the work, the following brief summary should suffice.

Die Meistersinger is set in sixteenth-century Nuremberg, where the young knight Walther arrives and aims to win the hand of Eva through his victory in a singing contest held by a local guild of master singers. The leader of the master singers is Hans Sachs, a local cobbler and poet, who engineers the union of Walther and Eva. Sachs teaches Walther to modify his passionate, free-form love songs in order to hew more closely to the traditional rules that the master singers have established for judging performance. Walther hates the rules established by the masters, and he yearns to find freedom by fleeing from the town with Eva. Sachs explains to Walther that young lovers sing with the passionate ignorance and bliss of spring, but that youthful passions wane with the hardships of fall and winter; the masters' art provides a form and discipline that enables men to continue to sing of love even as they suffer life's hardships. At the same time, Sachs must demonstrate to the guild that, when suitably controlled, Walther's innovative brilliance can enrich their traditions. To do this, Sachs must stoically relinquish his own love for Eva, while deftly manipulating the passions of the townsfolk. This last point proves to be key: because Sachs is uniquely free of the oppressive force of his own passions, he can direct those of the other characters. Through the course of the plot Sachs realizes that, when left to their own devices, the villagers will be overwhelmed by the ubiquitous power of "*Wahn*"—illusion, or madness. Early in act 3 Sachs delivers a monologue that begins "*Wahn! Wahn! Überall Wahn!*" and concludes that, since the power of *Wahn* cannot be escaped, he will have to "guide the madness," putting *Wahn* into the service of "noble works."

Sachs elaborates on this point in the next scene. He tells Walther, who has just awakened, that he should sing of what he has been dreaming, since "the poet's task is to mark and record his dreams," which are the source of our "truest illusion" (*wahrster Wahn*). Emboldened by this, Walther sings passionately, and then Sachs modifies Walther's passionate expressions to fit them within the rules of the master singers. The scheme succeeds: Walther wins the hand of Eva with the song, and Sachs has thereby shown how *Wahn* can be manipulated for the benefit of his beloved town.

Die Meistersinger can initially appear somewhat out of place in the Wagner canon. It is a sort of "romantic comedy," while none of his other operas is even remotely lighthearted; it is his only opera that does not feature any deaths or supernatural elements; its characters are ordinary people, not epic heroes. But *Die Meistersinger* is not an anomaly. Wagner wrote it along with *Tristan und Isolde*—that is to say, after his discovery of Schopenhauer, and before completing the *Ring*. And Wagner actually makes *Tristan* and *Die Meistersinger* refer to one another: in act 3, after Eva suggests to Hans Sachs that she might be willing to marry him, Sachs demurs, explaining that he knows the tale of Tristan and Isolde (and at this point Wagner has strains from that opera filter into the scene), and he wants to avoid the fate of King Marke, the older man to whom Isolde was betrothed, but whom she could not really love.[7] So Sachs is the one character in the opera who is familiar with the Schopenhauerian wisdom of *Tristan*—that is why he alone in the opera sings of the Schopenhauerian theme of *Wahn*. But precisely because Hans Sachs understands the illusions of love, he can manipulate them in others, and craft a world in which the illusions of love persist. Yet there is a difficulty with this resolution, which Wagner indicates at the end of the opera, when Sachs tries to induct Walther as a master singer, and Walther emphatically rejects the honor, proclaiming, "I would be blessed without being a master," while he (in Wagner's stage directions) "looks tenderly at Eva." Thus, Sachs has shown that *Wahn* can be manipulated so that others are able to live under the illusion of love—but is his own life, free of that illusion, one worth living? This is the problem of the founder or creator as it appears in Wagner.[8]

When Nietzsche refers to Hans Sachs in his early writings, he shows that he is aware of both Sachs's major task as a founder or creator (the manipulation of *Wahn* for the benefit of others), and the problem to which it gives rise (whether there is any satisfaction for the creator who manipulates the illusions of others—or whether such a life must be loveless, precisely because it has been disillusioned, while love requires illusion).

Thus, in section 1 of *The Birth of Tragedy*, Nietzsche comments that, according to Lucretius, it was in dreams that human beings first apprehended the superhuman, and adds that, if asked about "the secret of poetic procreation," Lucretius would have echoed Hans Sachs in saying that "the poet's task is to mark and record his dreams," and to interpret them, since they are the source of our "truest illusion" (*wahrster Wahn*). This is not meant as a criticism on Nietzsche's part: his position in *The Birth of Tragedy* is that life in general, and culture in particular, requires illusion and myth. Hans Sachs is, then, practically his first authority for this key point—and appropriately so, since the purpose of the essay is to exalt Wagner as the creator of a new, life-giving myth. That being said, the way in which Nietzsche frames this point implies that a most delicate balance has to be upheld: for it is not just any old illusion that the poet or creator works with here, but, rather, the "truest illusion."[9] By employing Wagner's notion of a "*wahrster Wahn*" so prominently, Nietzsche provokes one to ask: is it possible to speak of a "true" illusion unless one is somehow under its spell? The answer, I think, must be no—and that answer is suggested by what Nietzsche says in the next passage where he appeals to the words of Hans Sachs.

In section 7 of *Uses and Disadvantages of History for Life*, Nietzsche writes:

"It is only in love, only when shaded by the illusion [*Illusion*] produced by love, that is to say in the unconditional faith in right and perfection, that man is creative." On this basis, Nietzsche is able to make a remarkable claim: "he who destroys the illusions in himself and others is punished by nature," that is, condemned to a life of misery and stultification. The lesson, writes Nietzsche, is that

> [a]ll living things require an atmosphere around them, a mysterious misty vapor; if they are deprived of this envelope, if a religion, an art, a genius, is condemned to revolve as a star without atmosphere, we should no longer be surprised if they quickly wither and grow hard and unfruitful. It is the same with all great things, "which never succeed without some illusion [*Wahn*]," as Hans Sachs says in the *Meistersinger*.

This makes plain the early Nietzsche's assessment of the problem of the founder or creator: the founder/creator must manipulate the illusions of others, and, to accomplish this, he must to some degree be able and willing to become intoxicated by those illusions himself, as can occur under the influence of love. For the early Nietzsche, then, a creator can have love *or* truth, not both. But this conclusion is brought into question by *Thus Spoke Zarathustra*, which revisits the project of the founder or creator, but does so in order to determine whether it can join together love and truth.

ZARATHUSTRA'S LOVE: THE GREAT MIDDAY

The action of *Thus Spoke Zarathustra* consists of a series of attempts by its title character to teach human beings the meaning of their existence, while his own understanding of that meaning evolves in the process. Zarathustra's attempts at instruction are framed by his repeated retreats to and descents from a solitary existence on a mountain where his understanding develops in ways that are initially only alluded to rather than depicted or detailed. Solitude is, therefore, essential for Zarathustra, but at first (and for the largest part of the work) we see mainly Zarathustra's departures from solitude. And at the outset of the work Zarathustra makes clear that his fullest satisfaction is not to be found in solitude.

In the work's first few lines, where Zarathustra descends from his mountain, he asks of the sun whose overflowing illumination had sustained him in his solitude for ten years: "What would your happiness be, were it not for those for whom you shine?" Having ripened to the point of overflow himself with the benefit of the sun's sustenance, Zarathustra has become "overburdened with my wisdom," and so his happiness now depends on bestowing the fruit of that wisdom upon recipients who may benefit from it. Having grown tired of his solitude in this way, "Zarathustra wants to become human again" (in other words, Zarathustra is here exhibiting not just an idiosyncratic trait, but a constitutively human one—the need and the desire for others). As Zarathustra makes his journey back to society, he meets an old holy man in the forest, who cannot understand why Zarathustra is leaving his solitude. Zarathustra explains to the old man: "I love human beings." The old man is unimpressed, explaining that he himself went into the forest "because I loved human beings all too much": "Now I love God: human beings I love not. The human being is for me too incomplete an affair. Love of human beings would be the death of me." This remark inspires Zarathustra to make a second statement, modifying his first: "What did I say of love! I bring human beings a gift." The old man remains skeptical, and as the two part ways, Zarathustra says to himself: "Could it be possible? This old man in the forest has heard nothing of this yet, that *God* is *dead*!" The old holy man and Zarathustra have, then, this much in common: they are both moved by great love. In the old man's case, so much so that he had to stop loving human beings, since he found them to be so "incomplete" that, by loving them, he could only frustrate himself, and as a result he has redirected his love toward God.[10] Zarathustra does not have this option, as his remark to himself makes clear.[11] That is why he tells the old man that he is bringing human beings a gift: for the gift will not negate his love for human beings, but, rather, make it possible to fulfill that love by *making human beings worthy of his love*.[12]

The gift that Zarathustra brings to human beings, we learn a few lines later, is his teaching about the "Superhuman" (also sometimes translated as the "Overhuman": the *Übermensch*). Zarathustra speaks to the first crowd of people that he encounters this way: "*I teach you the Superhuman*. The human is something that shall be overcome. What have you done to overcome it?" This declaration clarifies the character of the love that led Zarathustra to return to society: he brings human beings a gift, but his gift to them is at the same time a demand placed on them. Human beings are not lovable, but they can and must make themselves so.[13] To that end, Zarathustra speaks to the people as follows, in section 3 of the prologue:

> Verily, a polluted stream is the human. One must be a veritable sea to absorb such a polluted stream without becoming unclean. Behold, I teach you the Superhuman: it is this sea, in this can your great despising submerge itself.

Thus, when Zarathustra tells the crowd that "the Superhuman is the meaning of the earth," this suggests that the Superhuman is what redeems the earth. Zarathustra's great capacity for love is, therefore, closely related to his great capacity for contempt. He loves what is able to correct, or redeem, that which inspires his contempt: "I love him who justifies those to come in the future and redeems those gone in the past."[14] In order to inspire just this sort of contempt among the assembled crowd, Zarathustra tells them of the repellent "last human," who does not know great contempt, and thus cannot experience great love, and so is incapable of transforming himself. The fate of this speech is complex: it has had the effect Zarathustra intended (generating revulsion at the prospect that modern society might be tending toward the generation of "last humans") among quite a few readers of *Thus Spoke Zarathustra* (most prominently, Max Weber),[15] but within the work itself the effect of the speech is very different: it is an abject failure, which leads the assembled crowd to exclaim their enthusiasm for becoming last humans, rather than overhumans. Zarathustra recognizes his failure, concludes that his solitude has left him ill equipped to mobilize the masses, and determines that he will have to move his operations to the margins of society, where he will cultivate a few select companions—and, even more important, where he will be able to observe and reflect anew on what moves and motivates human beings.[16] Zarathustra's initial denunciation of the modern world, therefore, leads him not so much to an antimodern project as to a reflection on *how* and *whether* such a project *could* become possible.[17] Zarathustra is compelled to reflect anew on what moves and motivates his own engagement with human beings, and to reconsider the spirit or the manner of his engagement with them—that is to say, to reconsider the spirit and manner of his love.[18]

This is not to say, however, that Zarathustra returns to solitude, or that his "gift" for human beings becomes any less central to his activity. To the contrary, a band of disciples grows up around Zarathustra, and at the end of part 1 Zarathustra delivers the culmination of his teaching for them: "a bestowing virtue is the highest virtue."[19] In his speech "On the Bestowing Virtue," Zarathustra makes clear that it is his own, defining virtue, which he understands as expressive of "the will of a lover" and identifies with "power" (thereby intimating thoughts that are elaborated in part 2's teaching on "the will to power").[20] Zarathustra also likens his virtue to the sun, and his use of the metaphor expands on his description of the sun in the prologue. A sun, for Zarathustra, has a need to shine forth over and shape others, though it does not need others in order to shine (in other words, its power does not depend on others, but its happiness does).[21] As this suggests, Zarathustra's virtue is dependent and independent in different ways: independent with regard to its power (which is produced internally), but dependent with regard to the conditions of its happiness (which is produced through its external relations with others). The sun's relations to others need not be "personal," however: it can benefit those over whom it shines even without having a particular, individual concern for (or even knowledge of) all those on whom it sheds its light.[22] Accordingly, while Zarathustra's project is designed to benefit the whole of humanity, it has by this point deliberately eschewed direct relations with the majority of human beings. Yet Zarathustra does still manifestly care for a specific group of others: his disciples, whom he instructs to put their "bestowing love" into the service of the earth (rather than turning away from it), and, to that end, direct their activity toward bringing about the Superhuman. Zarathustra, therefore, concludes his speech "On the Bestowing Virtue" by promising to return to his disciples when he is able to celebrate with them the "Great Midday" at which "the sun of his knowledge" will stand at its peak.[23]

In part 1, then, Zarathustra seems to succeed where he had failed in the prologue: he was unable to instruct the crowd, but he is able to deliver his message to a select circle, and he is, therefore, able to return to solitude, leaving the work that he has begun in the hands of others. But this solution makes his solitude even more difficult to bear, because now Zarathustra is deeply invested in hopes for a future that he has left for others to bring about. As a result, part 2 of the work begins with Zarathustra "full of impatience and desire for those whom he loved," and concerned that his teaching has been distorted and lies in danger. Zarathustra appears to be gripped by concern for the wider world even more strongly now than he was in the prologue, and so his love draws him down from his mountain once again: "A lake is within me, solitary and self-contained; but the river of my love draws it off—down to the sea!"[24] On his new expedition, however, Zarathustra will be less occupied with delivering teachings to disciples than with explaining, and exploring, his own self-understanding.[25] And, as a result, in part 2 Zarathustra not only elaborates further what is distinctive about his sort of wisdom, he now also reveals the distinctive challenges that it must wrestle with.

ZARATHUSTRA'S WISDOM: THE WILL TO POWER

The key discussion of Zarathustra's wisdom in part 2 occurs over a sequence of five chapters: "On the Famous Wise Men," "The Night-Song," "The Dance-Song," "The Grave-Song," and "On Self-Overcoming." This sequence begins with a speech addressing representatives of pseudo-wisdom, and ends with a speech addressed to "the wisest"; in between these two speeches are three songs, through which Zarathustra gives voice to his own experiences.[26]

At the beginning of the sequence, in the speech "On the Famous Wise Men," Zarathustra sketches the character of two alternatives to himself—primarily the "famous wise," but also the Free Spirits—and thereby shows why he and his task should not be confused with either of theirs. The "famous wise," Zarathustra observes, are those who have sought after truth only to the extent of finding it in objects of popular reverence, and so ultimately in "the people" themselves. This is not the way of Zarathustra, who seeks to transform popular understanding, rather than justify it. Zarathustra contrasts the posture of the famous wise with that of the Free Spirits.[27] The Free Spirits, he says, are distinguished by the intransigence of their "will to truth," an intransigence that has broken their "revering hearts," rendering them as solitaries to dwell in "deserts," "redeemed from Gods and adorations." From the depth of their deserts these "non-worshippers" on occasion will not be able to resist "squinting thirstily at the islands rich in springs, where living beings repose beneath dark trees," but their contempt for the idols that inevitably arise among such beings will only serve to confirm them in their "godless" isolation.

There is no doubt that Zarathustra views the Free Spirits as superior to the famous wise, and understands the Free Spirits' critical activity as providing a welcome corrective to the degradation of wisdom brought on by the popularized philosophy of the famous wise. Nevertheless, Zarathustra does not share in the Free Spirits' taste for a radically solitary existence, and the reason is indicated by his attribution of a "lion-will" to the Free Spirits. This recalls us to a speech from part 1, "On the Three Metamorphoses," in which Zarathustra identified the lion-will as emerging in the "loneliest desert," where it is driven to debunk all established idols, thereby clearing the ground for their replacement—but remaining incapable of furnishing that replacement itself.[28] Zarathustra is creative, as the lion-will is not, and he therefore escapes the sterile solitude of the Free Spirits, while equally avoiding the servile sociability of the famous wise, since Zarathustra is, as we have seen, like a sun that shines over others (rather than taking its strength from them).

But no sooner has Zarathustra's wisdom been distinguished from both the famous wise and the Free Spirits than his own self-understanding is thrown into question by the three songs that follow. Each of the songs deals in one way or another with a theme that belongs very much to Zarathustra (rather than to a Free Spirit): love. The three songs approach that theme from three different perspectives, each of which expresses a different aspect of Zarathustra, and each of which poses a distinctive challenge: in the first case; that of a godlike creator; in the second case, that of a philosopher; in the third case, that of the human, all too human.[29] The challenges can be outlined as follows.

The first song, "The Night-Song," presents the dilemma of the creator: a "sun" who bestows light on others, and precisely for that reason cannot experience the world as others do, and who longs to receive a gift of his own. "A desire for love is within me," Zarathustra sings here: love is needy, but the creator only satisfies that need in others, and is left unsatisfied as a result. Here Zarathustra confronts directly the problem that Hans Sachs was left with at the end of *Die Meistersinger*, and which makes clear that the fate of a "sun" (which Zarathustra had looked forward to earlier) may be a deeply frustrating one.[30] The third song, "The Grave-Song," presents not the problem of a creator who lacks the gift of love, but, rather, the problem of a more ordinary human who has experienced love—and the loss of it. In this song Zarathustra laments the "glances of love" from the "visions and apparitions of my youth," and how "quickly they died away." What Zarathustra laments, however, is not simply the passing away of his youthful "visions and apparitions," but also their lasting effect on him ("To this day I am the heir and rich earth of your love"): for now he has been disillusioned and known enmity, and the world seems tainted to him as a result ("All disgust I once vowed to renounce"; "Ah, whither has my noblest vow fled?").[31] In "Night-Song" and "Grave-Song," then, Zarathustra sings from two different perspectives, but each addresses a similar problem: the world seems deeply unsatisfactory because love has not been fulfilled. In the central song, "The Dance-Song," Nietzsche approaches the problem in a different way: here, love appears as a problem, but a hope is held out that the problem might be solved and the promise of love fulfilled. In this song Zarathustra sings as one who desires Wisdom, and who desires Wisdom because she reminds him so much of Life. Zarathustra is bewitched by Life because she appears to be "unfathomable."[32] Life protests that Zarathustra, like all men, makes her out to be something she is not ("you men call me 'the Profound' or 'the Loyal,' 'the Eternal,' 'the Mysterious' "). The failure to fathom Life has led men to falsify her—to attribute qualities to her that sound exalted, but that are in fact phantoms of Man's frustrated desire.[33] Thus, Wisdom chastises Zarathustra: "You will, you desire, you love, for that reason alone you *praise* Life!" Zarathustra does not tell Wisdom that he loves her because of what about her reminds him of Life, but then Life tells Zarathustra that she sees *herself* in his account of Wisdom. And yet Life also tells Zarathustra that she is not "unfathomable" (but only "changeable")—which suggests that perhaps she is lovable in a way he has failed to recognize. Has Zarathustra, then, learned that his love of Wisdom can (unexpectedly) be transformed into a love of Life, as she truly is (and as she has not been loved until now)? If so, then perhaps the promise of love *can* be fulfilled on the basis of a new appreciation of the *truth* about Life.

This possibility is taken up by the speech "On Self-Overcoming." Here a crucial advance in Zarathustra's understanding is laid out—and in a way that further clarifies his difference from the Free Spirits. In this speech Zarathustra reflects on the "will to truth" of which the Free Spirits were so proud. The will to truth, Zarathustra explains, has been a misnomer through which even the very wisest heretofore have misled both themselves and others about their activity. For at the root of all life is only *will to power*: that is to say, a will to constant self-overcoming, not directed toward any given end, and so eventually bound to oppose even that which it creates.[34] Zarathustra's whole speech "On Self-Overcoming" is addressed directly to "the wisest" (and there is no other speech where Zarathustra speaks exclusively to the wisest individuals). In this context Zarathustra stresses that most agents of the will to power have misunderstood it, and this has been true not only of "the unwise" or "the people," but also of the wisest themselves, whom Zarathustra admonishes in these terms: "You still want to create the world before which you can kneel: that is your ultimate hope and intoxication." Against such misunderstandings of the will to power, Zarathustra insists that no form of life will be able to avoid inviting and ultimately even demanding its own overcoming. Thus, Zarathustra reports to the wisest the claim of a personified Life: "And even you who understand are only a path and footstep of my will; verily, my will to power walks even on the feet of your will to truth!" After he has presented "the secret of Life," Zarathustra comments, "Thus did Life once teach me: and with this, you who are wisest, I go on to solve the riddle of your hearts." Zarathustra thereby rips away from "the wisest" their heretofore "ultimate hope and intoxication"—that is, the illusion that has sustained them until now (that they have been driven by a will to truth rather than will to power)—but he does so not to discredit their quest for truth, but to challenge them to face the truth more squarely.[35] Indeed, Zarathustra clearly intends his debunking of the wisest's self-understanding to be invigorating, not deflating: "there is many a house still to build!" the speech concludes. In other words: the coming into self-consciousness of the will to power is to be celebrated for the opportunities it makes possible, not lamented for the illusions that are left behind in the process.

To fully understand the role Zarathustra is set to play within this process of the will to power's historical evolution (the process of its coming into self-consciousness), we need to refer back to a speech from part 1, "On the Thousand Goals and One" (the first of the three speeches in which Zarathustra refers to the will to power). In that speech, the codes of good and evil ("values," as Zarathustra calls them) that define a given "people" or civilization are said to be "the voice of their will to power": a means through which the people collectively challenged and overcame itself, mastering ever more demanding tasks for the sake of some greater goal or ideal. Zarathustra is emphatic that such values initially emerged only through this sort of communal consciousness: "Creators were at first peoples and only later individuals; verily, the individual is itself just the most recent creation." As a result, Zarathustra explains, the individual "I" emerged at first only as the bad conscience and "going under" of a people: as calculating, self-seeking, "loveless." In these last respects the "I" that first acquires self-consciousness as the bad conscience of a people might call to mind the solitary, broken-hearted Free Spirits who are relentlessly at odds with the people. In the context of the speech, Zarathustra does not condemn the loveless "I," but he does pointedly observe, "It has always been lovers, and creators, that created good and evil," and concludes that "there is lacking the one goal. Humanity still has no goal. But say to me now, my brothers: if humanity still lacks a goal, does it not also lack—itself?" What Zarathustra thereby suggests is that human life is incomplete so long as it is only the life of the "I"; what is needed now is the self-conscious re-creation of something akin to the collective sense of "oneness" that peoples had before the "I" became ascendant.[36] Zarathustra himself aims to be just the sort of loving creator called for (in the prologue he had declared, "The time has now come for the human to set a goal for itself" and "I want to teach humans the meaning of their existence"). The task of deliberately re-creating a form of communal consciousness (albeit a radically new form) is another respect in which Zarathustra's activity must be distinguished from that of the Free Spirits, and it is a point to which I will return in due course. First, however, Zarathustra must comprehend the difficulty of this task for precisely the *individual* creator: for a self-conscious act of loving creation *now* (that is, after the proclamation of Zarathustra's wisdom) requires coming to terms with the truth of Life as will to power.

Zarathustra has shown, then, that various other avatars of wisdom need to be supplanted, and he has shown much of what their needed successor must look like, but he has not yet quite shown that he is up to the challenge himself. He grapples with the challenge directly for the first time near the end of part 2, in the chapter "On Redemption," which results in his whole teaching being thrown into crisis. The crisis comes about in the following way. Zarathustra is told that although his teaching has finally begun to win over the people, in order for them to fully accept his teaching, he must show that it can persuade even the crippled among them. Zarathustra then confides to his disciples that, for him, all human beings are decisively crippled because they represent incomplete or distorted expressions of their fullest potential ("I walk among human beings as among fragments of the future; that future which I envisage"). On this basis Zarathustra questions whether he could even bear to be human if, in striving to better himself, he did not also better the whole of humanity:

> This is all my composing and striving, that I compose into one and bring together what is fragment and riddle and cruel chance. And how could I bear to be human if the human being were not also a composer-poet and riddle-guesser and the redeemer of chance! To redeem that which has passed away and to re-create all "It was" into a "Thus I willed it!"—that alone should I call redemption.

Zarathustra's articulation of his will implies an intractable obstacle, which it faces in the "chance" (or "accident" [*Zufall*]) to which it is subject. For Zarathustra might will the creation of a great future, but he cannot unwill the conditions under which his own will was created. Thus, Zarathustra observes, "willing liberates," but at the same time "the will itself is still a prisoner," since it can only ever be "an angry spectator of all that is past." The failure to accept this fact ("the will's ill-will towards time") has been responsible for turning the will into an instrument of revenge, rather than of liberation: the will's conditioning has been felt as a "punishment," and this in turn was interpreted as somehow deserved, as "justice." Creative will may lie at the heart of life, but in order for this insight not to be understood negatively (in order for this insight to lead to a celebration life rather than a condemnation of it), the will must unconditionally embrace its own, unchosen conditioning:

> Has the will yet become its own redeemer and joy-bringer? Has it unlearned the spirit of revenge and all gnashing of teeth? And who has taught it reconciliation with time, something higher than any reconciliation? Something higher than any reconciliation the will that is will to power must will—yet how shall this happen? Who has yet taught it to will backwards and want back as well?

And here (after this, the work's final reference to the will to power) Nietzsche says that Zarathustra fell silent and began to look terrified. Zarathustra's terror at his unspoken thought is the subject of the remainder of the work, where it becomes clear that the solution to the problem that he has just identified must be to "will backwards" by willing the eternal return (the notion that every moment of his individual life and every aspect of human existence will repeat itself an infinite number of times).

As this suggests, the thought of the eternal return appears in the work as an extension of (or as a response to) Zarathustra's experience of the will to power: for if, as Zarathustra has come to realize, a will to self-overcoming lies at the heart of life, then that will is bound to be frustrated unless it can (not only accept but also) will the conditions in which it emerges.[37] In other words, if the will to power is the fundamental fact of life, then something like the eternal return is required, if life is to be judged as truly lovable for what it is—and, this is to say, if the affirmative and loving Zarathustra is to be judged as the highest exemplar of wisdom, rather than the critical and loveless Free Spirits.[38] In part 2 Zarathustra is not able to arrive at this judgment, and so his teaching and task and wisdom are all thrown into crisis. In part 3, however, Zarathustra does come to grips with the problem, by confronting directly the problem of the eternal return. Coming to grips with the eternal return compels Zarathustra, not necessarily to change his course of action, but certainly to modify the motive he attributes to it. In other words, the thought of the eternal return shows Zarathustra that he must engage in his project in a new spirit (if he is to engage in it at all). In effect, then, where part 2 shows us the thought of the eternal return emerging out of Zarathustra's reflection on the will to power, part 3 shows us the eternal return reflecting back onto the will to power.[39]

ZARATHUSTRA'S SOLITUDE: THE ETERNAL RETURN

In part 3 Zarathustra confronts the possibility, implied by the thought of the eternal return, that what he seeks most to transcend will return just as surely as the goal he is working to bring into being. The eternal return thereby forces Zarathustra to question his entire activity as a teacher of human beings, since it implies that the end he initially believed his instruction was advancing is not actually an end at all, but only a means to the repetition of the whole process: "All is the same, nothing is worthwhile, knowing chokes."[40] Confronted with this difficulty, Zarathustra is unable to affirm the eternal return, and so eventually retreats from society back to his mountaintop.

This move does not entail any diminution of Zarathustra's concern for the wider world, however. To the contrary: although Zarathustra attempts, in the first chapter of part 3, to "console his heart with hard sayings," by the end of the chapter he admits that the need to find something that he could love (and, relatedly, thoughts for the friends he has left behind) continue to have a strong hold over him. But Zarathustra here also identifies his love as a danger, precisely because, as a need, it longs not just for something but for *anything* on which it can bestow itself, and his move back to solitude is therefore to be understood as an attempt to shape and properly direct the love he feels, so that when he returns to the wider world, he can love what ought to be loved as it ought to be loved.[41]

Accordingly, when, for the first time in the entire work, we are finally shown at some length Zarathustra in the solitude of his mountain—in a chapter titled "The Return Home" (for Zarathustra declares here that solitude is his home)—that solitude appears to be a rather different existence from the deserts in which the disenchanted Free Spirits had secured their distance from all objects of reverence. For what Zarathustra experiences in his solitude proves to be a renewed openness toward and insight into the nature of all things: "Here the words and word-shrines of Being spring open for me; here all being wants to become word, here all becoming wants to learn from me how to speak." Zarathustra's retreat to solitude appears to entail not so much an escape from the world as the adoption of a different, architectonic perspective on it: a perspective that, far from devaluing human things, *revalues* them, giving them a new weight and so a renewed potential for reverence. This task is carried out in the speeches that follow, through which Zarathustra assumes the role of a creator, culminating in the longest speech in the work, "On Old and New Tablets." Here, as the title suggests, he conceives of his mission as a kind of modern Moses, announcing a new code for the conduct of all human life, speaking of his love again, and calling on his "brothers" to steel themselves for the defeat of the "last human" and the transition to the Superhuman, and thus bring about the "Great Midday" that he had promised at the end of part 1.

This is the fullest realization of Zarathustra's task (as laid out in the prologue) that we have yet seen. But although the Great Midday has again been announced, it does not yet appear to be at hand. Zarathustra's tablets are only "half-inscribed": there is still work to be done. And that is true not only for Zarathustra's "brothers" (whom he is not yet descending down to, let alone addressing directly), but for Zarathustra himself: for the problem that drove him into solitude (his inability to affirm the eternal return) still remains, and is indeed the subject of the very next chapter ("The Convalescent"), through which Zarathustra explains why he is still powerfully drawn to—but also still struggles with the challenge of—the activity of a prophetic lawgiver that he has just been enacting (without yet engaging in it directly by returning to human beings).[42]

"The Convalescent" begins with Zarathustra collapsing unconscious after a renewed struggle with the eternal return, only to be gradually resuscitated by the chatter of his animals—not their specific words, so much as their general sounds ("babbling"). "Words and tones," Zarathustra reflects, present the world as a garden at his disposal because they provide "seeming-bridges between what is eternally separated." But as pleasing and restorative as Zarathustra admits to finding this, he also asserts that such bridges do not actually exist: "For me—how could there be an outside-me? There is no outside me! But with all tones we forget that; how lovely it is that we forget!" Such forgetting naturally appears lovely to human beings because it furnishes them with "names and tones," which in turn allow them to "refresh themselves with things": Zarathustra seems to be referring to the process of naming through words, which is to say, creative/legislative activity by means of which "our love dances on colorful rainbows" (that is, expresses itself over the illusory bridges binding communities together). More generally, then, through this whole statement Zarathustra speaks from his recently adopted perspective as a founder: that is, a determinedly singular perspective, but one that is pleased by the appearance of human community which is facilitated through sound ("words," "tones," "names") and which thus makes the creative (evaluative) activity of the individual founder possible. So at this point it appears that, although there is a kind of illusion or self-forgetting entailed in creative activity, it is nevertheless something that pleases Zarathustra, as the expression of a kind of innate loving desire to stretch out beyond ourselves, and feel ourselves to be a part of something larger. In his sympathetic receptivity to this sentiment, Zarathustra's posture—even in his solitude—remains very different from that of a Free Spirit.[43]

That being said, Zarathustra is driven back to a much more starkly singular perspective when his animals reply by speaking to him of the eternal return—that is, from within the perspective created by the teaching they had heard him speak of earlier ("for those who think as we do all things are already dancing," the animals tell him). But where Zarathustra had spoken of a relatively moderate and thus, for him, also pleasing diminution of "individuality" through the apprehension of various sounds, the animals now present a much more radical challenge, by reminding Zarathustra of his own teaching: "Everything breaks, everything is joined anew; eternally is built the same house of Being." Hearing this, the would-be founder's sense of distinctness from what he rebelled against evaporates: "Naked I once saw them both, the greatest and the smallest human being: all-too-similar to each other, even the greatest!" The same teaching that comforts its would-be disciples and beneficiaries convulses its progenitor. Zarathustra, therefore, rebuffs his animals and the vulgarized version of his insight they regurgitate (addressing them as "You buffoons and barrel-organs," and asking, "have you simply made a hurdy-gurdy song of it all?"). For the animals, then, the "eternal return" teaching represents a solution ("Thus—*ends* Zarathustra's going under!" the animals imagine Zarathustra saying upon having accepted his task as teacher).[44] But for Zarathustra the teaching represents a problem, not because of any difficulty with the doctrine as a source of comfort or meaning for those who receive it (it has succeeded in providing a redemptive teaching for the animals), but because of the difficulties the doctrine creates specifically for the one who would teach it (Zarathustra's will is still as frustrated, or unredeemed, as it had been in the speech "On Redemption").[45]

This last observation can help us to see why Zarathustra remains in a position that is distinct from both the Free Spirits (whose solitude left them "redeemed from all adorations" and thus cut off from all society) and the famous wise (whose concern with society compelled them to serve it). For the exchange with the animals over the eternal return suggests that if Zarathustra is ever to assume the role of a teacher of the doctrine and descend from his mountain once more, it will have to be with the awareness that his teaching will inevitably be misunderstood and popularized in a manner that would spark the critical-destructive ire of a Free Spirit, and that this task could therefore only be taken on if it were somehow nevertheless aimed primarily at satisfying Zarathustra's *own* deepest desires. Only if this last condition were satisfied and kept constantly in mind would Zarathustra be able to go down from his mountain and still escape the charge of having become just the latest iteration of a famous wise man serving the many who do not share in his wisdom—while also remaining something more than a Free Spirit, who destroys without creating. Only at this point, then, does Zarathustra finally see clearly the challenge that he and his project face.

Zarathustra faces up to this challenge in the next, and final, three chapters of part 3. He does so, first, by ignoring his animals—feigning sleep so that they leave him to lie in a solitude where even they are not present (and in this state his thoughts no longer dwell on the demands or potential of the world below him). But even in his most solitary solitude Zarathustra proves to be not wholly alone, for he lies now in dialogue with his soul. The concern with his soul now appears to be what is most important to Zarathustra, as he speaks to it of the gifts that he has bestowed on it, eventually appearing to his soul as the sun had appeared to him in the prologue to the whole work—as the source of overflowing brilliance that had nourished its development. But this means that Zarathustra's soul now stands to him as he once stood to the sun: as overfull and in need of stretching itself out beyond itself. "O my soul," Zarathustra admonishes:

> I have given you all, and all my hands have become empty for you—and now? Now you say to me, smiling and heavy of heart: "Which of us should be thankful?—should not the giver be thankful that the taker has taken? Is bestowing not a need?"

Zarathustra seems to concede his soul's question, for he responds by according to it a task through which it may unburden its surplus of riches: "You must *sing*, O my soul!" and he indicates that the subject of these songs should be Dionysos, "your great redeemer" and the god with whom Nietzsche identified the eternal return.[46] "Better yet," Zarathustra adds by way of conclusion (since the last command could by itself be taken as a final gift to his soul), "sing to <u>me</u>, O my soul! And let me give thanks!" And then, in the next two chapters, we are given two songs through which Zarathustra is finally able to declare his love for Life and the eternity in which he lives.

Without venturing a detailed interpretation of the songs that follow Zarathustra's exchange with his soul, let me simply suggest the decisive respect in which that exchange provides the essential context for the songs. Zarathustra, at this point, no longer faces the problem of the creator as it had been outlined in "The Night-Song": his soul is now giving to, and receiving from, itself.[47] Hence Zarathustra's activity is no longer dependent on, or in the service of, another (whether the sun, his animals, or humankind). And *this* appears to be the proper context for the thought of the eternal return, which Zarathustra is now finally able to confront and affirm: as part of a reflection on the self, by the self, for itself.[48] That being the case, Zarathustra's world-affirmation will now have to be a product of his self-affirmation (whereas, in the speech "On Redemption," he had turned away from the thought of the eternal return precisely because he was so deeply frustrated by his own will).

Zarathustra's odyssey up until this point therefore progresses in roughly the following manner: because he acknowledges the will to power as the fundamental fact of human existence and, in particular, the fundamental fact driving his own activity as a teacher or leader of other human beings, he seems to be uniquely capable of being responsible—for others, and for his own activity. What almost crushes Zarathustra is his being forced to acknowledge the persistence of what he *cannot* be responsible for—and, in particular, the way in which the doctrine of the eternal return reveals the limits of what his will can accomplish. His attempt to teach or lead others therefore stands in need of being rethought in light of those limits. This is what Zarathustra begins to do at the end of part 3, where he learns to love Life as it is, rather than as his will would make it.

To this extent, the position Zarathustra arrives at by the end of part 3 should entail his having become distanced from, and no longer standing *in need of*, anything like the Great Midday.[49] An important indication of the progress in Zarathustra's understanding is that in part 4 he delivers a speech on "Midday," simply, which proves to be a phenomenon very different from the "Great Midday." The major contours of this contrast can be sketched in the following terms: the "Great Midday" that Zarathustra speaks of is a historical event, a transformation of the world that must be brought about, and on which his happiness depends; the "Midday" is a timeless and universal possibility, immanent in the world as it is, the enjoyment of which requires Zarathustra to depend on no one but himself.[50] This "Midday" might be compatible with a certain way of understanding the eternal return: that is to say, as a way of referring to Zarathustra's ability, in principle, to always return to himself, knowing that the world *as it is* is perfectly sufficient for his happiness.[51]

Zarathustra's "Midday" makes for an obvious point of comparison with aphorism 308 of *The Wanderer and His Shadow* ("At Midday"). Both passages describe a natural state of solitary happiness, and employ similar imagery.[52] But they do not describe an identical state of being: there is nothing in the earlier passage like the thought that "the world is perfect" (in fact, the earlier passage includes conspicuous reminders of the world's imperfection—"destruction, transience"—and it therefore offers only a "heavy happiness"). Nevertheless, in neither case does the state described appear to be lasting: in *The Wanderer* because "*life*" is said to draw one out of Midday's state of repose, and in *Zarathustra* because the title character forces *himself* out of that state. So in both *The Wanderer and His Shadow* and *Thus Spoke Zarathustra*, a certain sort of solitary "Midday" happiness is raised as a possibility, but not rested content with (almost Zarathustra's last words in part 4 are: "Am I striving then for *happiness*? I am striving for my *work*!"). For both Heinrich Meier and Robert Pippin, this reflects Zarathustra's ultimate failure to make decisive progress: he winds up back where he started, with his old hope to change the world (and the delusions and difficulties that hope entails).[53]

For present purposes, however, I want to shift the point of focus from determining the final position Zarathustra arrives at, and instead emphasize a crucial point about the general trajectory of his journey, and how his trajectory relates to that of the Free Spirits. For, whatever we make of the ending of *Zarathustra*, what we have seen so far should be sufficient to show that the respective journeys of the Free Spirits and Zarathustra circle around each other in the following manner: the Free Spirits begin as determinedly independent, dwelling in solitary deserts and steeling themselves to resist the allures of music or love, yet cannot ultimately avoid acknowledging the persistent allure of those features of "life" that they have cut themselves off from (as we saw in *WS* 308). Zarathustra, in contrast, begins as loving and seeking out others, but is drawn around to a renewed recognition of the need to care for and cultivate himself in solitude. In other words, the Free Spirits and Zarathustra *begin from* very different positions but are eventually led to admit the attraction of a position that stands closer to that of the other.

And, as for the question of how the positions of the two characters are ultimately to be reconciled or fit together, I will suggest now that the Free Spirit writings and *Thus Spoke Zarathustra* are best understood as *raising* that question, rather than as answering it themselves. They raise that question by introducing us to the characters, and making the points of contrast between them clear. But this picture must stand as incomplete until it is filled out by Nietzsche's late autobiographical writings, for those writings discuss more directly how Nietzsche understood the strengths and weaknesses of these characters, and those writings alone show us how Nietzsche retrospectively arbitrated between them. Before turning to those writings, however, let me recapitulate the major considerations that have brought us to them.

CONCLUDING REMARKS

Nietzsche initially developed the ideal of the Free Spirit as an embodiment of all that he wished to place in opposition to Richard Wagner and the Wagnerian project. Yet in working through the Free Spirit ideal, Nietzsche came to see that it would require an austere self-discipline, in order to maintain a strict demarcation between the Free Spirit's own, individual interests and the projects or aspirations of broader human community. Nietzsche's turn to Zarathustra therefore represents an attempt to engage more fully and sympathetically with many of the features of human life that the Free Spirits deny to themselves. Thus, Zarathustra sets out to have a lasting, creative impact on the world, and understands that project as an expression of his love. Yet Zarathustra does not take on this task in the manner that Wagner himself would have: for Zarathustra does not set out to self-consciously teach the world a life-giving illusion; instead, he sets out to teach the world the truth of the will to power as the fundamental fact of life. Yet precisely in becoming the teacher of the will to power, and in making it the foundation for his creative project, Zarathustra is forced to confront the limits of the will, and hence of his ability to reshape the world. As a result, Zarathustra is made to wrestle with a question that Nietzsche had learned (thanks to the case of Wagner) must be confronted by every philosopher: namely, whether the world can be loved for what it is, not what the lover would make it. The notion of the eternal return is a way of raising this question, since it suggests that what one most abhors about the world must be affirmed insofar as it is woven up with the fabric of existence (in other words, by playing out his longing for redemption *of* the world, Zarathustra is redeemed *from* that very longing). In sum, Zarathustra must be what Wagner could not be: one whose creative activity is an expression of world-affirmation, not world-denial. And, at the same time, insofar as Zarathustra knows how to love the world for what it truly is, his position must also differ from the strict self-discipline—the determinedly detached and debunking posture—of the Free Spirits. The example of Zarathustra therefore seems to promise a more fully satisfying way of living than the example of either Wagner or the Free Spirits.

But to what extent are we entitled to conclude that the promise of this fictional creation can be fulfilled? The best way to answer that question may be by asking to what extent Nietzsche judged his own creative activity as "the poet of *Zarathustra*" (*EH* TSZ 4) to be superior to his activity as a Free Spirit and Wanderer. Nietzsche himself invites us to ask this question because in his late autobiographical self-assessments he differentiates between the experiences that lay behind his creation of the character of the Free Spirits versus the experiences behind his creation of Zarathustra (and in each instance Nietzsche assimilates himself to his characters to a considerable degree). And in the process he helps readers to see—with a directness and detail that would not be available if either the Free Spirit writings or *Thus Spoke Zarathustra* were taken on their own—a decisive point: namely, that while each character reflects a *necessary* aspect of his thought, neither is the *definitive* manifestation of that thought. Instead, each character turns out to constitute an essential, but partial, component of Nietzsche's overall *health*.

* 3 *

Health

CHAPTER FIVE

The Prospects for Self-Knowledge in *Ecce Homo* and the 1886 Prefaces

> What I write here is not my teaching but my study; and it is not a lesson for others, it is for me. Yet, for all that, you should not be ungrateful to me for publishing it. What is useful to me may also accidentally be useful to another.
>
> —MONTAIGNE, *Essays*

The Free Spirit and Zarathustra represent two different approaches to the conduct and understanding of life. Nietzsche developed these figures at different moments in his life, and they reflect different modes of life. But this means that these distinctive figures are ultimately linked together by the life of Nietzsche himself. And Nietzsche, in his late autobiographical writings, drew attention to that fact, and accounted for it.

Nietzsche's autobiography, *Ecce Homo*, includes a chapter titled, "Why I Write Such Good Books." This chapter includes ten subchapters, each of which offers a commentary on one of his books, covering nearly his entire career (only *The Antichrist*, *Nietzsche contra Wagner*, and *Ecce Homo* itself are not included). The longest of those commentaries are the subchapters devoted to *Thus Spoke Zarathustra* and *Human, All Too Human* (all three installments of which are dealt with in a single subchapter). These subchapters stand out not only for their length but also because they focus on describing the *composition* of each work—explaining how each work fits into a particular moment of Nietzsche's life (whereas other subchapters focus more on discussing the content of the text at issue, or some general theme related to the text). In this way, Nietzsche makes clear to readers that the works that introduced the figures of the Free Spirit and Zarathustra are works closely bound up with specific moments of his life. And the connection between these two subchapters is not only a matter of form, it is also a matter of substance, because when discussing these two landmarks of his career, Nietzsche places a special emphasis on one of the central features of his life and of his thought: his *health*.

It would not be unfair to say that *the* theme that links together every stage of Nietzsche's career, and in terms of which his entire career ought to be assessed, is the theme of health.[1] We have already seen Nietzsche suggest as much: "Every art, every philosophy, may be considered a remedy and aid in the service of either growing or declining life" (*NCW* "We Antipodes"). And we have seen examples of this principle: Wagner is "one of my illnesses"; when Zarathustra moves toward the affirmation of the eternal return, he is "the convalescent." But in several places Nietzsche also makes use of the notion of health as a prism through which to gauge his own thought and his own career. This theme is especially prominent in the preface he wrote in 1886 for the reissue of *The Joyful Wissenschaft*. In section 1 of that preface Nietzsche remarks that the work expresses "the gratitude of a convalescent," one who has been "all of a sudden attacked by hope, by hope for health, by the *intoxication* of recovery." Nietzsche begins to elaborate on this thought, only to be interrupted in section 2 by an objector, who protests, "But let us leave Mr. Nietzsche: what is it to us that Mr. Nietzsche has got well again?" "Mr. Nietzsche" replies: "A psychologist knows few questions as attractive as that concerning the relation between health and philosophy," because a philosophy born of health will differ in essential ways from a philosophy born of sickness. As Nietzsche remarks in section 3: "A philosopher who has passed through many kinds of health, and keeps passing through them again and again, has passed through an equal number of philosophies." To understand any given philosophy, one must therefore understand the person (including the physical constitution) that produced it: "we philosophers are not free to separate soul from body as the common people do; we are even less free to separate soul from spirit." In view of these remarks, a reader might infer that Mr. Nietzsche's "philosophies" of the Free Spirit and Zarathustra represent different kinds of health that he encountered over the course of his life. This chapter will offer support for that thought.

What Nietzsche shows in his autobiographical self-assessments is that *Human, All Too Human* and *Thus Spoke Zarathustra* amount to turning points in his *thought* because they reflect turning points in his *life*, involving above all changes in his *health* around the time that he wrote each text. Nietzsche's retrospective accounts show that the two works embody different kinds of health, and different stages in his "physiological" (and therefore personal and philosophic) development. To state what is at issue here a bit schematically, Nietzsche's self-account has the following structure: for Nietzsche, *good health* is associated with *forgetting of oneself* (a process that can be seen at work in *Thus Spoke Zarathustra*), while *ill health* is associated with *returning to oneself* (a process that can be seen at work in *Human, All Too Human*). And the major lesson of the autobiographical writings proves to be not the superiority of Zarathustra to the Free Spirits, or vice versa—but, rather, the necessity of each for Nietzsche as tools in a process of examining and enriching his self-understanding ever more deeply. The reader is thereby led to recognize that Nietzsche possesses a perspective that grows out of—but is ultimately more comprehensive than—that of the two major characters he created. Let me, therefore, examine in turn how, first, *Human, All Too Human* and, then, *Thus Spoke Zarathustra* contributed, in their different ways, to the distinctive character of Mr. Nietzsche.

THE HISTORY OF *HUMAN, ALL TOO HUMAN*

In part 1 we saw that an evolution in Nietzsche's understanding of the Free Spirit project occurred *within* the original three installments of *Human, All Too Human*. But there is a still further and no less crucial addition to Nietzsche's understanding of that project: one that occurs in his *retrospective* assessments of *Human, All Too Human*. To that extent, the work assumed a fourth and final form when Nietzsche reissued the original three installments under a single cover in 1886. For that final edition Nietzsche indicated that a change had taken place in his understanding by revising the prefatory material that introduced the work.

Human, All Too Human had no proper preface when it was originally published in 1878. The original publication did, however, have three pieces of introductory material. In the 1878 edition we find, first, a dedication "to the memory of Voltaire," followed by a short statement explaining that "the book would not have been given to the public at this time" had the pending anniversary of Voltaire's death not provoked in the author "the wish to offer a timely personal tribute to the greatest liberator of the human spirit." The dedication to Voltaire stands in implicit contrast to the dedication of Nietzsche's first book to Richard Wagner: the dedication of *The Birth of Tragedy* to Wagner reflected Nietzsche's then-closeness to Romanticism; the dedication of *Human, All Too Human* to Voltaire indicates his newfound sympathy for the Enlightenment.[2] In this way, *Human, All Too Human* made clear at the outset that it was presenting to the world a new Nietzsche.

The remarks on Voltaire are followed by an epigraph underneath the heading, "In Place of a Preface." The epigraph is taken from Descartes, and it reads as follows:

> For a time I reviewed the various occupations that people have in this life, and made the attempt to choose the best of them; and without wishing to

> say anything of the employment of others, I thought that I could not do better than to continue in the same one in which I found myself engaged, that is to say, in occupying my whole life in cultivating my reason, and advancing on the path of truth in accordance with the method I had prescribed to myself. For the fruits that I had already tasted on this path were such that, according to my judgment, nothing more sweet, nothing more innocent, could be found in this life; and every day discovering by means of it truths that seemed to me of some importance and not generally known. Then finally my soul was so filled with joy that all remaining things could no longer touch it.[3]

Like the dedication to Voltaire, the epigraph suggests sympathy for the Enlightenment. It invokes a certain scientific spirit as a model for inquiry (exemplified by the Cartesian method), and it suggests that a distinct and deeply satisfying manner of living goes hand in hand with the scientific spirit.[4] The epigraph thereby indicates that *Human, All Too Human* marks Nietzsche's turn, not only toward modern philosophy, but, at the same time, toward philosophy as a way of life.[5] This notion of a "turn" to philosophy—a turn that represents a distinct moment in the course of one's life, involving critical reflection on one's whole life up until that point, and which, as a result of the reflection, lays the foundation for a properly philosophic way of living and understanding—has been reported on by other philosophers.[6] Nietzsche's Cartesian epigraph might be taken to indicate that with *Human, All Too Human* he follows their example and enters their company.

But there is a puzzle here, because when Nietzsche reissued *Human, All Too Human* in 1886, he removed all this introductory material. Not only that: the epigraph from Descartes, which had been presented "In Place of a Preface," was replaced with a properly titled "Preface." Why did Nietzsche make this change? The answer, I suggest, is this: between 1878 and 1886 Nietzsche realized that his initial turn to a philosophic life had been *somewhat* (although not *entirely*) misguided. As a result, *Human, All Too Human* had to be introduced anew, in order to take account of a principle not properly reflected by the work's original Cartesian epigraph—namely, that "philosophizing begins in error."[7]

The self-misunderstanding—the *necessary* lack of self-knowledge—that begins any spiritual-intellectual quest is an important theme of the mature Nietzsche. We have already seen that in *On the Genealogy of Morality* Nietzsche suggests that *Human, All Too Human* exhibited a self-misunderstanding typical of philosophers (overestimating the degree of one's independence).

However, in the 1886 prefaces to *Human, All Too Human* Nietzsche exposes not only his errors, but something more: how he was able to learn from those errors, and thereby gradually come to understand and live more fully in accord with what he in fact was.[8] Nietzsche's 1886 prefaces therefore not only reintroduce his earlier work, they also reinterpret that work and give it a new meaning by recasting his earlier efforts as provisional steps in an evolving odyssey of self-knowledge.[9]

This is true not only of the 1886 prefaces but of *Ecce Homo* as well. The two sets of autobiographical texts supplement each other in this regard. In *Ecce Homo* Nietzsche shows that his achievement in *Human, All Too Human* was *determined*, to a degree that he did not previously recognize or stress, by specific features of his nature (his health). The 1886 prefaces make note of this same issue (they also stress the matter of health), but they draw out more fully a crucial consequence: namely, that because Nietzsche did not initially face up to just how "idiosyncratic" the experiences behind his *Book for Free Spirits* were (that is to say, dependent on his particular nature), he was led in that work to overstate the extent to which his experience was something that could be shared with others. Thus, when the 1886 prefaces and *Ecce Homo* are taken together, they suggest that because the Free Spirit project of *Human, All Too Human* was spurred and structured by forces lying outside of any deliberate design of Nietzsche's (that is, because it was the product of states of health that were given, not chosen), the prescriptiveness of that project (the degree to which it could provide a template for other, potential Free Spirits) appears much more ambiguous in retrospect than it did initially—and while Nietzsche continues to leave open the *possibility* that the work could still serve that purpose, he now has a *justification* of it that has disabused itself of the illusion that it is (or must eventually become) part of an enterprise that is engaged in with others. This point lies at the heart of the new meaning that Nietzsche is able to retrospectively give to his Free Spirit project, and I now want to unpack the point at length by working through the relevant texts.

The "Return to Myself"

Human, All Too Human is part of a "return *to myself*" on Nietzsche's part (*EH* HH 4), and *Ecce Homo* explains how that return was accomplished. The answer turns out to be more complex, and far more ambiguously prescriptive, than a reader could have readily guessed on the basis of *Human, All Too Human* itself.

We have already seen that in *Ecce Homo* Nietzsche characterizes *Human, All Too Human* as "the monument of a crisis" (that is, the crisis caused by the break with Wagner). Immediately after making that statement, he adds: "It calls itself a book for *free* spirits: practically every sentence in it expresses a victory—with it I liberated myself from what in my nature *did not belong to me*" (*EH* HH 1). And, shortly after: "There is no other way for the phrase 'free spirit' to be understood here: a spirit that has *become free*, that has seized possession of itself again." These formulations make clear that a Free Spirit is one that has freed itself *of* something, and to that extent it is defined by what it opposes: this is consistent with how Nietzsche had characterized the Free Spirit in *Human, All Too Human*, and with his most obvious purpose in that work (debunking his old Schopenhauerian and Wagnerian idols).[10] Yet Nietzsche's formulation here places the emphasis on what the Free Spirit opposes, not in the world at large, but *in itself*: "I liberated myself from what in my nature *did not belong to me*." This suggests that when Nietzsche refers to the Free Spirit as one "that has seized possession of itself again," this involves first and foremost an internal victory of one part of the self over another.

A certain version of this thought had been a theme of *The Wanderer and His Shadow*, where the Free Spirit had been directed to care for "the closest things" that can be easily lost from view without the aid of a strong self-discipline (and the category of "the closest things" would certainly include the issue of "health" that figures so prominently in Nietzsche's retrospective self-assessments). But *Ecce Homo* brings this concern to light in a different way than one might have expected on the basis of *The Wanderer*. For what Nietzsche explains in retrospect is that the crisis his earlier work entailed was not *primarily* a change in philosophical orientation that enabled him to devote more attention to "physiological" concerns (in other words, a turn away from the "first and last things" of metaphysics, and then toward "the closest things," such as health). Instead, Nietzsche now asserts, his philosophical development was *compelled* by his physiological evolution: the physiology, rather than independently arrived-at philosophic commitments, is what is now presented as primary. In other words: in *Ecce Homo* philosophy appears to be a consequence of physiology, not vice versa. This point would not have been at all clear if *Human, All Too Human* were taken on its own (in any of its three installments), but the claim is characteristic of Nietzsche's later writings,[11] and it reflects the extent to which Nietzsche came to see philosophy (along with all human activity) as a matter of compulsion, rather than of choice.

In *Ecce Homo* both Nietzsche's attraction to Wagner *and* his break with the composer appear to be symptomatic first and foremost. For instance, when Nietzsche alludes to the genesis of *Human, All Too Human* in his flight from the Bayreuth Festival, he remarks on his state of mind:

> The decision that was taking shape in me at that time was not just a break with Wagner—I was registering a general aberration of my instinct, and individual mistakes, whether Wagner or my professorship in Basel, were only a sign. I was overcome by an *impatience* with myself; I realized it was high time to reflect on *myself*. (*EH* HH 3)

This remark contrasts in a revealing way with the epigraph from Descartes that Nietzsche had included in the original publication of *Human, All Too Human*. In that epigraph Descartes described setting out to justify the satisfying way of life that he had already found. But Nietzsche's remarks in *Ecce Homo* emphasize that *Human, All Too Human* was *not* the product of the satisfying way of life that he had discovered at the time he wrote the work—but, rather (and more negatively), a product of his consuming *dissatisfaction* with life as he knew it, along with the gnawing and growing awareness that he had failed to sufficiently reflect on himself. In other words, at the time when Nietzsche set out on the journey of *Human, All Too Human*, he did not really know what was good for himself (he lacked self-knowledge). So whereas Descartes describes his decision to continue along contentedly in the manner of life that he was already enjoying, the Nietzsche of *Ecce Homo* will explain that he had to be *compelled to take on* the activity of *Human, All Too Human*, almost by force:

> Now that *bad* inheritance from my father's side came to my assistance in a way that I cannot admire enough, and just at the right time—basically a predestination to an early death. *Illness slowly released me.* (*EH* HH 4)

Nietzsche elaborates on this last thought:

> Illness gave me the right to completely overturn all my habits; it allowed me, *compelled* me, to forget; it bestowed on me the gift of *having* to remain idle, lie still, wait, and be patient . . . But that is what thinking is! (*EH* HH 4; cf. *GS* 295)

Nietzsche's illness thereby forced him to put an end to the career as a classical scholar that he had chosen for himself ("All by themselves my eyes put an end to all my bookwormery, otherwise known as philology"), with an unexpected but welcome result:

> That nethermost self, as if buried alive, as if made mute beneath the constant *need* to pay heed to other selves (—which is what reading is!) awoke slowly, shyly, hesitantly—but finally *it spoke again*. (*EH* HH 4)[12]

In other words, Nietzsche's illness forced a new way of life onto him and, in the process, enabled him to see his nature more clearly (its needs and inclinations), and better understand how to serve it.

To spell out what is at issue here: Nietzsche's point is that during his youthful academic career, precisely because he was in relatively good health in a narrow sense (comparatively physically vigorous), he was not compelled to pay careful attention to his most personal needs, and he therefore gladly (as if "selflessly") submitted himself to the routines of others, without even realizing how much they were at odds with his own inclinations. (Nietzsche remarks that during his time as a professor "there was a complete lack of the subtler kind of selfishness, a commanding instinct's *care*; it was treating oneself as equivalent to everyone else, a *selflessness*, a forgetting of one's distance" [*EH* Clever 3].) So his good health made him forget himself, until a confrontation with ill health brought him back to himself.

From the vantage point that Nietzsche acquired as a result of his illness, he was able to realize that his former attraction to Wagner was not solely the result of qualities intrinsic to either the composer or himself, but was actually a consequence of the sort of life that he had chosen for himself at the time when he encountered Wagner: a life of academic busywork that gave no regard to his own nature or cultivation. He describes the predicament that he faced:

> Ten years behind me when quite simply the *nourishment* of my spirit had been at a standstill, when I had learnt nothing more that was useable, when I had forgotten a ridiculous amount about a hotchpotch of fusty erudition. Crawling through ancient metricians with meticulous precision and bad eyes—things had got that bad with me! (EH *HH* 3)

Looking at that predicament in retrospect, Nietzsche sees that his youthful situation was far from unique. Many of his most talented contemporaries, upon reaching adulthood, found themselves consumed by a life of busywork: a situation that is typical of modern life in "a so-called 'profession'" (something that Nietzsche defines here as "an activity chosen contrary to one's instinct" [*EH* HH 3]). A soul that finds itself living a life that is not suited to its most authentic needs will develop a new and perverse sort of need: the "need to have one's feeling of emptiness and hunger *anaesthetized*." Such souls in Nietzsche's time, therefore, gratefully found escape for "*five or six hours*" through Wagner's "narcotic art" (*EH* HH 3).[13] Wagner's operas spoke to the needs created by this particular "professional" way of life: "art in the age of work," as Nietzsche had put it in *The Wanderer and His Shadow*, referring to art designed as an escape from dreary workaday life (entertainment), rather than as an expression and extension of the passions of a truly fulfilling life, as art would have existed in healthier civilizations.[14] Analyzing this phenomenon from a newfound distance, Nietzsche came to see his earlier enchantment with Wagner as nothing other than a typical symptom of the age: "When I looked around me more carefully I discovered that a large number of young men face the same crisis: one perversity positively *compels* a second" (*EH* HH 3). In other words, Nietzsche had been driven to place his work (classical research) into the service of Wagner (with his quasi-neoclassicism), not so much as the result of misunderstanding Wagner, as because of Nietzsche's own failure to understand what kind of work (what way of life) was most appropriate for him.[15] When illness made it impossible for him to continue with that work, his attachment to Wagner atrophied along with it. And instead of seeking a narcotic escape from his natural infirmities, he was driven to overcome them:

> I have never been so happy with myself as in my life's periods of greatest illness and pain: you need only take a look at *Daybreak* or *The Wanderer and His Shadow* to understand what this 'return *to myself*' was: the highest kind of *recuperation*! . . . The other kind simply followed on from this. (*EH* HH 4)[16]

In this way, Nietzsche's illness liberated him from a life that suppressed and distorted his nature, and thereby helped him to see that his health actually required embracing the pain of his physical ailments.

Nietzsche's approach to health as reflecting something more thoroughgoing than one's most immediate physical or psychological state is anticipated in chapter 1 of *Ecce Homo*, in another passage that reflects on his recovery from the sickness that he had fallen into around the time of Bayreuth: "I took myself in hand, I made myself healthy again: the prerequisite for this—as every physiologist will concede—is *that one is basically healthy*. A typically morbid being cannot become healthy, still less make itself healthy; for a typically healthy person, conversely, being ill can be an energetic *stimulant* to living, to living more" (*EH* Wise 2). In other words: a fully consistent life cannot be one that is free from illness, but instead must be a life that confronts one's inevitable illnesses in a manner productive of a more fundamental kind of health.[17] At all events, health for Nietzsche is not the absence of illness to fight, but rather the ability to fight one's illnesses, and emerge all the better as a result.[18] The process that produced *Human, All Too Human* serves as his case in point, reflecting his willingness to embrace pain and struggle in order to return to the fullest form of health he was capable of.

By showing how his physiological and philosophical states engaged in a sort of dialectical development with one another, Nietzsche could seem to be indicating to the reader how to fulfill the promise of *Ecce Homo*'s subtitle: *How to Become What You Are*. But there is a deep ambiguity involved here, because, as we have seen, Nietzsche consistently stresses the way in which his constitution conditioned and *compelled* his development—saving him from his own ("intentional") choices, and uncovering aspects of his nature that he was not conscious of. Nietzsche seems, at most, to have participated in this process, rather than controlling it.[19] That being the case, can it be sensible to take Nietzsche's account of his development as "prescriptive" (a kind of self-help manual offered to readers)?[20]

Nietzsche's presentation seems deliberately ambiguous on this point. The ambiguity stands out even more clearly in the 1886 prefaces to *Human, All Too Human*, which present as *the* puzzle or problem of the work whether it could serve to create (or propagate) other Free Spirits (since Nietzsche, although with that work he withdrew from the Wagnerian project of cultural creation, did so in the expectation that he would be doing so in the company of a few gifted, and similarly independent-minded, fellow travelers). The prefaces indicate that Nietzsche initially overestimated the work's ability to accomplish exactly that—and as a result he now values the work primarily for the contribution it has to make to enriching his own, entirely independent self-understanding, irrespective of any help that the work may (or may not) offer to others (and, to this extent, the prefaces show Nietzsche returning to himself in an even more thorough-going way than he did when writing *Human, All Too Human*).

The Hope for Friends

Nietzsche wrote two prefaces for *Human, All Too Human*: one for the first volume (containing the first "installment" of the work), and one for the second volume (containing the next two installments: *Assorted Opinions and Maxims* and *The Wanderer and His Shadow*). The first of the two prefaces is especially important. In an incisive discussion of the first preface, Paul Franco notes that Nietzsche described it to his publisher as "an essential contribution to the understanding of my books and of the hard to understand self-development lying at their foundation."[21] Nietzsche's private statements always have to be taken cautiously, but in this case I think the text bears out the assertion of the letter, because the preface proves to be the text in which Nietzsche makes most explicit that his earlier work had to be corrected (and indicates how he corrected it).

Nietzsche opens the preface with a comment on his entire oeuvre (as it existed at that point in time, which is to say, from *The Birth of Tragedy* through *Beyond Good and Evil*). "All my writings," Nietzsche reports having been told by others, seem to contain "a persistent invitation to the overturning of habitual evaluations and valued habits," and thus to provoke a certain "mistrust" regarding morality. This, he says, makes his writings rather hard to take—even, Nietzsche now admits, for himself, reporting that he has sometimes had to "recuperate from myself, as it were to induce a temporary self-forgetting." This is why, "where I could not find what I *needed*, I had to artificially enforce, falsify and invent a suitable fiction for myself," and "perhaps in this regard I might be reproached with having employed a certain amount of 'art,'" since he could not face the truth of life. This was a form of "self-deception," Nietzsche frankly states, but it was also a form of self-preservation—since "life is, after all, not a product of morality: it *wants* deception, it *lives* on deception." The failure to face up to this fact of life is an error that the *Genealogy* had stressed is characteristic of Free Spirits; a more mature philosophy faces up to the necessity of just such errors and deceptions.[22]

In section 1 of the preface, Nietzsche makes a general statement about the kind of self-deception that was most persistently at issue for him: "What I again and again needed most for my cure and self-restoration, however, was the belief that I was *not* thus isolated, not alone in *seeing* as I did." He makes this self-indictment more concrete by mentioning several examples of this tendency, taken from his early period: the self-deception regarding the potential of Schopenhauer and Wagner, "likewise with the Greeks, likewise with the Germans and their future—and perhaps a whole long list could be made of such likewises?" Nietzsche does not provide a "whole long list" of similar cases. But he does add one further example, in the first sentence of section 2:

> Thus when I needed to I once also *invented* for myself the "free spirits" to whom this melancholy-valiant book with the title *Human, All Too Human*

> is dedicated: "free spirits" of this kind did not exist, do not exist—but, as I have said, I had need of them at that time if I was to keep in good spirits while surrounded by ills.

So the creation of the "free spirits" in *Human, All Too Human* amounted to a work of "art" on Nietzsche's part, no less than his earlier elevation of Schopenhauer and Wagner. In both instances, Nietzsche deceived himself about the potential of the characters he celebrated, making it seem as if he were associating himself with causes that were more powerful than they really were, and that had more in common with him than they really did: in the case of Schopenhauer and Wagner, Nietzsche deceived himself about the character of his "friends" in order to be able to believe that he *had* friends,[23] and although he eventually disabused himself of that delusion with regard to Schopenhauer and Wagner, the underlying tendency carried over into the project of *Human, All Too Human* insofar as in that work he convinced himself (against the available evidence) that he was part of a band of "free spirits" that "did not exist, do not exist."[24]

But immediately after making this admission, Nietzsche adds "[t]hat free spirits of this kind *could* one day exist"; regarding *that* possibility, he writes at the conclusion of section 2:

> *I* would want to be the last to doubt that. I see them already *coming*, slowly, slowly; and perhaps I shall do something to speed their coming if I describe under what vicissitudes, upon what paths, I *see* them coming?

No sooner, then, has Nietzsche suggested that the "free spirits" of *Human, All Too Human* were an illusion, a work of "art" (so much so that he refers to them only with scare quotes), than he shifts to prophesying the coming of Free Spirits proper (without scare quotes). Even here, however, there is an ambiguity: Nietzsche says that he *wants* to be the last to doubt this prophecy; and although he says that he will describe how he sees them approaching, he also says that doing so may only *perhaps* hasten their arrival. But if Nietzsche thereby casts a shadow of doubt over the advent of Free Spirits, then what is the point of his discussion here? Is he gingerly acknowledging to the reader that he may be deceiving himself about this whole matter once again, imagining that he has (or will soon have) friends where the available evidence suggests otherwise?[25] And, in any case, if *Human, All Too Human* stands revealed as an exercise in self-deception (since Nietzsche has admitted that at the time of that work his hope for friends required "art," to help him evade the reality of his situation), then of what value can the work be now?

This last question is far from an idle one: Nietzsche dated the preface "Spring 1886," but his correspondence from January of that year shows him considering having all remaining copies of *Human, All Too Human* destroyed (planning to replace it with a kind of second edition—the work that became *Beyond Good and Evil*).[26] At any rate, the first two sections of the preface force one to ask: to what extent were the Free Spirits of *Human, All Too Human* a work of "art" on Nietzsche's part (a bit of wishful thinking, a life-sustaining illusion)? And to what extent did the Free Spirits *become* a reality for him? Moreover: does a Free Spirit ultimately *require* "friends"? Is gaining one's independence from the powers that reign around one a sufficient and satisfactory accomplishment, or must one become part of a broader movement of similarly inclined individuals?[27] If so, to what extent does Nietzsche think that his writings can help to bring about that outcome?

Nietzsche's 1886 preface provokes the reader to ask these questions, but he does not answer them directly. Instead, he uses sections 3–7 of the preface to offer the reader a narrative about how a Free Spirit *would* emerge and evolve. Nietzsche's narrative of a prospective Free Spirit's emergence and evolution mirrors aspects of his own odyssey that we have already seen: the process begins with a "great liberation" from objects of youthful reverence, followed by a long, solitary project of critical examination and reevaluation of popular ideals, leading to a more mature state of self-mastery through which the Free Spirit moves back toward a state of always imperfect but ever improving health, from which perspective they are able to understand life and their place within it anew.

Nietzsche's narrative here is somewhat tricky to assess, because it seems to be attempting to simultaneously capture his own experience along with that of other (potential) Free Spirits. Thus, in section 7, Nietzsche says that a Free Spirit will eventually be led, through reflecting on their own case, to make the following "generalization":

> "What has happened to me," he says to himself, "must happen to everyone in whom a *task* wants to be embodied and 'come into the world.'"

But, in the eighth and final section of the preface, Nietzsche highlights not the "generalizable" aspect of this process, but its reflection on his case in particular:

> No psychologist or reader of signs will have a moment's difficulty in recognizing to what stage in the evolution just described the present book belongs (or has been *placed*—).

The difficulty here is somewhat greater than Nietzsche claims: I agree with Paul Franco that the narrative Nietzsche provides is general enough that it would be a mistake to interpret it as a simple chronology of his career, with precise names and dates to be filled in by the reader (or, at any rate, by a "reader of signs").[28] But, as Franco also helps to show, Nietzsche's narrative does have certain broad stages, within which one can identify features that call to mind different parts of his career.[29] One of the most significant of those features is the theme of discipline. I have already argued that a certain kind of self-discipline is integral to the Free Spirit project, but in the 1886 prefaces we see the need for discipline not only reiterated, but now also cast in terms that open up the possibility that Nietzsche is proposing a regimen of discipline that could generate the sort of "friends" that he imagined for himself at the outset of the Free Spirit project.

The Imposition of Discipline

The theme of discipline emerges in the prefaces in the following way: in section 3 of the first preface Nietzsche describes how the Free Spirit emerges through a "great liberation," which "is at the same time a sickness that can destroy the man who has it," and inspires a radical questioning of all things and a turn to solitude. This picture broadly maps onto the first installment of *Human, All Too Human*, since the notion of a "great liberation" recalls the dedication of the original volume to the "great liberator" (Voltaire), and since that work was bound up with an illness that almost destroyed Nietzsche, as well as with his flight away from Bayreuth and into solitude. Next—in section 4 of the preface—Nietzsche explains that the "sickly isolation" that follows from the "great liberation" is succeeded by a "*mature* freedom of spirit which is equally self-mastery and discipline of the heart." This allusion to "self-mastery and discipline of the heart" seems to point in two directions at once. On the one hand, it points forward to the "*mature* freedom of spirit," which transcends the early stages of the "great liberation."[30] On the other hand, it points backward to elements of *Human, All Too Human* ("that monument to a rigorous self-discipline" [*EH* HH 5]), and particularly the final installment of that work, *The Wanderer and His Shadow* (where discipline of the heart was a crucial theme).[31] Nietzsche himself draws attention to this latter connection, because in the preface to volume 2 of the 1886 edition (that is, the volume containing *Assorted Opinions and Maxims* and *The Wanderer and His Shadow*), he makes the theme of discipline prominent, and he does so in terms that make clear that discipline is not only the end result of that project, but also a means to be adopted for the purpose of *becoming* a Free Spirit.

The key statement comes in section 2 of the second preface, where Nietzsche comments on his decision to bring *Human, All Too Human*, *Assorted Opinions and Maxims*, and *The Wanderer and His Shadow* together under a single cover:

> [P]erhaps taken together they will teach their precepts more powerfully and clearly—they are *precepts of health* that may be recommended to the more spiritual natures of the generation just coming up as a *disciplina voluntatis* [discipline of the will].

In the next several sections Nietzsche lays out just such precepts of health, but drawing them not from *Human, All Too Human*, *Assorted Opinions and Maxims*, or *The Wanderer and His Shadow* directly, but instead from a description of his experiences around the time that he wrote those works. For instance, in section 3 he recounts that after his disillusionment with Wagner drove him into illness and isolation, "I began thoroughly and fundamentally *forbidding* myself all Romantic music," in order to impose a new direction and discipline onto the desires of his spirit. In that same context he advises others to learn from his example, issuing the injunction "*cave musicam!*" (beware of music!). Then, in section 4, he stresses that taking this step was an act of self-denial on his part:

> I thus, and not without a sullen wrathfulness, took sides *against* myself and *for* everything painful and difficult precisely for *me*:—thus again I found my way to that courageous pessimism that is the antithesis of all romantic mendacity, and also, as it seems to me today, the way to "myself," to *my* task.

And this, he declares, is not only the way to *his* task:

> Illness is the answer, every time <u>we</u> wish to doubt our right to *our* task—when we begin to make things easier for ourselves in any way.

In this manner, Nietzsche highlights the importance of a *disciplina voluntatis* not only for the purpose of describing his own experience in executing the project of self-discipline and self-determination whose monument was *Human, All Too Human*, but also for the purpose of prescribing a course of action for anyone who wants to engage in a similar project. To that extent, the 1886 prefaces might be taken as proposing a way to create what they charge that *Human, All Too Human* itself had too readily assumed already existed: fellow Free Spirits.[32]

To be sure, Nietzsche's proposal here is ambiguous precisely because it shifts so obliquely between describing his own case and prescribing that of others.[33] Still, the prescriptive element of his rhetoric is lent weight by its thematic connections to the political posture of his later writings. What I have in mind is this: Nietzsche's struggles with illness (and the self-disciplined regimen that they compelled him to develop) points to ways in which the soul can be spurred to train and condition itself through successive stages of self-overcoming. But since not everyone experiences the same struggles with their health that Nietzsche did, one way of inducing a similar effect among a broader swath of people might involve the adoption of an intensively demanding, extensively stratified social structure.[34]

To that end, we should note that the *disciplina voluntatis* appears twice in Nietzsche's writings (in texts that were written only a few months apart). It makes its first appearance in the preface to *Human, All Too Human*, quoted above. Its second appearance is in book 5 of *The Joyful Wissenschaft*. In the first case, the context is more "personal" (concerned with the cultivation of one's self); in the second case, the context is more "political" (concerned with the cultivation of a broader culture). But these two concerns (self-cultivation and cultural cultivation) can be connected to one another, since the latter passage suggests that the establishment of a *disciplina voluntatis* is part of a larger effort to create a cultural horizon in light of which individuals can understand themselves, and which they can direct their activity toward:

> The true invention of the religion-founders is first to establish a certain way of life and everyday customs that work as a *disciplina voluntatis* while at the same time removing boredom; and then to give just this life an *interpretation* that makes it appear illuminated by the highest worth, so that henceforth it becomes a good for which one fights and under certain circumstances even gives one's life. (*GS* 353)

When Nietzsche's two references to the *disciplina voluntatis* are taken together, then, the following possibilities present themselves: (1) that a discipline of the will could generate Free Spirits; (2) that this form of discipline operates not only at the individual level but also through the work of religion-founders who give meaning to, and shape the way of life of, larger communities.[35]

With his remarks on the *disciplina voluntatis*, then, Nietzsche raises possibilities that are quite different from what he had originally proposed in *Human, All Too Human* (since, as we saw in chapter 2, that work aimed to insulate the activity of Free Spirits from all manner of social authorities, and thereby assumed a roughly libertarian bent). But those possibilities are raised throughout Nietzsche's later writings, particularly insofar as they contend that the life of the mind (including the work of philosophers) can actually benefit from social orders that combine aristocratic and theocratic elements.[36] For instance, an aphorism from *Beyond Good and Evil* (a text that Nietzsche composed only a few months before the two texts dealing with the *disciplina voluntatis*) outlines how a "philosopher will make use of religion for his project of cultivation and education," not only because individuals who "incline to a more withdrawn and contemplative life through their higher spirituality" can find a protective shelter under the aegis of religious authority, and not only because it offers "contentment" to the lower classes, but because for those in society's ascending classes, "religion offers them sufficient occasions and temptations to walk through the paths of higher spirituality and to test the feelings of great self-overcoming, of silence and solitude" (*BGE* 61).[37] In the same work, Nietzsche identifies potential spurs to self-overcoming not only in religion but also in politics: he writes admiringly of the intensely competitive *agon* of the Greek *polis*, and suggests that the greatest achievements of the Greek world were the product of a decaying aristocracy, speculating that the decay of the modern world might present attractive possibilities for those who experience a war within themselves (a struggle among their own instincts), if they find a way to join that internal battle to the political conflicts of the wider world, in a new life-affirming contest of self-overcoming (*BGE* 200, 262, see also 257–59).[38] A later text expresses a similar thought, with another analogy drawn between self-overcoming at the individual level and the collective level: "How is freedom to be measured, in individuals as well as nations? By the resistance which must be overcome, the efforts it costs to stay *on top*. The highest type of free men would need to be sought in the place where the greatest resistance is constantly being overcome" (*TI* Skirmishes 38). In short, Nietzsche displays an interest in religio-political orders that could serve to discipline the will and direct it to self-overcoming, and that interest complements his call for a "*disciplina voluntatis*" among "the more spiritual natures of the generation just coming up."

As the passage quoted above from *GS* 353 indicates, however, a society structured in this way would require goals worth sacrificing oneself *for*, and providing such a goal points beyond the project of Free Spirits, and toward that of Zarathustra (who, as we have seen, is—or at least toys with being—the sort of constructive-creative religion-founder that is called for following the "death of God"). In view of that larger project, Nietzsche's later writings make the Free Spirits transitional to (and decisively lower than) future philosopher-legislators (see *BGE* 44, 211)—and the writings that follow Nietzsche's Free Spirit trilogy (above all, *Thus Spoke Zarathustra*) can be read as an attempt of his own to engage in such philosophic legislation (as they have been read most extensively in a series of studies by Laurence Lampert).[39]

For the purposes of the present discussion, however, what is of the greatest importance is that even when Nietzsche's writings shift their point of focus away from the figure of the Free Spirit and toward Zarathustra, that shift—and the political posture it entails—is intelligible as an *outgrowth* of Nietzsche's reflections on the process that produced *Human, All Too Human*, insofar as those reflections led him to stress the indispensability for that process of his having been forced to wrestle with a strong source of resistance (and even a threat to his existence) in the form of ill health (and the capacity for self-mastery and self-overcoming that he developed as a consequence). This self-assessment on Nietzsche's part helps to explain why in later writings he ceased to recommend the sort of "libertarian" political program that had been suggested in *Human, All Too Human* (because he wished to place more emphasis on the need to encounter deadly threatening forms of resistance, and embrace struggle in a program of self-overcoming).[40] We can, therefore, conclude that although the political position that Nietzsche ultimately arrived at is an unnerving one, and one whose advisability ought to be interrogated with humane skepticism, it is by no means an incongruous anomaly, discontinuous with the more significant features of his thought.[41] To the contrary, Nietzsche's politics can be understood as the result of a reflection on his innermost experience of the world.[42]

But this still leaves open the question: to what extent did Nietzsche require or expect that a program of discipline could serve to generate a new class of Free Spirits? That Nietzsche often employs a highly exhortative rhetoric (Beware of music! Illness is the answer!) can make him appear hopeful in this regard, but that fact should not distract from the qualifications and provisos that are generally found in the same context. To that end, we saw that in the second of the 1886 prefaces Nietzsche in effect hedges his bets by switching back and forth between giving a retrospective description of his own experience and prescribing a future course of action for others. And the aphorism in *The Joyful Wissenschaft* on religion-founders and the *disciplina voluntatis* states more plainly why all expectations about what a program of discipline can accomplish ought to be circumscribed:

> The true invention of the religion-founders is first to establish a certain way of life and everyday customs that work as a *disciplina voluntatis* while at the same time removing boredom; and then to give just this life an *interpretation* that makes it appear illuminated by the highest worth, so that henceforth it becomes a good for which one fights and under certain circumstances even gives one's life. Actually, the second invention is the more important: the first, the way of life, was usually already in place, though alongside other ways of life and without any consciousness of its special worth. The significance, the originality of the religion-founder usually lies in his *seeing* and *selecting* this way of life, in his *guessing* for the first time what it can be used for and how it can be interpreted. (*GS* 353)

This makes clear that religion-founders can discipline a given life form but not simply will a new form of life into existence. If we apply this principle to Nietzsche, it would suggest that although his exhortative rhetoric offers guidelines to others about how certain potential can best be developed, it cannot and does not pretend to create potential where there is none.[43]

This thought has implications for how we read Nietzsche's mature understanding of his work. For if even a program of strict discipline is limited and uncertain in what it can accomplish, then Nietzsche could not confidently justify his writings in terms of the "friends" that they would eventually win for him. Nietzsche acknowledges as much in *Ecce Homo*, when he comments as follows about his post-*Zarathustra* writings: "From then on [that is, from *Thus Spoke Zarathustra* on] all my writings are fish-hooks: perhaps I am as good as anyone at fishing? . . . If nothing was *caught*, then I am not to blame. *There weren't any fish . . .*" (*EH* BGE 1). Nietzsche is not to blame because the results of his fishing expedition are not entirely within his control, irrespective of his abilities as a fisherman. But does this mean that his efforts are (at least potentially) in vain?

This question can be asked about Nietzsche's oeuvre as a whole, but it needs to be asked about *Human, All Too Human* in particular, since that work—far from having been written on the understanding that despite all best efforts it might bring up no "fish"—was composed (as the 1886 prefaces explain) on the basis of an implicit trust in the possibility of finding friends through the work. If that trust was misplaced, must the work count as a failure? To answer these questions, we need to return to the first of the 1886 prefaces, which explains how the project that began with *Human, All Too Human* eventually came to a state of fruition.

The Return to Health

We have already seen that the first preface offers a narrative of the Free Spirit's emergence and subsequent development. However, we left off in section 4, with the "*mature* freedom of spirit which is equally self-mastery and discipline of the heart." But this "maturity" turns out not to be the last of the stages that Nietzsche's narrative of the Free Spirit passes through. It shades into, or sets the stage for, a further stage—a return to health, which Nietzsche describes (in sections 4 and 5 of the preface) as a gradual and complex process of "convalescence," as a result of which the Free Spirit "again draws near to life."[44] Nietzsche's narrative of the Free Spirit therefore includes at least the following major stages: the "great liberation," the stage of solitary "self-mastery and discipline of the heart," and a return to health and to life.

The moment of being drawn closer to life had been somewhat anticipated by what we saw near the end of *The Wanderer and His Shadow*, in the aphorism "At Midday" (where a reengagement with "life" was looked forward to, if not begun in earnest). But the 1886 prefaces make clear that a reengagement with life is not the end of the story. The Free Spirit's development is now pushed a stage further, in section 6 of the preface, where Nietzsche explains that a Free Spirit may "finally" be able to "unveil the riddle" of the "great liberation" by attaining mastery over itself *and its own virtues*, that is, by instrumentalizing those virtues, deploying them for its own ends, in view of its newfound awareness of "the problem of *order of rank*." Nietzsche's account of the Free Spirit's development concludes with that problem ("*our* problem," he calls it, at the end of section 7), so that the three major stages of the Free Spirit odyssey already identified (the "great liberation"; the solitary "self-mastery and discipline of the heart"; the return to health and to life) gain at least a fourth in this confrontation with the problem of rank-ordering.

However, in section 7 of the preface Nietzsche in effect reframes the steps along this path so that they appear not as discrete events, but as all part and parcel of a broader process through which a Free Spirit comes to grasp the nature of the *task* that defines its distinctive place and mission in the world. The statement that opens section 7 is worth quoting at length:

> This is how the free spirit elucidates to himself that riddle of liberation, and inasmuch as he generalizes his own case ends by adjudicating on what he has experienced thus. "What has happened to me," he says to himself, "must happen to everyone in whom a *task* wants to be embodied and 'come into the world.'" The secret force and necessity of this task will rule among and in the individual facets of his destiny like an unconscious pregnancy—long before he has caught sight of this task itself or knows its name. Our vocation commands and disposes of us even when we do not yet know it; it is the future that regulates our today.

The road that begins with the "great liberation" therefore seems to culminate in the discovery of the "task" (which would then function as the end in the service of which one's virtues would be ordered and directed). Nietzsche underscores this thought in the preface to volume 2, where the recovery of the task is presented as the crowning moment of the Free Spirit odyssey (for example, at the end of section 5 of that preface: "Finally our reward is the *greatest* of life's gifts, perhaps the greatest thing it is able to give of any kind—we are given *our task* back").

Having reached the end of Nietzsche's account of the Free Spirit odyssey, we can now return to, and reconsider, a remark from the eighth and final section of the preface:

> No psychologist or reader of signs will have a moment's difficulty in recognizing to what stage in the evolution just described the present book belongs (or has been *placed*—).

I have already suggested that (even though the preface does not seem designed to provide a perfectly precise chronology of Nietzsche's career) there are reasonable grounds for concluding that the main text of *Human, All Too Human* (in all three of its installments, minus the 1886 prefaces) belongs mainly to the early stages of the evolution described by the preface: that is to say, it is the result of a great liberation and consequent sickness, solitude and self-discipline, and it sets the stage for the first steps of recovery that followed. But although I think that drawing this conclusion is accurate enough so far as it goes, it is also inadequate, because it does not account for a critical detail: namely, that although *at first* Nietzsche says that *Human, All Too Human* "belongs" to a particular stage of the evolution that he has just been describing, he then *adds*, in parentheses, that the work has been "*placed*" at that stage. This implies that the book takes on a new meaning in retrospect—and can *only* be properly defined in retrospect.

This moment—the moment of retrospective self-definition—was alluded to in section 7 of the preface: immediately after describing the emergence of "the problem of order of rank" along with the coming-to-consciousness of the "task," Nietzsche referred to that moment as "the midday of our life" and observed that "only now" (that is, only at that midday) does the Free Spirit comprehend how all of their earlier experiences were a necessary preparation for arriving at this moment. The degree of self-possession and clarity about one's place in the world present at this stage seems to constitute a step beyond *The Wanderer*'s "midday"; it fits much more with the state that Nietzsche had arrived at by the time of his autobiographical writings.

As this suggests, the moment of retrospective reinterpretation—through which initially apparently discrete events and experiences acquire new meaning as a result of the contribution they are now understood to have made to the emergence of a "task" that unites and defines all that one has undergone—is an essential part of any Free Spirit odyssey. To flesh out this thought, consider again the following statement from section 7 of the preface:

> This is how the free spirit elucidates to himself that riddle of liberation, and inasmuch as he generalizes his own case ends by adjudicating on what he has experienced thus. "What has happened to me," he says to himself, "must happen to everyone in whom a *task* wants to be embodied and 'come into the world.'" The secret force and necessity of this task will rule among and in the individual facets of his destiny like an unconscious pregnancy—long before he has caught sight of this task itself or knows its name. Our vocation commands and disposes of us even when we do not yet know it; it is the future that regulates our today.

The decisive image here is the "unconscious pregnancy": one's "task" is like the child that is cared for through a gestation period during which it shares in and gives shape to all of one's activity, but cannot yet be known in a full sense. The metaphor of pregnancy is an important one for Nietzsche, and its appearance here brings to mind the complex dynamics of closeness and separateness, awareness and uncertainty, sovereignty and receptivity, at play in one's relation to one's task.[45] But the metaphor as used here suggests an even more radical state of affairs, since it is an "unconscious pregnancy": in other words, one begins not having caught sight of one's task and not even having acquired a clear sense of its presence (even though it is already sharing in and shaping one's activity). That is why the Free Spirit's initial liberation is a "riddle": because it is an essentially embryonic state whose influence on its host can only be comprehended (or even recognized) after it has matured.[46]

If we apply this principle to Nietzsche, then, we can conclude that *Human, All Too Human* was *Nietzsche*'s "unconscious pregnancy" (the "great liberation" that marked the first step toward the recovery of his task, and which was shaped by that task, although he was not then aware of it)—and the preface is the "future" that is now "regulating" (by interpreting) the "today" that the main text represents ("placing" it in a particular stage of an evolution that he is only now able to give a proper account of, now that his task stands before him in full view). This means that the culmination of the Free Spirit project is to be found not within the original Free Spirit writings, but in Nietzsche's retrospective assessments of those writings. Through those assessments he is able to define *Human, All Too Human* as part of a larger project (and, as a result, the preface alludes to phrases and themes that figure prominently in writings from the period of *Zarathustra*).[47] And, accordingly, through those assessments he is able to *place* his earlier work within an evolution whose contours have become clear to him only in retrospect.[48]

This explains why Nietzsche did not have to destroy his old book (as he had originally planned to do), but why he did have to replace its preface: he could give the work a new significance by giving it a new interpretation, which makes sense of the Free Spirit's development retrospectively, through the lens that Nietzsche is now—and only now—able to provide the text. Once the work is understood to have this kind of dual existence and dual meaning, it is possible to understand why Nietzsche's preface can simultaneously indict *Human, All Too Human* for having "artfully" (self-deludingly) invented "free spirits" that did not in fact exist, and yet nevertheless say that such "free spirits" still *could* "one day exist": for Nietzsche has (since originally writing *Human, All Too Human*) reconstructed the imperfect beginning of his Free Spirit project as its genuine and necessary beginning.[49] In this way, the 1886 prefaces make *Human, All Too Human* into an even more rigorous return to oneself than the original work itself.

In sum, Nietzsche's 1886 prefaces show that he has a roughly generalizable account of the coming-to-be of a Free Spirit: Begin with objects of powerful reverence (that is, as a "fettered spirit")! Experience the shock of a great liberation, and set yourself apart, going even into solitude! Embrace struggle, self-discipline, even self-denial! Attain self-mastery and bring your true task into the world! But even as Nietzsche issues these exhortations, the first of the prefaces suggests that although he would surely welcome other Free Spirits being generated through such a process, he does not need to "invent" them to make his account meaningful, because it is now in the first place a self-account. In other words, the 1886 preface suggests that Nietzsche deceived himself about the existence of fellow Free Spirits when he wrote *Human, All Too Human* (and to that extent, it was based on a self-misunderstanding, insofar as it did not appreciate its own need for "art," that is, Nietzsche's need to evade the reality about his situation in the world), but the preface also indicates that Nietzsche no longer needs to deceive himself about that question.

To put this point another way: Nietzsche wrote *A Book for Free Spirits*, but his preface makes it into *A Book for (and about) a Free Spirit*, that is, a book *for* and *about* himself (or, at least, the preface allows these two meanings of the work to coexist in a way that they had not before). This is to say that Nietzsche can ultimately affirm the sentiment of one of his favorite writers, Montaigne (as quoted in the epigraph to this chapter): what he writes may be useful to others, but it would have to be so "accidentally" (since its becoming so depends on forces outside his control), and so it is to be understood as useful for himself first and foremost.

But this thought has to be nuanced in an important respect: for, as we have just seen, the trajectory of a Free Spirit leads up to the recovery of an individual "task." And although the 1886 prefaces persistently allude to the emergence of the task, they do not fully explain it. *Ecce Homo* remedies that situation by showing that the task that incubates in the Free Spirit writings is brought fully into the world only through *Thus Spoke Zarathustra*—and that this process entails a stretching-beyond-oneself that puts it at some distance from the returning-to-oneself of *Human, All Too Human*. Let us see how that works.

THE HISTORY OF *THUS SPOKE ZARATHUSTRA*

Ecce Homo defines Nietzsche's task and shows how his various writings contributed to its realization. In this account, everything leads toward *Thus Spoke Zarathustra*, and Nietzsche's task is to some degree equated with Zarathustra's.

The first key statement occurs in the same section where Nietzsche explains "how to become what you are": in this context, he refers to how one's life trains one in stages to take up one's "dominant task"—which (switching to the context of his own life) he refers to as "the task of *revaluing values*." Then, when commenting on the works of the Free Spirit period, Nietzsche explains how they each contributed to the emergence of this task, leading up to *Zarathustra*: first, in *Human, All Too Human*, by launching a critique of morality that was a necessary ground-clearing exercise for the revaluation of values (*EH* HH 6);[50] next, in *Daybreak*, by becoming more conscious of the necessity of that task of revaluation, which Nietzsche refers to in these terms:

> My task, that of preparing the way for a moment of highest self-contemplation on humanity's part, a *great noon-day* when it will look back and look ahead, when it will step out from under the dominance of chance and the priests and for the first time ask the question "why?" "what for?" *as a whole*. (*EH* D 2)

The overall characterization of this task (especially the language of the "great noon-day") points ahead to *Thus Spoke Zarathustra*. Indeed, in his next commentary, on *The Joyful Wissenschaft*, Nietzsche says as much: this work, he says, is written on the basis of a new hope that looks to be realized through the work of *Zarathustra*.[51] And, in the final section of the subchapter on *Zarathustra*, Nietzsche directly identifies his task with the task of his creation ("At one point Zarathustra strictly specifies his task—it is mine, too"; "he is *yes-saying* to the point of justifying, of redeeming even all that is past").[52] Finally, he declares that with *Zarathustra* complete, "the yes-saying part of my task was solved" (*EH* BGE 1).

However, this last formulation indicates that while *Zarathustra* is the capstone of one part of a process, it is not the end of it. And *Ecce Homo* shows why the work of *Zarathustra* had to be supplemented: namely, because the creation of *Zarathustra* involved a self-forgetting on Nietzsche's part that had to be followed by another return-to-himself, but a return now conducted on the basis of understanding that this process of self-forgetting and self-return constituted a permanent and productive characteristic of his life and thought. Let me spell out each of these points in turn.

The Turn to "Being-Outside-Oneself"

Nietzsche stresses that *Thus Spoke Zarathustra* is a "yes-saying" work, along with its predecessors, *Daybreak* and *The Joyful Wissenschaft* (and in this respect they all stand apart from *Human, All Too Human*).[53] But this seems to be true in a new way of *Zarathustra*, because Nietzsche highlights something new that is said "yes" to here. The second sentence of the subchapter devoted to the work states what that is: "The basic conception of the work—*the thought of eternal return*, the highest possible formula of affirmation—belongs to the August of 1881."

This is an artful formulation, which conveys a dual meaning: in the first place, it means that the eternal return is the key concept to be *found in the text* (where it is Zarathustra's formula of affirmation); but it also refers to the way in which the concept *occurred to Nietzsche himself* (how he, as the creator of the text, conceived of it). At various points throughout the subchapter, the lines between creature (Zarathustra) and creator (Nietzsche) become blurred, and that is related to the fact that at several points Nietzsche presents the work itself—and its "basic conception," in particular—as not exactly "belonging to" either himself or his creation. Instead, both appear as vectors for something altogether uncannier (and, to that extent, when Nietzsche says that "the basic conception of the work" is something that "belongs to the August of 1881," this could be taken fairly literally—what is fundamental here is the property of something other than Nietzsche himself).

The uncanny aspect of the work is indicated in several ways. To begin with, immediately after Nietzsche identifies the eternal return as the "basic conception" of *Zarathustra*, he notes that when "this thought came to me" in a hike through the woods, he "dashed it off" on a single sheet of paper with the caption: "6000 feet beyond man and time." This unusual formulation suggests something at the least out of the ordinary, and possibly something outside of the order of nature.[54]

Even more strikingly, throughout the remainder of section 1 of the subchapter Nietzsche frames his discussion within a context that is *musical*. This appears in several ways. First, he observes that his apprehension of Zarathustra's "basic conception" (the eternal return) carried with it "an omen": "a sudden and profoundly decisive alteration in my taste, in music above all." Then he adds, "*Zarathustra* as a whole may perhaps be counted as music." Finally, he remarks that in the period between 1881 and 1883 (that is, in the period after the eternal return first occurred to him on the mountain "6000 feet beyond man and time"), he composed a piece of music (the "Hymn to Life"), and he discusses this work at greater length than the book he wrote at the same time (*The Joyful Wissenschaft*). Furthermore, after having completed *Thus Spoke Zarathustra*, Nietzsche often chose to refer back to it in songs (as in the "Aftersong" concluding *Beyond Good and Evil*, and in the appendix of songs written for the reissue of *The Joyful Wissenschaft*). At all events, then, Nietzsche seems to stress that *Thus Spoke Zarathustra* and its "basic conception" have a kind of nondiscursive status, possibly a sub- or suprarational one (their "omen" having been a change in *taste*—in music, above all).

The musical dimension of this picture is significant, since (as we have seen earlier) in *Human, All Too Human* (for example, in aphorism 153) Nietzsche had identified music as one of the primary dangers that Free Spirits had to determinedly guard against, due to its potential to inspire mystical and metaphysical sympathies, and in the second of the 1886 prefaces to the work he warned even more emphatically, "Beware of Music!" But since Nietzsche's account of *Thus Spoke Zarathustra* makes so prominent, from the outset, that the basic conception of that work was bound up with a turn back to music on his part, we might recall a statement of Zarathustra's: "How could there be an outside-me? There is no outside me! But with all tones we forget that; how lovely it is that we forget!" And in *Ecce Homo* Nietzsche himself suggests that the musical turn of *Zarathustra* entailed a new kind of openness to what lay beyond himself: to begin with, at the end of section 1 of the relevant subchapter he describes the daily hikes that he would take when he lived along the Bay of Rapallo, "not far from Genoa," and comments, "On these two routes the whole first part of *Zarathustra* came to me, especially Zarathustra himself, as a type: or rather, he *ambushed me*." So Zarathustra (or his "type") seems to have come to Nietzsche as if from outside himself.[55]

But while Nietzsche at first only hints at the possibility that *Thus Spoke Zarathustra* is some sort of revelatory rather than strictly rational text, in section 3 of the subchapter that possibility is presented much more directly and dramatically. Section 3 takes up the hints of section 1, but in a way that immediately strikes the reader as discontinuous because, whereas the surrounding sections are placed within a detailed chronology (mentioning many exact places, dates, and events from Nietzsche's life), section 3 points outside of that whole chronology by opening with the question: "Does anyone, at the end of the nineteenth century, have any idea of what poets in strong ages called *inspiration*?" (In the next section Nietzsche will refer to himself as "the poet of *Zarathustra*.") Nietzsche explains what he means by "inspiration": "the sense of being just an incarnation, just a mouthpiece, just a medium for overpowering forces." "The notion of revelation," he comments, "provides a simple description of the facts of the matter." Nietzsche then provides a more detailed, phenomenological account of this phenomenon, encapsulating it with a striking neologism that he introduces here: "a perfect being-outside-yourself" (*ein vollkommnes Ausser-sich-sein*). The notion of "being-outside-yourself" as described here recalls something of the ecstatic experience of art that Nietzsche had once described in *The Birth of Tragedy*.[56] And, in a fragment from 1869 that reads as a draft for *The Birth of Tragedy*, Nietzsche characterizes Dionysian revelries as an "*Ausser-sich-sein*," entailing a dissolution of individual identity related to the process whereby poets come to believe in their own creations (*KSA* 1:521).[57]

Could something like this have happened with Nietzsche and his Zarathustra? Nietzsche suggests as much toward the end of section 3, where he shifts from describing the general phenomenon of "inspiration" to offer an observation about the description that he has just given: "it really seems—to recall a phrase of Zarathustra's [from the chapter on "The Return Home"]—as though the things themselves were stepping forward and offering themselves for allegorical purposes." Then, as if recalling Zarathustra's experience for himself, Nietzsche provides in parentheses a direct quotation of the most "metaphysical" passage of that same chapter ("Here the words and word-shrines of all Being spring open for you . . ."). But then, immediately outside of the parentheses, Nietzsche emphatically asserts: "This is *my* experience of inspiration." So Nietzsche's account of *his own* experience of inspiration shades into the experience of *his character* Zarathustra, and it is not entirely clear where Nietzsche ends and where Zarathustra begins. The reader is thereby left with the impression that *Zarathustra* was the product of an immersion in the kinds of inspired experiences that Nietzsche has just outlined—and, insofar as those are timeless experiences (or, at least, typical of "strong ages"), Nietzsche seems to be recommending them to the reader, as an encounter worth seeking out, or at least remaining open to (perhaps by regularly indulging oneself in the stimulus of music, for example).[58]

This experience of "being-outside-yourself"—the sense of being a part of, or a vehicle for, something beyond or greater than oneself—seems to stand at a distance from the "return to myself" that characterized *Human, All Too Human* (with its self-disciplined concentration - especially in *The Wanderer and His Shadow* - on what is "closest").[59] To that extent, Nietzsche's account of revelation serves to underline the fundamental gulf that separates these two landmarks of his career: *Human, All Too Human* marked his return to, and focus on, his most individual self; *Zarathustra* represents a receptivity to and immersion in what lies beyond himself.

The Turn to "Great Health"

That being said, while these two key moments of Nietzsche's career are very different, they are not simply discontinuous. For in *Ecce Homo* Nietzsche indicates that he possesses a perspective that enables him, in successive steps, to reach beyond, and then reflect back on, himself (including his creation of *Zarathustra*). That perspective is made possible by what he calls his "great health."[60]

The perspective of the great health is introduced in section 2 of *Ecce Homo*'s subchapter on *Zarathustra*. The context of the section is complex. It is set up in the following way: in the last sentence of section 1, Nietzsche gives his description of the circumstances under which Zarathustra "*ambushed*" him, referring to Zarathustra in that context as a "type" ("the whole first part of *Zarathustra* came to me, especially Zarathustra himself, as a type"). This notion of Zarathustra as a "type" is picked up in the first sentence of section 2, which reads: "To understand this type [that is, Zarathustra] you first need to be clear about its physiological precondition, which is what I call *great health*." That Nietzsche refers here to Zarathustra as a "type" *to be understood* suggests that a critical distance from the character of Zarathustra is being adopted. So whereas in section 1 Nietzsche characterized his enterprise in *Zarathustra* as one of nondiscursive or subrational inspiration (a suggestion intensified by section 3), in section 2 he points toward a vantage point from which that entire enterprise can be analyzed and evaluated. This impression is reinforced when we find that the remainder of section 2 consists of an aphorism reproduced (with minor modification) from book 5 of *The Joyful Wissenschaft*, where it appeared as the penultimate aphorism (no. 382) under the title of "The Great Health." Now, book 5 of *The Joyful Wissenschaft* was composed *after* Nietzsche had completed *Zarathustra*. In other words, in the midst of presenting *Zarathustra* as an example of the experience of "being-outside-oneself," Nietzsche introduces a perspective that stands apart from *that* whole experience.

There is one more point of context to mention here (and it will require me to momentarily descend into what might appear to be minutiae, though the relevance of these details should become clear in due course): as already noted, the aphorism on "The Great Health" originally appeared near the end of book 5 of *The Joyful Wissenschaft*—that is, in the second edition of the work (published in 1887). The aphorism concludes with the phrase "the tragedy *begins*." This phrase echoes the final aphorism to the *first* edition of the work (published in 1882). In the first edition, the work had concluded with an aphorism that presented the opening section of the preface to *Thus Spoke Zarathustra*, under the title "*Incipit Tragoedia*." So both editions of *The Joyful Wissenschaft* more or less conclude with an aphorism declaring that "the tragedy begins," a phrase that is to be understood as directing readers to *Thus Spoke Zarathustra*. But the second edition of the work complicates the meaning of that phrase. For in the preface to the second edition, Nietzsche writes as follows: "*Incipit tragoedia*, we read at the end of this suspiciously innocent book. Beware! Something utterly wicked and mischievous is being announced here: *incipit parodia*, no doubt." In other words: *after* completing *Zarathustra* Nietzsche can refer back to it in a way that suggests that what had originally seemed a "tragedy" may now also appear as a "parody." Looking back on *Zarathustra* makes it look somehow new. How that works is clarified by the aphorism on "great health," which is presented next.

The aphorism on "great health" outlines a series of experiences that a certain sort of person will pass through (and which, as already noted, are presented in *Ecce Homo* as the "physiological precondition" necessary to understand the "type" Zarathustra). Since the discussion is highly compressed and figurative, it may be helpful to quote from the aphorism directly, beginning with its first words:

> We who are new, nameless, hard to understand, we premature births of a yet unproven future, we require for a new end a new means, too, namely a new health, one that is stronger, craftier, tougher, bolder, merrier than all healths have been so far. Anyone whose soul thirsts to have experienced the entire compass of previous values and desiderata and to have circumnavigated the entire coastline of this "Mediterranean" of the ideal, anyone who wants to know from the adventures of his ownmost experience how it feels to be a conqueror and discoverer of the ideal, likewise to be an artist, a saint, a legislator, a sage, a scholar, a pious man, an old-style religious hermit: for this he is in need of one thing above all else, *great health*—of the kind you not only have but also still constantly acquire and have to acquire because time and again you give it up, have to give it up . . .

So: the "physiological precondition" of *Thus Spoke Zarathustra* is a "great health" that requires one to feel from "his ownmost experience how it feels to be a conqueror and discoverer of the ideal," and so also "an artist, a saint, a legislator, a sage, a scholar, a pious man, an old-style religious hermit." The aphorism goes on to comment on the result of immersing oneself in such experiences:

> How could we, after such prospects and with such a ravenous hunger in our knowledge and conscience, still be satisfied with *present-day man*? It is bad enough, but unavoidable, that we now observe his most worthy objectives and hopes with a seriousness that is difficult to maintain, and perhaps no longer even look.

But, Nietzsche continues, this turn away from "present-day man" is compensated for by a promised alternative: the "overflowing abundance" of a spirit that has seen through the old idols, so that their transcendence is accompanied by their replacement with a new "human-superhuman" ideal, which sets itself up against "all previous earthly seriousness," making it appear ridiculous—a "parody." But this is itself no laughing matter, for with the new ideal, Nietzsche stresses, "*the great seriousness* at last begins"—or, as the aphorism concludes, "the tragedy begins": *Thus Spoke Zarathustra* begins (see further *GM* II.24–25).

This all suggests that *Thus Spoke Zarathustra* is the product of a "great health" that enabled Nietzsche to experience for himself what it would entail to discover new ideals, and thus to know something of the experience of artists, legislators, and an array of religious types. In that light, it becomes clearer why Nietzsche places the creation of *Zarathustra* in an "inspired" context: the turn to what lies outside himself, including the possibility of something like divine inspiration, was an essential part of the experience of the work (both its composition and its content). Because the "great health" brings with it the possibility of a new "great seriousness"—because it is able to envision alternatives to "present-day man," and to inspire new acts of creation—Nietzsche's thought poses a permanent challenge to our world (and to any other world).

But although this constitutes *part of* Nietzsche's overall health, is it his final, or definitive, state of health? *No*: the great health is, Nietzsche says, "of the kind you not only have but also still constantly acquire and have to acquire because time and again <u>you give it up, have to give it up</u>."[61] Nietzsche's own experience illustrates the point. For, in the first line of section 4 of the subchapter (immediately after the section where he describes the experience of "revelation," and calls it "*my* experience," and associates it with the experience of "poets in <u>strong</u> ages," as well as with the experience of Zarathustra, whose experience seems to shade into his own), Nietzsche writes: "Afterwards I lay ill for a few weeks in Genoa." And then, in the next several sections, Nietzsche describes how, as the creator of *Zarathustra*, he came to terms with his work of creation—a necessary experience for any creator, recuperating by abjuring (at least temporarily) the role of the creator (see further *EH* BGE 2).[62] In other words, after the being-outside-himself of the "great health," Nietzsche's ill health brought him back, again, to himself.

For Nietzsche, then, the relationship between health and sickness is essentially interactive, and the "great health" therefore always stops short of being the "great*est* health."[63] This thought is consistent with Nietzsche's remarks in the first preface for *Human, All Too Human*: there he described (in section 4 of the preface) "that tremendous overflowing certainty and health which may not dispense even with sickness, as a means and fish-hook of knowledge,"[64] and (in section 5) he explained that "to become sick in the manner of these free spirits, to remain sick for a long time and then, slowly, slowly, to become healthy, by which I mean 'healthier'" can be considered a "*cure.*" In other words, the only cure that Nietzsche looks forward to is one that entails always returning to illness, but doing so in order to confront challenges that spur him to become continually "healthier."[65]

In sum: the moment of health and reaching beyond oneself is an essential part of Nietzsche's experience and understanding of the world, but it is not, cannot be, and is not desired as the whole of that experience or understanding. It is, rather, part of an ongoing development and interplay between health and illness, as he indicates in both the aphorism on "The Great Health" (where he describes it as a health that has to be constantly given up and reacquired), and the first preface to *Human, All Too Human* (where he stresses that he must always be getting "healthier"). To this extent, Nietzsche's thought can be characterized as dialectical, although it is a dialectic to be carried out primarily with (or within) oneself: for the dynamic of health and illness is, for Nietzsche, such that one can be led continually away from and back toward oneself, and thereby continually be exploring and learning from oneself.[66]

Concluding Remarks

Hardly anyone would aspire to lead Nietzsche's life. His achievements as an author and his posthumous fame might be appealing, but his life is another matter: after some youthful success as a student (which did not satisfy him much, in any case), he lived through a series of crippling illnesses, professional failures, and personal isolation, cut short by a sudden collapse at the age of forty-four. Nietzsche did not attempt to conceal the challenges that he faced. To the contrary: he drew attention to those challenges by equipping his books with an extensive autobiographical apparatus. And through those autobiographies Nietzsche showed how his books learned from and responded to the challenges that he faced in his life (from struggling with his health, to finding his work so often ignored or misunderstood, to confronting the missteps and self-misunderstandings that were bound up with different stages of his career).

Although Nietzsche went to great lengths to show how his books grew out of his life, readers can take some comfort in knowing that he did not recommend that others attempt to follow the exact path of his life; in fact, he insisted that an accomplishment such as his could only be arrived at by forging a path of one's own.[1] But he was still able to offer a few points of guidance for readers wishing to make their own way.

What Nietzsche offered were two characters who represent compelling but different ways of life: on the one hand, the Free Spirit, who is characterized by a drive to acquire maximal independence, and who adopts a strict self-discipline in order to maintain that independence; on the other hand, Zarathustra, who is characterized by a loving desire to creatively engage with the wider world, but who must confront the challenge of loving the world for what it is (rather than for what his will would make it). The experience of the Free Spirit is part of a return-to-oneself (concentrating on and caring for what is closest to, most personal about, oneself), while the experience of Zarathustra entails a kind of being-outside-oneself (forgetting or losing oneself within a larger whole).

I have argued that for Nietzsche neither one of these characters represents a complete, final, or altogether superior approach to life. What is key for Nietzsche is that both are *justified*: they are justified for the contributions they make to a larger process of learning ever more fully what one is. That is why Nietzsche sees an aspect of his overall health in each character: he made use of both, in order to think through (and get through) different periods of his life. And, as a result, he was able to think through the meaning of health—as well as the possibilities for independence, and the potential of love—from multiple and contrasting perspectives.

The task that Nietzsche executed in this manner was uniquely his own, but his account of the process outlines a general structure of self-exploration and self-realization that others may learn from to one degree or another. And he suggests some of the most important lessons to be learned along the way: protect your independence through a stringent self-discipline that minimizes your dependence on others as much as possible; eventually realize, however, that you have overestimated the degree to which you are or ever can be wholly independent, and once you have recognized that tension in your existence, strive to affirm it rather than escape or resent it; open yourself up to the capacity for love that connects you to others, and wait to uncover within yourself a task through which you can challenge yourself by actively engaging with the wider world; occasionally forget yourself by immersing yourself in a plethora of human possibilities that you are not; learn to love the world for what it is, rather than for what you can make it; learn the necessity of your own mistakes and suffering; learn that there is no end to this process, but only a process to be repeated, through which you can come to know yourself ever more deeply (although never completely).

For the most part, Nietzsche does not present his lessons in a didactic or doctrinal way. Instead, through the characters of the Free Spirit and Zarathustra he gives us a picture of what would otherwise be much more difficult to see: how those lessons could be learned, step by step, by an individual who was passionately determined to live out a drive to independence, or a desire for love, or the need to understand and serve the conditions of their own health.

In the end, however, Nietzsche makes no promises. He suggests that his work can be viewed as an experiment and a temptation.[2] It is therefore fitting that, in his autobiographical writings, he shows that he used his writings not so much to teach others as to learn for himself, through the work of articulating and reflecting on his experience of the world, and he leaves it to readers to test his account of his life against their own. And this leads me to a final conclusion: to read Nietzsche's writings within the context set by his autobiographies is to recognize that his work was not intended primarily as a doctrinal or metaphysical philosophic system, or as a literary achievement, or as a revolutionary manifesto. Those dimensions may be found within Nietzsche's writings, but his writings were first and foremost part of his own project of acquiring self-knowledge, and his work therefore ought to be judged first and foremost on the basis of how effectively (or deficiently) his writings help readers to acquire such knowledge for themselves.

NOTES

INTRODUCTORY REMARKS

1. For this quotation, and the criticism of reading more generally, see *EH* Clever 3, 8; *HH* 4.

2. See *D* Preface 5; *GM* Preface 8.

3. "What a philosopher is, that is hard to learn, because it cannot be taught: one must 'know' it, from experience" (*BGE* 213). See also *BGE* 6, 204, 292; as well as *D* 481; *GS* Preface 1.

4. "My writings speak *only* of my overcomings: 'I' am in them, together with everything that was inimical to me"; "But it has always required time, recovery, distancing, before the desire awoke within me to skin, exploit, expose, 'exhibit' (or whatever one wants to call it) for the sake of knowledge something I had experienced or survived, some fact or fate of my life" (*HH* vol. 2, Preface, section 1).

5. For some of Nietzsche's published commendations of these authors, see *AOM* 408; *GS* 92, 95; *SE* 2, 8; *TI* Expeditions 45; *WS* 86. On Nietzsche's reading more generally, see Brobjer, *Nietzsche's Philosophical Context*, 7–8, 23–25, 49, 115n49, 182n72).

6. *SE* 8. Nietzsche would have agreed with Pierre Hadot: "We ought not to forget that many a philosophical demonstration derives its evidential force not so much from abstract reasoning as from an experience which is at the same time a spiritual exercise" (*Philosophy as a Way of Life*, 107). Hadot makes this point primarily in reference to ancient philosophy, but he notes that Nietzsche shares the ancient understanding in this respect (272).

7. Consider his remark to a correspondent: "It is absolutely unnecessary, and not even desirable, for you to argue in my favor: on the contrary, a dose of curiosity as if you were looking at an alien plant, with an ironic resistance, would strike me as an incomparably more intelligent attitude towards me" (letter to Carl Fuchs, July 29, 1888). See also *EH* Destiny 1: "I have a terrible fear of being declared *holy* one day . . ."

8. Since it is quite common for Nietzsche's self-assessments to be given short shrift (including in scholarship that I have found in many respects quite instructive), a list of examples would quickly become unwieldy, but I have flagged some important instances in the notes as they arise (for instance, in these introductory remarks, see notes 14, 16, 21, and 43).

9. Abbey, *Nietzsche's Middle Period*, xii. For a recent example of this, see Stern's introduction to *The New Cambridge Companion to Nietzsche*, 5–12, which gives an overview of Nietzsche's career that "follows the convention" established by Salome, without noting her as the architect of that convention.

10. For what follows, see Salome, *Nietzsche* (especially 8, 33, 73, 88, 98–99). My synopsis is designed to highlight features of Salome's account that have become common currency.

11. Abbey, *Nietzsche's Middle Period*, 87, and Young, *Friedrich Nietzsche*, 242–43, both apply the positivist label to these writings with reference to their enthusiasm for modern science.

12. Thus, Jaspers follows Salome's periodization scheme (although without crediting her directly), and comments that the third period entails "a new faith . . . [that] expresses itself only symbolically and in a visionary manner" (*Nietzsche*, 44); and, according to Arnhart (who does credit Salome, and explicitly builds on her argument), *Zarathustra* "looks like Nietzsche's attempt to devise poetic imagery that will satisfy the transcending yearnings of atheists like himself who still have religious longings" (*Political Questions*, 438).

13. On the suspicion toward Nietzsche's later works that Salome's scheme helped to engender, see Behler, "Nietzsche in the Twentieth-Century," 286–87.

14. For instance, when Karl Löwith endorses Salome's scheme, he somewhat misleadingly remarks: "This division into periods is no mere external schematization that one could, without damage to one's understanding of Nietzsche's system, replace with another, better scheme. Rather, the periodic division is confirmed in its full significance by Nietzsche himself" (*Nietzsche's Philosophy of the Eternal Recurrence of the Same*, 23).

15. It should be acknowledged that Salome did not have access to one of Nietzsche's most important autobiographical statements, *Ecce Homo*, since it was not made public until a decade after her study. But her schema has endured long past that publication.

16. Martin Heidegger's approach to Nietzsche stands as an important case in point. Heidegger once began a course on Aristotle by issuing the following instruction to his students: "Regarding the personality of a philosopher, our only interest is that he was born at a certain time, that he worked, and that he died. The character of the philosopher, and issues of that sort, will not be addressed here" (*Basic Concepts of Aristotelian Philosophy*, 4). Aristotle's terse manner of writing, along with the absence of reliable biographical records, lends itself to such an approach, but Nietzsche would seem to be a very different case. Nevertheless, a decade after his course on Aristotle, Heidegger began a course on Nietzsche with an echo of his earlier injunction, telling students to disregard the well-known literature dealing with Nietzsche's biography (and scholarly literature more generally), since "whoever does not have the courage and perseverance of thought required to become involved in Nietzsche's own writings need not read anything *about* him either" (*Nietzsche*, vol. 1, 10–11). Yet precisely if one focuses one's energies on becoming involved in Nietzsche's own writings, one will be led into an appreciation of the ways in which "the character of the philosopher, and issues of that sort" did shape his thought, because Nietzsche tells us so much about exactly this matter. But this fact is not particularly evident from Heidegger's interpretation, because Heidegger focused, not on Nietzsche's published writings, but on his unpublished notes, in order to try and reconstruct from those notes a "system" (located within the history of metaphysics), which Heidegger was convinced that Nietzsche wanted to write. The autobiographical commentaries Nietzsche

appended to his books show greater direct interest in psychological than ontological questions, but Heidegger displays no interest in those commentaries (when Heidegger does refer to one of the retrospective prefaces, he winds up examining an unpublished fragmentary draft of that preface; see *Nietzsche*, vol. 3, 248). It seems to me more sensible to follow Heidegger's principle than his practice: that is, to focus attention on "Nietzsche's own writings," but to recognize that in making this the point of focus, we learn a great deal about Nietzsche's character and life, and their relation to his writings. The result should not be to "reduce" Nietzsche to his biography. To the contrary, the results presented in this study should demonstrate that Nietzsche's books are illuminating when taken on their own terms: they do not have to be read as the antechamber to some unpublished philosophy, because they represent a well-defined and self-contained project of their own (and, as a result, I have referred to Nietzsche's unpublished notes in only a few cases, where they seem to elaborate a thought that is stated more succinctly in the materials prepared for publication).

17. On the hermeneutical work that Nietzsche deliberately left for readers to complete on their own, see Lampert, *Nietzsche's Task*, 283–84; and Lampert, *What a Philosopher Is*, 208–9.

18. For a fuller account, I recommend consulting Schaberg's extremely valuable study, *The Nietzsche Canon: A Publication History and Bibliobiography*.

19. See *EH* BGE 1.

20. The distinct status of the Free Spirit and Zarathustra is most obvious from the fact that they are named in the very titles of the works that introduce them. Nietzsche has one other work whose title includes character names, *The Wanderer and His Shadow*, but these are both aspects of the Free Spirit. Richard Wagner is another "character" who appears in several of Nietzsche's titles, but Nietzsche did not create Wagner.

21. The approach to Nietzsche's thought that I am proposing here can be contrasted with that of Alexander Nehamas, whose influential study *Nietzsche, Life as Literature*, argues that Nietzsche made himself into the main character of his writings, turning his life into a literary artwork (playing the Plato to his own Socrates, Nehamas suggests [137, 194–99, 227–28, 234]). This general thesis shares something with my own, but the way in which Nehamas pursues his thesis has several problems from my point of view. First, Nehamas concludes that the character of Nietzsche is "so specific and idiosyncratic" that it cannot provide a model for anyone else's life (233), apart from supporting a commitment to creative self-fashioning (8). So the model that Nietzsche offers is quite indeterminate and unbounded for Nehamas: he calls it "aesthetic" because he thinks that Nietzsche "is so willing and even eager to leave the content of his ideal life unspecified" (166), limiting himself instead to showing us how to "give style" to whatever life we might choose (38–39, 185, 191; see also 222: "it is hard to avoid the suspicion that Nietzsche has little of positive value to say"). One reason that Nehamas can reach this conclusion is that he does not treat the Free Spirit and Zarathustra as characters who grow out of Nietzsche's life and experiences, and who represent concrete and demanding models of how to live (at one point Nehamas remarks that "Nietzsche's own conception [of a free spirit] stops short of being very specific" [132; see also 226]). Moreover, although I agree that Nietzsche made a kind of literary character out of himself, Nehamas does not really help us to understand how Nietzsche went about that task, because he overlooks most of what Nietzsche says about how his life informs his work. At one point Nehamas expresses "the suspicion that only the 'biog-

raphy' that emerges through Nietzsche's works, and not the 'life' out of which they grow, is of any importance" (199). This would be fair enough, if Nehamas did not neglect so much of what Nietzsche says *in his works* about the life out of which they grow. Thus, Nehamas focuses his attention on Nietzsche's writings from *Thus Spoke Zarathustra* onward, but he explicitly disregards their relationship to earlier writings, noting that "my practice leaves many questions about Nietzsche's development unanswered, for whole books could be written not only about these questions but also about the views Nietzsche expressed in these works" (9). But Nietzsche's later writings actually raise such questions repeatedly, and that is because Nietzsche makes clear that the "character" that he fashions out of himself in the later writings is one that has grown out of (learned from and responded to) problems laid out by his earlier works, so interpreting the later works in isolation leaves out much of importance. Nehamas justifies his procedure by denying that any particular relationship among Nietzsche's writings can or should be determined (10), taking the view that Nietzsche ("intellectually unable to engage in long, sustained argument") was merely concerned with presenting the same set of problems again and again "from as many points of view as possible," and not with developing solutions to those problems (231). At every turn, then, Nehamas's concern is with "the magnificent character" who appears in Nietzsche's writings, to the exclusion of "the miserable little man who wrote them" (234). I think that Robert Pippin (*Interanimations*, 153) is, therefore, right to suggest that a more appropriate subtitle for Nehamas's study would have been "Literature *Instead of* Life." But such a prospect would have horrified Nietzsche (as his skepticism about the value of books indicates). To be sure, Nietzsche invested a tremendous amount of his life in his work as an author, but he used his books to present and evaluate determinate and demanding possibilities about how best to conduct one's life (the Free Spirit and Zarathustra being major options), and he did not view his achievements as an author as something distinct and separable from the achievements and experiences of his life taken as a whole. In sum: I believe that for Nietzsche an author's work is derivative from their life (not vice versa), and so the work cannot be understood as superior to the life that makes the work possible. Nehamas's contrary position may be compelling in its own right (for a thoughtful defense, see Anderson and Landy, "Philosophy as Self-Fashioning"), but in that case it needs to be considered as an *alternative* to Nietzsche's position, not as an extension of it.

22. Pinker, *Enlightenment Now*, 445–49; also 33 (Pinker's assessment draws heavily on the lengthier critique by Wolin, *The Seductions of Unreason*).

23. For some examples, see Aschheim, *The Nietzsche Legacy in Germany*, 6–25, 37–41, 114–18; Parkes, "Nietzsche and East Asian Thought," 360–61; Ratner-Rosenhagen, *American Nietzsche*, 29–36, 149–60, 172–92, 257–60; Rosenthal, *New Myth, New World: From Nietzsche to Stalinism*, 28–32, 68–94; Sevea, *The Political Philosophy of Muhammad Iqbal*, 102–3.

24. Pinker, *Enlightenment Now*, 446 (Nietzsche was "a lively stylist" with "literary panache").

25. See further the concerns about Nietzsche put forward by Philippa Foot, *Moral Dilemmas*, 158; as well as by Beiner, *Dangerous Minds*, 62–63; and Gillespie, *Nietzsche's Final Teaching*, 198–99.

26. This conflict is dramatized in a landmark American drama, Eugene O'Neill's *Long Day's Journey into Night*. In the autobiographical play a character representing the young O'Neill outrages his family with his keen interest in Nietzsche.

27. On Elisabeth Förster-Nietzsche, see Diethe, *Nietzsche's Sister and "The Will to Power."*

28. See Kaufmann, *Nietzsche: Philosopher, Psychologist, Antichrist*, 418 (Kaufmann's book was originally published in 1950, and is now in its fifth edition, published in 2013).

29. See Nehamas, *Nietzsche: Life as Literature*; and Foucault, "Nietzsche, History, Genealogy." Foucault became interested in questions of self-care and self-creation late in his career, but he did not directly link that interest to his reading of Nietzsche. Although the reading of Nietzsche as primarily a theorist of private, personal self-improvement dissociated him somewhat from politics, it also had an influence that extended beyond the studies of academic specialists, which can be seen at work in the 2004 film *Eternal Sunshine of the Spotless Mind* (or, more recently, in John Kaag's *Hiking with Nietzsche*, which presents Nietzsche's thought as a kind of self-help manual for a general audience).

30. Williams, *Shame and Necessity*, 10–11.

31. For this description, see Brobjer, "The Absence of Political Ideals in Nietzsche's Writings," 313, 315.

32. See Detwiler, *Nietzsche and the Politics of Aristocratic Radicalism*. The paradoxical formula of an "aristocratic radical" was coined by one of Nietzsche's first readers, George Brandes; Nietzsche called it "the cleverest thing that I have yet read about myself."

33. For a strong statement of this position, see Pangle, "The Roots of Contemporary Nihilism and Its Political Consequences according to Nietzsche"; and Pangle, "The 'Warrior Spirit' as an Inlet to the Political Philosophy of Nietzsche's *Zarathustra*."

34. Detwiler, *Nietzsche and the Politics of Aristocratic Radicalism*, 5.

35. Beiner, *Dangerous Minds*, 39 (emphasis in original).

36. Gillespie, *Nietzsche's Final Teaching*, ix.

37. Pinker, *Enlightenment Now*, 452, 446.

38. Gillespie, *Nietzsche's Final Teaching*, xiv.

39. Beiner, *Dangerous Minds*, 5, 14 (emphasis in original).

40. A somewhat different recent assessment is offered by Drochon's *Nietzsche's Great Politics*, which agrees with the first two propositions (and, to that end, provides the most detailed case since Detwiler for reading Nietzsche as a political thinker), but is more equivocal with respect to the third proposition, since although Drochon contends that "there *is* a Nietzschean politics," he also argues that "it is first and foremost a politics for the nineteenth century" (22). That claim seems to me to stand at some tension with a further claim Drochon makes, to the effect that Nietzsche's late writings are "dictated by the logic of a total revolution: having presented his philosophy, he is moving into politics, he is getting ready to 'rule the world.' What Nietzsche means by this is that once Christianity is no longer the only dominant form of morality, his philosophy will be able to direct certain segments of society" (151). I agree that Nietzsche's late writings suggest something along those lines, but I think it follows that the power of his thought has to be assessed in precisely those more "millenarian" terms: has Nietzsche discovered a new meaning of human existence (moving beyond the Enlightenment, beyond Christianity, beyond "Platonism"—beyond good and evil), and devised a way to shape and direct human life in accordance with that meaning? Is it plausible to think that such a goal could be realized (or even coherently conceived)? I think that Nietzsche knew quite well that a major source of his appeal to readers would be his skill at playing with the millenarian "logic of

a total revolution" (as is quite rightly stressed by Beiner, *Dangerous Minds*, 7–11, 43, 47, 54–58). But if that logic is compelling, it will not be compelling only (or even primarily) in the context of the nineteenth century. Thus, it is striking that although Drochon advises readers interested in Nietzsche's political philosophy to look for it primarily in *Beyond Good and Evil*, together with the thumbnail sketches of a political movement that are found in private notes and letters (47–48, 184), he does not mention Nietzsche's epistolary warning that "people *may* be able to read [*Beyond Good and Evil*] around the year 2000" (letter to Malwida von Meysenbug, September 24, 1886). Accordingly, Drochon tends to look for Nietzsche's political philosophy in comparatively prosaic (and unpublished) public policy prescriptions. The appeal of those prescriptions certainly is constricted by time and place (which may be why Nietzsche did not publish them), but if Nietzsche's political vision was not so narrowly limited to the nineteenth century, then his thought may remain compelling regardless (see note 42, below).

41. See *EH* Dynamite 1.

42. On Goldman and Nietzsche, see Ferguson, *Emma Goldman*, 160–61 (quoting Goldman's comment that "[Nietzsche's] aristocracy was neither of birth nor purse, it was of the spirit"). As a further example of Nietzsche's protean political appeal, we can add that the anarchist Goldman was joined in her admiration for Nietzsche by the conservative American president Richard Nixon, who made a point of reading Nietzsche during political campaigns, explaining that Nietzsche bolstered his conviction that "without struggle, man grows soft and life becomes meaningless" (Crowley, *Nixon in Winter*, 351–52). These remarks by Goldman and Nixon make clear that they were drawn to the political *spirit* or *character* held up by Nietzsche, not to his political proposals in the more narrow sense of precise public policy positions. (It would, therefore, be a mistake for anyone interested in Nietzsche's influence, including his political influence, to focus their attention narrowly on those "public policy" positions; for instance, if Nietzsche praises the Laws of Manu, what matters most is the *ethos* that it exemplifies, not the exact rules that it prescribes.) It is also worth noting that Nietzsche's appeal, for either Goldman or Nixon, is not that of a teacher of nihilism; for both, Nietzsche is an invigorating thinker because he holds out the hope that even after the "death of God," modern life can still be *meaningful* (on this point, see Heidegger, *Nietzsche*, vol. 1, 66).

43. As will become increasingly clear over the course of this study, I think that an essential principle for any interpretation of Nietzsche is given by his statement, "Psychology is now once again the path to the fundamental problems" (*BGE* 23). Two major readings of Nietzsche that use this statement as a starting point, and think through its importance for his whole project, are Parkes, *Composing the Soul*, and Pippin, *Nietzsche, Psychology, and First Philosophy*. These are both illuminating studies, but they tend to investigate Nietzsche's reflections on psychology in a general sense, rather than taking what seems to me to be the indispensable step of examining in a systematic way what Nietzsche says about how his own psychology (and thus his own life) shaped his writings (although the importance of the issue is noted by Parkes: see, for example, *Composing the Soul*, 13, 123, 408n76).

44. Although Nietzsche scholarship generally takes a more nuanced view than the one I am objecting to here, the less nuanced view is probably the more broadly influential one. It is visible not only in the case of Steven Pinker (see note 22, above), but also in prominent authors ranging from Bertrand Russell (*Power*, 211) to Simone de Beauvoir (*The Ethics of Ambiguity*,

72) to Charles Taylor (*The Ethics of Authenticity*, 65–66) to Dierdre McCloskey (*The Bourgeois Virtues*, 394) (and see also Heidegger, *Nietzsche*, vol. 2, 215–16). It is especially prevalent in a resilient tendency to characterize Nietzsche's thought as a modern-day iteration of the "might makes right" teachings of the Platonic characters Callicles and Thrasymachus (for example, see Barney, "Callicles and Thrasymachus"; Deleuze, *Nietzsche and Philosophy*, 54; Dodds, *Plato's Gorgias*, 388; Flanagan, *The Geography of Morals*, 17; Hobbs, *Plato and the Hero*, 151; Ryan, *On Politics*, 52). To be sure, what I am referring to here as the "less nuanced view" has an important degree of prima facie plausibility, but readers who doubt that a rhetorical bomb-thrower like Nietzsche could have aimed, on a certain level of argument, to temper rather than merely to inflame might consider an admonition that appears in Proust: "It is true that the qualities Mme de Villeparisis especially favored, such as levelheadedness and moderation, had nothing very inspiring about them; but, to be able to talk about moderation in an entirely convincing way, moderation itself is not enough, and certain of a writer's qualities that entail a somewhat immoderate sense of inspiration are needed" (*The Guermantes Way*, 178–79). I think that a similar judgment informs Nietzsche's way of writing.

45. For a summary and criticism of these tendencies, see Drochon, *Nietzsche's Great Politics*, 72–74; as well as Beiner, *Dangerous Minds*.

CHAPTER 1

1. As Robert Pippin observes, "Many contemporary philosophers want to ask of Friedrich Nietzsche questions he himself does not directly address, to make use of what he does say, what he does seem committed to, to try to figure out what he would say, or what he must be committed to, in spite of his silence about various issues, all in a more conventional philosophical language" (*Nietzsche, Psychology, and First Philosophy*, xiii). For further reflection on appropriations of Nietzsche, consider Stern, " 'Some Third Thing': Nietzsche's Words and the Principle of Charity."

2. This statement appeared on the back of the title page to the first edition of the *Genealogy* (see William Schaberg, *The Nietzsche Canon*, 149). Nietzsche characterizes all his writings from *Beyond Good and Evil* onward as "fishhooks" in *EH* BGE 1.

3. Davis, *The Autobiography of Philosophy*, 48.

4. On Nietzsche's addressee in this section, see further Hatab, *Nietzsche's "On the Genealogy of Morality": An Introduction*, 25–27.

5. This is one of the oldest objections that philosophers have faced: Aristophanes directed it at Socrates in *The Clouds*, and Plato has Socrates outline the same problem in a famous passage referring to Thales (*Theaetetus* 173c–75e; also *Philebus* 48a–50d), whom Aristotle identifies as the first of the natural philosophers (*Metaphysics* 983b18). That this problem was so well known early in the philosophic tradition does not diminish the force of Nietzsche's treatment of it. To the contrary: the fact that the classical treatment of that problem (whether by Socrates, Plato, or Aristotle) has become part of a "philosophic tradition" renders that treatment problematic, for insofar as it becomes part of received wisdom—an orthodoxy in which certain answers are taken for granted and certain questions are left unasked—it functions as an obstacle to genuine self-knowledge, rather than a challenge to be discovered and wrestled with in its

elemental form. Nietzsche, therefore, sets out to clear a new path to self-knowledge partly by dismantling the authority of the whole "tradition" through his genealogies and polemics (not least of all by calling into question the authority of Socrates and Plato).

6. At least until the eighth and last section of the preface, which takes a new turn, instructing the reader in the "*art* of reading" necessary to appreciate the text.

7. Davis, *The Autobiography of Philosophy*, 35.

8. Thus, while Ken Gemes helps to explain how self-knowledge functions as a central concern of the *Genealogy*, he nonetheless concludes that after the first section of the preface, "the whole theme of being strangers to ourselves is quickly and quietly dropped" ("'We Remain of Necessity Strangers to Ourselves': The Key Message of Nietzsche's *Genealogy*," 192). Janaway calls the first section "detached and disconcerting" (*Beyond Selflessness*, 16).

9. Although Gemes (see note 8, above) overlooks the connection between these questions in the preface, I believe he correctly identifies why, as a general matter, Nietzsche carries out his commentary on self-knowledge only "indirectly," under cover of a commentary on morality: because, although Nietzsche's remarks on morality are rather ostentatiously shocking, they are actually *much less shocking* than what he has to say about self-knowledge (consider *GS* 335: "the saying 'Know Thyself,' addressed to human beings by a god, is near to malicious"). A would-be knower (or anyone else) will be open to being "shocked" regarding morality before they are open to being shocked regarding the state of their self-knowledge (they might even enjoy the former, but certainly not the latter). Nietzsche therefore hooks a few readers into the painful questioning of their self-knowledge by drawing them in with the enticing bait of his questions about morality.

10. It seems to me that Janaway invites confusion when he writes, "Nietzsche states that his ideas have not fundamentally changed in the ten years since *Human, All Too Human*" (*Beyond Selflessness*, 19). As a general matter, Nietzsche holds that each person exhibits a certain degree of "fundamental" consistency (see *BGE* 231), and that is true of himself here as well (thus his language about the "common root" from which all his thoughts spring). But Janaway's formulation encourages the reader to gloss over the possibility that any significant development has occurred in the ten years between *Human, All Too Human* and the *Genealogy*. Nietzsche suggests otherwise when he expresses his hope that his thoughts will prove to have become "more mature, stronger, brighter, more perfect," and he will go on to speak more plainly about the shortcomings of *Human, All Too Human*. Still, it is better to recognize—as Janaway does—that Nietzsche wants the reader to appreciate a fundamental continuity in his thought, than to conclude—as Raymond Geuss (*Changing the Subject*, 193) does—that Nietzsche is so unconcerned with finding any kind of "consistency" behind the various "masks" put on by a given philosopher that "it is a mistake even to ask 'who is the *real* Nietzsche?'" For Geuss's Nietzsche, "the true philosopher knows that beneath any mask there may well lie not a natural face but another mask. In fact, beneath the mask there may be further masks, all the way down as far as we can reach" (192). Nietzsche would agree with the first sentence, but not the second: if he thought there was not anything to philosophy beyond a multitude of masks, he could not have cast his own work in terms of a "common root," or written autobiographies that tried to help his readers identify the "root" that lay beneath the masks that he adopted over the course of his career. Also relevant to this point are letters that Nietzsche wrote in December 1882 to

Hans von Bülow and Erwin Rohde. In these letters Nietzsche admits that he has constructed a "second nature" for himself, but defends that procedure on the grounds that it has enabled him to enter into "genuine *possession*" of his "first nature" (so the mask of the second nature conceals, and serves, an enduring core).

11. Otherwise detailed commentaries on the *Genealogy* do not have much (or anything) to say about the list of references that Nietzsche provides in the fourth section of the preface. For instance, in a section-by-section commentary on the preface, Conway remarks only that the references are meant to illustrate "the superior, unsentimental explanations that his [Nietzsche's] own books provide of the moral phenomena under investigation in GM," as compared to the efforts of his friend Paul Rée (*Nietzsche's 'On the Genealogy of Morals': A Reader's Guide*, 23). This is true enough, but it is insufficient, because Nietzsche has just gone out of his way to criticize the book in which these passages appeared, so the evolution of his own thought is at issue here, not just his disagreement with Rée. And, as we will now see, the list of references that Nietzsche gives clarifies the self-criticism he is making.

12. This is most obvious if one considers the instance that appears, at first glance, to be most incongruous: the inclusion of a reference to *Daybreak* (that is, a book that Nietzsche wrote *after* completing the three installments of *Human, All Too Human—HH*, *AOM*, and *WS*) in the midst of three references to *The Wanderer and His Shadow*. But if one refers to the texts, the connection is clear: *D* 112 concludes by stressing the "equilibrium" necessary to justice; the next reference (*WS* 22) has the title "Principle of Equilibrium" and elaborates on the connection of equilibrium to justice.

13. Nietzsche makes this point emphatically and often, for example: "[W]e continue on with custom and morality: which latter is nothing other than simply a feeling for the whole content of those customs under which we live and have been raised—and raised, indeed, not as an individual, but as a member of the whole, as a cipher in a majority" (*AOM* 89). "Morality is first of all a means of preserving the community and warding off its destruction; then it is a means of preserving the community at a certain height and in a certain quality of its existence" (*WS* 44). "Whenever we encounter a morality we find an evaluation and ranking of human drives and actions. These evaluations and rankings are always the expression of the needs of a community and a herd"; "With morality the individual is instructed to be a function of the herd"; "Morality is herd-instinct in the individual" (*GS* 116). For further discussion of this issue, see Richardson, *Nietzsche's New Darwinism*, 85–94.

14. For Nietzsche's view of natural neediness as the key factor in the development of community, see *GS* 354.

15. "Socrates and Plato are right: whatever man does he always does the good, that is to say, that which seems to him good (useful) according to the relative degree of his intellect, the measure of his rationality" (*HH* 102). Also see *HH* 107: "there is no difference in kind between good and evil actions, but at most in degree."

16. This point is important because (as Nietzsche stresses in the preface to *GM*) *HH* was partly a response to arguments by his friend Paul Rée suggesting that morality was originally associated with "altruistic" actions that benefited the community, in contrast to immoral, egoistic actions that reflected only self-interest. But Nietzsche rejects precisely this duality (see Franco, *Nietzsche's Enlightenment*, 25–26). Nietzsche does not treat actions benefiting the community

as part of a distinct class of behavior, with a unique goal and motivation ("selfless" rather than "selfish"). It is crucial for Nietzsche that all actions are at their root *attempts* by individuals to secure their own good, so that actions are to be evaluated with respect to the *effectiveness* with which they accomplish that goal: "Nowadays there is a thoroughly erroneous moral theory which is celebrated especially in England: it claims that judgments of 'good' and 'evil' sum up experiences of what is 'expedient' and 'inexpedient'; that what is called good preserves the species while what is called evil harms it. In truth, however, the evil drives are just as expedient, species-preserving, and indispensable as the good ones—they just serve a different function" (*GS* 4).

17. As this suggests, since morality is an instrument of community, and since any functioning community requires custom, the "morality of requital" precedes the "morality of custom" in a logical rather than a temporal sense (see also *D* 9: "Everywhere that a community, and consequently a morality of custom exists").

18. Nietzsche calls the morality of custom "the longest epoch of the human race" in *GM* II.2 (and refers the reader to *D* 9, which makes the same point). In *D* 16 Nietzsche states "the first proposition of civilization": "any custom is better than no custom," so that initially custom need be no more than a "perpetual compulsion to practice custom." Nietzsche's sources for this point are helpfully discussed by Franco, *Nietzsche's Enlightenment*, 63–66 (finding that Nietzsche was "drawing heavily on the most advanced anthropological knowledge of his day"). For more recent scholarship that offers a similar account, see Henrich, *The Secret of Our Success*, chap. 9.

19. As this suggests, Nietzsche sees that "an important species of pleasure, and thus an important source of morality, originates in habit" (*HH* 97). "Pleasure in custom" therefore constitutes one of the most attractive ties binding us to society—but this more civilized experience of morality is possible only after a long process of harsh and painful domestication (on this point, see also *D* 16, 18; *BGE* 229; *GM* II.2–3, III.9). From Nietzsche's point of view, the harsher varieties of custom have the advantage of making its true purpose clearer (reshaping individuals so that they can be reliably subordinated to their communities).

20. Nietzsche elaborates this point in a later text: "That is how education always proceeds: it tries to condition the individual through various attractions and advantages to adopt a way of thinking and behaving that, when it has become habit, drive, and passion, rules in him and over him *against his ultimate advantage* but 'for the common good.'" (*GS* 21).

21. To make sense of this point, one needs to know that for Nietzsche "forgetting" is not a passive act, where thoughts happen to slip from our mind through laziness and oversight; it is an *activity* that the mind imposes on itself, with effort and purpose (*GM* II.1; see also *HL* 1)—in this case for the purpose of making morality operate more effectively within ourselves, and thus within our broader communities. For a recent account of forgetting—in the form of self-deception—that supports Nietzsche's assessment of it as an active capacity that shapes our existence, see von Hippel and Trivers, "The Evolution and Psychology of Self-Deception."

22. Nietzsche's fullest discussion of this problem is *GS* 354. The theme of language as an instrument of communal valuations (that is, of a specific morality) appears throughout his writings (an overview is provided by Richardson, "Nietzsche, Language, Community"). A discussion of the problem that builds on Nietzsche's arguments in order to illuminate how the most

famous philosophic moralism—the Platonic theory of the Ideas—self-consciously builds on the "systematically misleading" (that is to say, systematically moralizing) character of language is offered by Lampert, *How Philosophy Became Socratic*, 334–36.

23. *GS* 344, quoted in *GM* III.24.

24. On Nietzsche's allusion to Odysseus, see further Lampert, *Nietzsche and Modern Times*, 319–24.

25. Pippin puts the point well: "according to Nietzsche, after Socrates (and all that he embodies and represents), 'knowing the truth' had come to matter very much—matter too much for our own good, Nietzsche wants to say; too much was expected of it" (*Interanimations*, 193).

26. An example of this phenomenon can be found in a book on self-deception by Robert Trivers (whose pioneering work stands behind the popularization of evolutionary biology by Richard Dawkins, Steven Pinker, and others). Trivers comments as follows on the relationship between truth and justice in scientific research (referring here to both the physical and the social sciences): "The usual assumption within academia is that we will derive a theory of justice from our larger theory of truth. But what if our prior stance regarding justice impedes our search for the truth? For example, an unconscious bias toward an unjust stance will invite cognitive biases in favor of this stance . . . In short, injustice invites self-deception, unconsciousness, and inability to perceive reality, while justice has the opposite effect. This can be a very pervasive effect in life. That is, we can construct a social theory—at the microlevel marriage, family, job; at the macrolevel society, war, etc.—and think we are pursuing the truth objectively, but we may only be fleshing out our biases. This suggests that an early attachment to fairness or justice may be a lifelong aid in discerning truth regarding social reality" (Trivers, *The Folly of Fools*, 304). So Trivers begins by asking a seemingly "Nietzschean" question (how do our moral commitments subconsciously shape our orientation toward the truth?), but then he winds up suggesting that "truth" and "justice" must ultimately be in some kind of fundamental harmony ("injustice" distorts our ability to recognize truth; "justice has the opposite effect"). But what sort of cosmic alignment of truth and justice would be necessary to ensure that a commitment to justice will reliably constitute "a lifelong aid in discerning truth," and not carry any of the dangers of "self-deception, unconsciousness, and inability to perceive reality"? This inadvertent disclosure of Trivers's faith in the old Platonist moral fire would surely have caused Nietzsche to smile.

27. Although he is by no means opposed to this sort of scientific work: "Of course even among the scholars of today there are enough steady and modest working folk who like their littler corner and therefore, because they like it there, from time to time speak up rather immodestly with the demand that one *should* be satisfied in general today, above all in the sciences—there is so much useful that needs doing precisely there. I won't contradict; least of all do I want to ruin the pleasure these honest workers take in their craft: for I enjoy their work" (*GM* III.23).

28. Franco, *Nietzsche's Enlightenment*, 211; also see Janaway, *Beyond Selflessness*, 237.

29. Philosophy is defined by its *independence* from early in Nietzsche's career to the end. Thus, early on Nietzsche opposed the modern, Hegelian view of philosophy to the example set by Schopenhauer, making the following observation: "in the end the supposed child of his time proves to be only its stepchild" (*SE* 3; also see *HL* 9). That is, the philosopher is not produced by the world in which he happens to live, but is a rebellious outlier whose true kin lie across

the boundaries of time and space. And, near the beginning of one of his very last books, Nietzsche remarked: "To live alone, you must be an animal or a God—says Aristotle. He left out the third case: you must be both—*a philosopher* . . ." (*TI* Maxims 3). Nietzsche's identification of independence as the aim of philosophy is consistent, although his understanding of how it is achieved evolves.

30. In a notebook entry, Nietzsche comments on the title of Schopenhauer's magnum opus: "'The World as Will and Representation'—translated in a close and personal way back into Schopenhauerian: 'The World as Sex-Drive and Tranquility'" (*KSA* 12:44 [1885/1/148]).

31. Consider section 8: "These are no unbribed witnesses and judges of the *value* of the ascetic ideal, these philosophers! They are thinking of *themselves*,—what is 'the saint' to them! They are thinking all the while of what is most indispensable precisely *to them*: freedom from compulsion, disturbance, noise." And "at the mention of the ascetic ideal they think, all in all, of the lighthearted asceticism of an animal that has been deified and become fully fledged, that roams more than rests above life." This outlook stands in contrast to one that Nietzsche sketches in the second section of the essay, characteristic of "all better-formed, more high-spirited mortals who are far from counting their labile balance between 'animal and angel' among the arguments against existence,—the subtlest and brightest, like Goethe, like Hafiz, have even seen in this one *more* enticement to life."

32. Consider the outlook of Goethe and Hafiz as described in note 31, above.

CHAPTER 2

1. See, in particular, Franco, *Nietzsche's Enlightenment: The Free Spirit Trilogy of the Middle Period*, which is an especially valuable guide to this series of writings.

2. This correspondence is noted by Werner Dannhauser, *Nietzsche's View of Socrates*, 164–66; and Franco, *Nietzsche's Enlightenment*, 15.

3. Ansell-Pearson, *Nietzsche's Search for Philosophy*, is attentive to the subtle combination of continuity and change that characterizes the *All Too Human* trilogy—although Ansell-Pearson tends to assimilate *AOM* and *WS*, whereas I will argue that the latter marks a more decisive turning point. Nevertheless, I cannot associate myself with Young's description of *WS* as an initially "*entirely* independent work" that was only brought together with *HH* and *AOM* in 1886 because "Nietzsche was concerned at the time to divide his past work into periods" (*Friedrich Nietzsche*, 277; emphasis added). The fact that *HH*, *AOM*, and *WS* are all organized according to the same chapter structure shows that they were linked together from the outset. And this fact is crucial for understanding the way in which *WS* serves to self-consciously revise the conclusions of the earlier volumes. Furthermore, as I noted in my introduction, above, Nietzsche does not really divide his work into "periods" (particularly not in the sense that has worked its way into scholarship following the suggestion of Lou Salome), although he does provide thematic categorizations for his works (the "Free Spirit" trilogy; the "yes-saying" versus "no-saying" works; those before and after *Zarathustra*)—but those categories are cross-cutting, and so do not amount to a "periodization."

4. Franco, in his generally authoritative study of the works of the "middle period," focuses his attention almost entirely on *HH*, justifying his neglect of *AOM* and *WS* in a note

that cites Nietzsche's own descriptions of these works as "continuations," "supplements," or "appendices" to *HH* (Franco, *Nietzsche's Enlightenment*, 233–34n8). In my judgment, those statements must be weighed against several facts. First, within the text of *Ecce Homo* Nietzsche refers to *WS* as an independent entity, and as a work that represents a distinct moment in his life and thought (see *EH* Wise 1 and *HH* 4); by contrast, *AOM* is never singled out for discussion. Similarly, in the fourth section of the preface to the *Genealogy*—where Nietzsche gives the series of references to *Human, All Too Human* for the reader to consult—he refers to *AOM* only as "Volume II," but he refers to *WS* by its unique title. And, in a notebook fragment from 1884, Nietzsche lists all of his writings up that point, with *WS* placed as a separate entry, in between *HH* and *D* (*KSA* 11:351 [1884/29/65]). Moreover, if one looks at the cover page of the first editions of *AOM* and *WS*, one can see plainly that, from the outset, Nietzsche highlighted the status of the former writing as a mere "continuation," and gave the latter a more independent status. Thus, the top half of the cover page for *AOM* has *Human, All Too Human* written in a large typeface, dominating the page, with *A Book for Free Spirits* on the next line in smaller type, followed by Nietzsche's own name near the center of the page. Below all of this one reads, *Appendix*: *Assorted Opinions and Maxims*. By contrast, on its successor volume we find an uncluttered title page, dominated by the words *The Wanderer and His Shadow* in large print (with no reference to *Human, All Too Human* anywhere on the page). So the original title pages suggest that *WS* stands on its own in a way that *AOM* does not. (The cover pages can be viewed in Schaberg, *The Nietzsche Canon*, 71, 75.) This is in keeping with the fact that, in later writings, "The Wanderer" (along with "the Shadow") would remain an important character in Nietzsche's writings: for example, *GS* 287, 309, 380; *TSZ*, "On Great Events" (toward the end, where Zarathustra is asked: "You have surely heard something of the Wanderer and his Shadow?"), as well as several chapters in part 4 of *TSZ*. There is, then, considerable reason to conclude that *The Wanderer* introduces an important new character-type into Nietzsche's writings. There is no innovation of comparable significance in *AOM*. (The very last aphorism of *HH* is titled "The Wanderer," but the figure makes this single appearance only at the end of the volume, and the Shadow does not appear at all.)

5. As Lampert, *What a Philosopher Is*, 126, remarks, "When Nietzsche began publishing autobiographical accounts of his writings, he consistently pointed back to one crisis event as the turning point in his becoming himself," namely, the break with Wagner.

6. For further discussion of this point, see Daniel Conway, *Nietzsche and the Political*, 43–44.

7. For detailed accounts, see Blue, *The Making of Friedrich Nietzsche*, 300; Hollinrake, *Nietzsche, Wagner, and the Philosophy of Pessimism*, 62; Magee, *The Tristan Chord*, 176. Although both Wagner and Nietzsche took to Schopenhauer with a rare passion, they did so in somewhat different spirits: Wagner had discovered Schopenhauer in middle age, and thought that Schopenhauer's philosophy more or less sufficed to explain all that he had experienced of the world until that point; Nietzsche discovered Schopenhauer while he was still a student (around the age of twenty), and although he was deeply captivated by the discovery, he never accorded Schopenhauer the kind of status as a final authority that Wagner did. In short, for the young Nietzsche, Schopenhauer represented a new challenge, and thus a beginning; for the older Wagner, Schopenhauer represented a kind of final confirmation, and thus an end point.

Nietzsche was not in a position to realize this fact about Wagner until he was older himself (as I will discuss in chapter 3).

8. See further Shaw, *Nietzsche's Political Skepticism*, 42–43.

9. For a more detailed account of Schopenhauer's role in convincing Nietzsche that a truly revolutionary transformation was only possible through culture, see Church, *Infinite Autonomy*, 179; and Church, "Two Concepts of Culture in the Early Nietzsche," 336–41.

10. *KSA* 7:756 [1874/32/10], 7:788 [1874/33/4].

11. Consider, in a related vein, *RWB* 4: "One can be undecided which name to accord to [Wagner], whether he should be called a poet or a sculptor or a musician"; "Wagner is never more Wagner than when difficulties multiply tenfold and he can rule over great affairs with the joy of a lawgiver. To subdue contending masses to a single rhythm, to subject a multiplicity of demands and desires to the rule of a single will—these are the tasks for which he feels he was born, in the performance of which he feels himself free."

12. Regarding Wagner's ambitions for his *Gesamtkunstwerk*, see Carnegy, *Wagner and the Art of the Theatre*, 46–51; Magee, *The Tristan Chord*, 86–93; Shaw, *Nietzsche's Political Skepticism*, 47–48; Young, *Friedrich Nietzsche*, 113–17.

13. On this turn from myth to truth, see Franco, *Nietzsche's Enlightenment*, 2–11; and Lampert, *The Enduring Importance of Leo Strauss*, 253–57. On Nietzsche's (qualified) sympathy for Enlightenment, also see Montinari, *Reading Nietzsche*, 51–52.

14. Franco's *Nietzsche's Enlightenment* is particularly helpful for clarifying the ways in which Nietzsche's project in the "middle period" (and even beyond) was meant to be compatible with the Enlightenment, rather than a wholesale rejection of it.

15. Franco demonstrates that this "problem of culture" is the unifying thread of Nietzsche's reflection in the work, in the wake of his disenchantment with Wagner (*Nietzsche's Enlightenment*, 13–55). Brief but incisive remarks on this aspect of the work are also made by Lampert, *The Enduring Importance of Leo Strauss*, 257–59.

16. See also Franco, *Nietzsche's Enlightenment*, 50–51; as well as Franco, "Tocqueville and Nietzsche on the Problem of Human Greatness in Democracy," 461–63.

17. See again, Franco, *Nietzsche's Enlightenment*, 52–53. On the theme of freedom and its political implications, see Shaw, *Nietzsche's Political Skepticism*, 27–31; on Nietzsche as a theorist of freedom more generally, see Church, *Nietzsche's Culture of Humanity*, 56–60.

18. In order to draw out the significance of Nietzsche's argument here, consider that in the twentieth century Friedrich Hayek quoted *Thus Spoke Zarathustra* as a definitive statement of "the spirit of collectivism," in opposition to Hayek's own "individualistic view of man" (*The Road to Serfdom*, 144). The quote Hayek selects is well suited to his purpose (as we will see in chapter 4, below), but this is to say that there is a tension between what we find in *Zarathustra* and what we find in the writings of the Free Spirit.

19. "In contrast to Bismarckian *Machtpolitik*, which aspired to shape aggressively a national identity, the new man of Nietzsche, that 'free spirit' who believes in *Geist, Geist Über Alles*, is free from any blind loyalty" (Golomb, "'Will to Power': Does it Lead to the 'Coldest of All Cold Monsters'?" 547). See also Detwiler, *Nietzsche and the Politics of Aristocratic Radicalism*, 172–73.

20. For further detail on this point, see Schaberg, *The Nietzsche Canon*, 58–59.

21. Nietzsche's concern here may not have been limited to his personal relationship with Wagner. He was best known and most respected in the circle of Wagnerians, so he may not have wanted to alienate potential readers.

22. For an illuminating account of Nietzsche's travels during this period and their relationship to his work (and the development of the Free Spirit ideal in particular), see D'Iorio, *Nietzsche's Journey to Sorrento*.

23. See the very incisive discussion by D'Iorio, *Nietzsche's Journey to Sorrento*, 91–96 and 101–12.

24. For an account of the development of the Free Spirit in Nietzsche's notebooks leading up to *Human, All Too Human*, see Large, "Nietzsche's *Helmbrecht*; Or, How to Philosophise with a Ploughshare." On the relevant notebooks, also see Lampert, *What a Philosopher Is*, 128–30.

25. See Abbey, *Nietzsche's Middle Period*, 27–28; Mullin, "Nietzsche's Free Spirit," 394.

26. The association of the term "free spirit" with such un-Nietzschean sentiments is a good argument for translating *Freigeist* as "free mind." Nevertheless, I adopt "free spirit" partly because my argument will stress that a great deal of what is at issue for these characters concerns their spirit in its *relation* to qualities of mind. Ultimately, however, no perfect translation is possible, so the reader should simply be advised of the dual sense of *Freigeist*as referring to both "spirit" and "mind."

27. Hutter, *Shaping the Future*, 179–99; also 7, 71.

28. See further Ansell-Pearson, *Nietzsche's Search for Philosophy*, 28, 18 (remarking that in *HH* and its successor volumes, "Nietzsche is committed to a philosophical hermeneutics whose chief aim is to cool down the human mind"). Berry, *Nietzsche and the Ancient Skeptical Tradition*, 84–86, adds helpful detail to this picture by showing that Nietzsche's position in *HH* was influenced by Montaigne's deflationary skepticism.

29. As already noted, the aphorisms of *WS* (like those of *AOM*) follow a thematic sequence that mirrors the chapter divisions of *HH*. Thus, *WS* 1–17 corresponds to *HH*, chap. 1.

30. In Ansell-Pearson's striking formulation, "Nietzsche sees the primary effects of genuine knowledge to be one of disappointment" (*Nietzsche's Search for Philosophy*, 8).

31. "There is every reason to believe that Nietzsche regarded his discovery and advocacy of the closest things as one of his principal philosophical teachings" (del Caro, *Grounding the Nietzsche Rhetoric of Earth*, 220; see also Abbey, *Nietzsche's Middle Period*, 99–101; Ansell-Pearson, *Nietzsche's Search for Philosophy*, 105). Appreciating this aspect of Nietzsche's thought at a minimum complicates attempts to present him as the ultimate antimodern opponent of the supposed "drabness, conformity, and philistinism of the new bourgeois order" (Smith, *Modernity and Its Discontents*, 173, also 17–19, 225, 251, 328; as well as Fukuyama, *The End of History and the Last Man*, 188). It is true enough that Nietzsche's ideal is not "bourgeois" (although he virtually never uses that term, but see *D* 173–75). Nevertheless (and notwithstanding the first few pages of *Thus Spoke Zarathustra*), Nietzsche's thought as a whole is not based on some knee-jerk contempt for creature comforts, or a would-be heroic disregard for the simple, everyday goods the new bourgeois order helps to make possible. To the contrary, Nietzsche's thought is grounded on a painstaking attention to the basic core of needs that every human being shares, and attempts to learn from a careful analysis of those needs what our humanity truly consists of and what it requires of us.

32. See Abbey, *Nietzsche's Middle Period*, 117; Dannhauser, *Nietzsche's View of Socrates*, 160.

33. On the points of overlap and divergence between these two authors, see Velkley, *Being after Rousseau*, 23.

34. In *TI* the first few aphorisms of the chapter "The Problem of Socrates" describe Socrates as "ugly," "stunted," "rabble," a "decadent," a "monster," a "criminal," and a "buffoon," who contained "all the bad vices and desires."

35. Nietzsche is referring to Diogenes Laertius, *Lives of the Eminent Philosophers* 2.21, which reports that Socrates was the first to focus philosophy on the concerns of ordinary life (privileging moral over natural philosophy). The Homeric quotation Socrates was said to favor is from *Odyssey* IV.392. The notion that Socrates was responsible for redirecting philosophy toward "the human things" was a commonplace in the ancient world (see Cicero, *Tusculan Disputations* 5.10–11). It finds support in Plato (*Phaedo* 96a–99d) and Xenophon (*Memorabilia* 1.1.11–16).

36. An illustration of how these two sets of interests come to be conflated can be found in Pericles's famous funeral oration (as reported by Thucydides), which locates the site of individuals' distinction precisely in the sacrifice of what is closest to them (their own bodies) for the sake of the greater whole of which they are a part (the Athenian city): "Beholding every day the power of the city in action, and becoming erotic lovers of it, and when to you it seems great, reflecting that men of daring who knew what had to be done and who possessed a sense of awe in their actions, acquired these things; and when they failed in any attempt, did not think they ought therefore to deprive the city of their virtue, but offered it the noblest contribution. *For by giving in common their bodies, they took individually the praise which is ageless*—and the most distinguished tomb: not that in which they lie, but that in which their fame is left forever remembered on every opportune occasion in speech and in deed" (Thucydides 2.43.1–2; compare 1.70.5–6, where the Corinthian ambassadors admiringly remark that the Athenians "use their bodies as if they were least their own, for the sake of the city"). This example highlights how it is possible to become confused about, and cease to properly care for, one's individual good: not by forgetting it altogether, but by believing that it can only be fulfilled through a sort of temporary, transactional sacrifice to a community that will then bestow back on us ("individually") a greater good than we would be able to acquire on our own (in this case, promising individual soldiers the quasi-immortality of fame in exchange for sacrificing their mortal—corporeal—being to the good of the community).

37. Corresponding to chapter 3 of *HH* ("The Religious Life").

38. As Villa observes, in *WS* Socrates and Nietzsche are aligned as "enemies of the ideal of their respective times and places," and as "paradigms of the independent, nondogmatic life" (*Socratic Citizenship*, 163; see also Dannhauser, *Nietzsche's View of Socrates*, 163).

39. Nietzsche never wavered in judging this "agonistic" aspect of Socrates as indispensable to his appeal (see *TI* "Problem" 8), even if in later works he emphasized its corrupting effect on Athenian youths. In this as in other respects, Nietzsche's "normative" assessment of Socrates seems to change later in his career, even though his assessment of the facts of Socrates's character remains consistent with points that he first established in *WS*.

40. In aphorism 72 Nietzsche says that he detects "a touch of Attic irony and love of jesting" in Socrates's claim to be a "divine missionary"; in aphorism 86 he commends Socrates's "joy-

ful kind of seriousness and *wisdom full of roguish tricks*" (consider Xenophon, *Memorabilia* 1.3.8, 4.1.1; and Xenophon, *Symposium* 4.29, on how Socrates "mixed the playful with the serious"). This is another point on which Nietzsche's assessment of Socrates remained consistent for the rest of his career: see *BGE* 191 on Socrates as a "great, secret-rich ironic"; and *TI* "Problem" 9 on Socrates as a "great ironist." Pierre Hadot remarks that "what philosophers have least retained from the model presented by Socrates" is his "irony and humor"—although Hadot then cites *WS* 86 as evidence that Nietzsche, for one, "was well aware of this [aspect of Socrates]" (*What Is Ancient Philosophy?* 50). Nietzsche is not alone in concluding that Socrates's skeptical response to the Delphic oracle is an ironic testament to his heterodoxy, and even disbelief, rather than proof of his piety: see Foucault, *The Courage of Truth*, 81–83; Leibowitz, *The Ironic Defense of Socrates*, 60–102.

41. Nietzsche had already referred to Socrates as a Free Spirit in *HH* 433, 437. In the first of these aphorisms, Nietzsche seems to be referring to Socrates's relationship with Xanthippe as depicted by Xenophon (*Memorabilia* 2.2.7–14; *Symposium* 2.10). Nietzsche's point here seems to be that Socrates's independence from his marriage was one aspect of his independence from society. Or, as he put this point later in his career, when elaborating on the "independence" that philosophers pursue: "A married philosopher belongs to *comedy*, that is my proposition: and that exception, the mischievous Socrates, appears to have married ironically, in order to demonstrate this proposition" (*GM* III.7).

42. See further Ansell-Pearson, *Nietzsche's Search for Philosophy*, 41, 43.

43. "Epicurus has been alive at all times and is living now, unknown to those who have called and call themselves Epicureans, and enjoying no reputation among philosophers. He has, moreover, forgotten his own name: it was the heaviest weight he ever threw off" (*WS* 227).

44. On Nietzsche's ideal of friendship, see Hutter, *Shaping the Future*, 79–82; compare Abbey, *Nietzsche's Middle Period*, 123–29.

45. Poussin made two versions of this painting, and Nietzsche's description is of the second (which was made in 1637–38). Poussin's significance for Nietzsche (including the way in which Poussin's painting "poignantly juxtaposes pastoral beauty with intimations of mortality") is discussed helpfully by Shapiro, *Archaeologies of Vision*, 5–58; see also Ansell-Pearson, *Nietzsche's Search for Philosophy*, 138–40.

46. On the importance of Nietzsche's walks during this period, see D'Iorio, *Nietzsche's Journey to Sorrento*, 55–56, 66–67; and Lampert, *What a Philosopher Is*, 139. See also Nietzsche's general counsel: "Only thoughts which come from *walking* have any value" (*TI* Maxims 34); "*Sit* as little as possible; do not believe any idea that was not born in the open air and of free movement" (*EH* Clever 1).

47. Robert Pippin notes that there are places when "even the resolutely prosaic Kant" writes about metaphysical speculation in terms of erotic desire (*Hegel on Self-Consciousness*, 56). Nietzsche, I am now suggesting, would not have been surprised by this (we will begin to see why that is the case in what follows, and the issue will be elaborated further in chapter 3).

48. Whether (worldly) "revolution" or (other-worldly) "redemption" is the goal is a question that changes over the course of Wagner's career. From Nietzsche's perspective, however, the two goals are the same, because they are both life-denying. I discuss this issue at length in chapter 3.

49. As we have seen, this argument first shows up in *The Birth of Tragedy*. In chapter 4 we will see that this pleasing illusion is part of Zarathustra's experience as a prophet/legislator, and in chapter 5 we will see that in the 1886 prefaces to *Human, All Too Human* Nietzsche makes explicit that the turn in his thought which that work represents is partly the result of his turn against music at the time that he wrote it.

50. See Gillespie, *Nihilism before Nietzsche*, 213–14, 233–40; and Strong, *Politics without Vision*, 70.

51. Nietzsche argues that the human tendency to overestimate what can truly be held in common is ultimately derived from our capacity for language, which necessarily exaggerates such commonalities, and thereby serves as the root of metaphysics (*GS* 354–55). Music is an extension of this phenomenon, as suggested by Zarathustra: "[A]re words and tones [*Worte und Töne*] not rainbows and seeming bridges between what is eternally separated?" (see my discussion of this passage in chapter 4).

52. On the "Rousseauian" ideal, see *TI* Skirmishes 48.

53. A similar thought is suggested by a remark that Nietzsche made in a letter written shortly after his break with Wagner, just as he was beginning his work on *HH*. Characterizing himself to his correspondent as a "free spirit," he explains that this means that he is "a person who desires nothing more than to lose some comforting belief every day, who seeks and finds his happiness in a liberation of the spirit that increases daily." But then he adds: "It may be that I *want* to be more of a free spirit than I am *able* to be!" (letter to Louise Ott, September 22, 1876).

54. This thought may shed light on a remark from one of Nietzsche's letters, where he comments critically on the "development" of one of his favorite authors, Ralph Waldo Emerson: "I don't know how much I would give if I could effect a change in the past and give such a glorious great nature, rich in soul and spirit, *strict* discipline, a *truly scientific* culture. As it stands, in Emerson we have **lost** a *philosopher*!" (letter to Franz Overbeck, December 22, 1884). Parkes, *Composing the Soul*, 37, finds this remark puzzling and uncharitable, but Lampert, *What a Philosopher Is*, 89, suggests that Emerson's transcendentalist spiritualism may have been at issue. I would add that Emerson's failure in this regard may not have been simply the failure to undergo a sufficiently rigorous and scientific educational program (as Lampert proposes); it may run more deeply, since the "discipline" that Nietzsche calls for is above all a self-discipline required by the *nature* of the *heart*.

55. For an elaboration of this thought, consider *GS* 59 and *BGE* 229–30.

56. Gillespie, *Nietzsche's Final Teaching*, 43–48. See also the similar suggestions by Reginster, *The Affirmation of Life*, 51–52; and Rosen, *The Mask of Enlightenment*, 162–63. Nietzsche would eventually refer to himself as "the poet of *Zarathustra*" (*EH* TSZ 4) and comment that "*Zarathustra* as a whole may perhaps be counted as music" (*EH* TSZ 1).

57. Gillespie seems to take this view when he suggests that Nietzsche never wavered from the goal (first set out during his Wagnerian period, and culminating in *Zarathustra* and later works) of revivifying the "Dionysian" (*Nihilism before Nietzsche*, 215–16). This seems to me to underestimate the threat that *Human, All Too Human* identifies as emanating from the "Dionysian." That recognition is what leads Nietzsche to stress the role that self-restraint must play in the Free Spirit project.

58. Nehamas, *The Art of Living*, 131.

59. Nehamas, *The Art of Living*, 155–56, treats *WS* 86 as a reflection on the Platonic Socrates, even though his quotation of the aphorism includes Nietzsche's reference to "die Memorabilien des Sokrates." I don't see how this disregard of the allusion to Xenophon can be justified in light of Nietzsche's notes from the same period. This disregard has consequences: since Nehamas does not connect *WS* 86 to Xenophon, he does not see that Nietzsche's assessment of Socrates's "*Weisheit voller Schelmenstreiche* [wisdom full of roguish tricks]" in that aphorism is at odds with his own assessment of the Xenophontic Socrates as "a conventional teacher," "innocuous," "with very little of the irony of his Platonic counterpart," who has provided posterity with "greater and deeper" food for thought (*The Art of Living*, 107; see also *Virtues of Authenticity*, 94–95). So for Nehamas Plato's dialogues are clearly more valuable than Xenophon's—but for Nietzsche that was not so clearly the case, as we are about to see.

60. See Dannhauser, *Nietzsche's View of Socrates*, 97.

61. For what follows, see *KSA* 8:94–95 [1875/5/192], 8:327 [1876/18/47], 8:505 [1878/28/11], 8:584 [1879/41/2]; letter to Carl von Gersdorff, May 26, 1876.

62. See *KSA* 8:94–95 [1875/5/192]; with Xenophon, *Memorabilia* 1.2.6.

63. See Xenophon, *Memorabilia* 1.2.1–6, 1.5, 1.6, *Apology* 16 *Oeconomicus* 2.7–8.

64. See, e.g., Xenophon, *Memorabilia* 1.2.23: "All things that are both noble and good are matters of training . . . For the pleasures growing in the same body together with the soul persuade the soul not to be moderate but instead to gratify themselves and the body as quickly as possible" (that is, persuasion/mind, pleasure/body, and soul compete for control, rather than organizing themselves into a harmonious hierarchy; see also 1.3.9–13). Thus, in the *Memorabilia* Socrates makes self-control (*enkrateia*) the very "foundation of virtue" (1.5.4; see also 2.1, 4.5).

65. On the self-sufficiency of philosophy, see Aristotle, *Politics* 1267a10–12; Aristotle, *Nicomachean Ethics* 1177a25–b; Nietzsche, *TI* Maxims 3 ("To live alone you must be an animal or a god—says Aristotle. He left out the third case: you must be both—*a philosopher*. . . .").

66. In Nietzsche's final treatment of "The Problem of Socrates" (in *Twilight of the Idols*) he alludes to this "theological" interpretation of Socrates's appeal in a complex way. First, Nietzsche quotes a "famous physiognomic judgment," according to which Socrates was a "monster in the face, monster in the soul," and then mentions that Socrates's friends were offended by this judgment. The source for this anecdote is Cicero, *On Fate* 5.10, where the physiognomic judgment is rebuked by Alcibiades. In Plato's *Symposium*, when Alcibiades likens Socrates to a Silenus, he emphasizes that those famously ugly creatures are reputed to have gods within them. For Alcibiades, then, Socrates's ugly exterior was at least partially compensated for by his quasi-divine interior. And, as Xenophon highlights (*Memorabilia* 1.1.2–5), Socrates attracted young friends partly with talk of his mysterious *daimonion*. Nietzsche reminds us of this point in "The Problem of Socrates": "Let us also not forget those auditory hallucinations which, as 'the *daimonion* of Socrates', have taken on a religious interpretation." I think that Nietzsche wants us to recognize that the *daimonion* "took on" a religious significance because of how Socrates was misunderstood by Alcibiades (and others). Nietzsche blames Plato for perpetuating (and exacerbating) this sort of misunderstanding, and saw Xenophon as a corrective to it. (As one scholar remarks, "Plato's Alcibiades in the *Symposium*, by contrasting Socrates' external ugliness to an internal, spiritual beauty, paradigmatically articulates the turn away from

a Homeric visual regime, a turn which becomes central to the Western evaluation of the non-corporeal over the physical" (Goldhill, "The Seductions of the Gaze," 110; see also Foucault, *The Use of Pleasure*, 20).

67. "[Socrates] is at heart a mystic and there is something 'other-worldly' about him" (Taylor, *Plato: The Man and His Work*, 211; compare Hadot, *What Is Ancient Philosophy?* 46–49).

68. See the comparison of the two portrayals of Socrates made by Huss ("The Dancing Sokrates and the Laughing Xenophon," 402n61): "Xenophon's Sokrates differs greatly from the Sokrates presented in Plato's *Symposium*. Neither is he an almost superhuman genius who endures cold and heat as well as any quantity of alcohol without being physically damaged, nor is he inspired by a divine or semidivine notion of eros. He remains the down-to-earth Sokrates known from the *Memorabilia* and *Oeconomicus*: practical, straightforward, and sometimes quite bourgeois." The comparatively all too human character of Xenophon's Socrates can also be seen in a contrast that Nietzsche would likely have appreciated, as follows: both Plato and Xenophon show us Socrates engaged in a very similar refutation of a sophist. In each case, the sophist initially espouses an amoral relativism, but is forced to back down from it when Socrates applies a thorough-going standard of utility to measure the nobility of an everyday object, finally registering the sophist's outrage (and thus revealing the hollowness of his purported amoralism) when that standard is used to speak of the nobility of some sort of pot. But there is a key difference in the respective reports of Plato and Xenophon in this matter. In the Platonic case, the pot is a generic pot (*Greater Hippias* 288c–d, 290d–e). In the Xenophontic case, it is a chamber pot (*Memorabilia* 3.8.4–6). This contrast supports the accusation, from the later stages of Nietzsche's career, that Plato "ennobled" the utilitarian Socrates (*BGE* 190; consider Plato's *Second Letter* 314b, which declares that his writings will give the world a Socrates made "beautiful and new"). In the later writings Nietzsche seems to be engaged in a competition with Plato for the fate of civilization, and therefore appears to view Plato with a mixture of censure and admiration (*BGE* Preface; *GS* 372). But in *The Wanderer and His Shadow*, at least, Nietzsche exhibits less affinity for the poetic Plato than for the prosaic Xenophon.

69. See *Memorabilia* 1.2.23 (quoted in note 64, above).

70. This suggestion is made by Huss, "The Dancing Sokrates and the Laughing Xenophon, or the Other *Symposium*," 404–5; also see Morrison, "Xenophon's Socrates as a Teacher," 190; as well as Foucault, *The Use of Pleasure*, 72–73.

71. In fact, in his *Symposium*, Xenophon shows us that (in direct contrast to the impression fostered by Plato's *Symposium*) Socrates himself was not quite so stoic in the face of beauty (Xenophon, *Symposium* 4.23–29). In the same dialogue, Xenophon presents Socrates's ascetically minded followers Hermogenes and Antisthenes (the latter went on to become the grandfather of the Stoic school of philosophy) as rather ridiculous fellows who did not understand Socrates very well (see 4.23 and 8.6). Moreover, a passage in the *Memorabilia* (3.11.7–14) suggests that Socrates's austere appearance was deliberately somewhat misleading or manipulative (and especially designed to mislead or manipulate students). In all these ways, Xenophon encourages us to view Socrates's austere exterior with a more skeptical eye than Plato does.

72. As a coda to these remarks, let me add that there is no need to conclude that Nietzsche's estimation of Socrates changed in any fundamental way in later writings: his praise of Socrates in *The Wanderer* is a tribute to the stern and austere, but still relatively down to earth and non-

dogmatic, portrait provided by Xenophon; it is the Platonic Socrates to which Nietzsche takes his hammer for the *Twilight of the Idols*. So while Alexander Nehamas (see note 59, above) and Pierre Hadot (*Philosophy as a Way of Life*, 169) contend that Nietzsche's view of Socrates is deeply conflicted and therefore subject to multiple fluctuations over the course of his career, I have indicated throughout this chapter that there is actually a great deal of continuity in Nietzsche's assessment of Socrates from *The Wanderer* onward (see notes 39, 40, 66, above). Changes in Nietzsche's assessment are more "normative" than "descriptive," and the normative shift can be explained as a consequence of the fact that in the later writings he is engaging in a civilizational contest with Plato (and his "new and beautiful" Socrates). But the Xenophontic Socrates is not a civilizational idol in the same way.

73. Identifying this movement in Nietzsche's thought (from the Free Spirit to Zarathustra) suggests a response to what Martha Nussbaum identifies as the deepest objection to Nietzsche: "What should we think about a human being who insists on caring deeply for nothing that he himself does not control; who refuses to love others in ways that open him to serious risks of pain and loss; who cultivates the hardness of self-command against all the reversals that life can bring? We could say, with Nietzsche, that this is a strong person. But there is clearly another way to see things. For there is a strength of a specifically human sort in the willingness to acknowledge some truths about one's situation: one's mortality, one's finitude, the limits and vulnerabilities of one's body, one's need for food and drink and shelter and friendship. There is a strength in the willingness to form attachments that can go wrong and cause deep pain, in the willingness to invest oneself in the world in a way that opens one's whole life up to the changes of the world" (Nussbaum, "Pity and Mercy: Nietzsche's Stoicism," 160). These are eloquent and important words, but not more so than Nietzsche's words in *WS* 308. Moreover—as I have tried to show—*The Wanderer* as a whole is Nietzsche's newfound recognition of many of the truths about the human situation noted by Nussbaum, and although the response to it that he suggests involves a certain hardness and closing oneself off, the tenability of that position is precisely what is questioned near the end (in aphorism 308). Moreover, in later writings (especially *Thus Spoke Zarathustra*) Nietzsche aimed to do greater justice to the opening-oneself-up-to-the-world that is entailed in a recognition of the human capacity for love. Nussbaum's criticism is echoed by Alasdair MacIntyre when he suggests that Nietzsche "isolated himself by ridding himself, so far as is humanly possible, of the commitments required by the virtues of acknowledged dependence" (*Dependent Rational Animals*, 162). To my mind this assessment, like Nussbaum's, misses the fact that Nietzsche's corpus deliberately constructs a tension between two competing positions (the Free Spirit versus Zarathustra). So where Nussbaum and MacIntyre find a certain tone-deafness in Nietzsche's thought, I see an abiding, unifying tension.

CHAPTER 3

1. Pippin shows that Nietzsche frequently employs imagery that suggests that philosophy needs to relearn how to love, and he argues that this imagery should be understood in terms of Platonic eros, since for Plato and Nietzsche alike philosophy is set in motion by a kind of erotic yearning or striving that reveals something fundamental about the nature of all human desire (*Nietzsche, Psychology, and First Philosophy*, 12–19, also 28–29, 36–38, 69). Pippin's study

concludes with these words: "[Nietzsche] might claim, like Socrates, to know only one thing beyond his own ignorance—something about the mysteries of human eros" (124). Lampert's commentary on *Beyond Good and Evil* arrives at a similar conclusion: "Nietzsche's philosophy is a love story" (*Nietzsche's Task*, 302). Regarding the place of eros in Nietzsche's psychology, also consider the discussion by Parkes, *Composing the Soul*, 105–6, 152–54, 231–47. As a student Nietzsche had taken a special interest in Plato's dialogue on eros, the *Symposium* (see Brobjer, *Nietzsche's Philosophical Context*, 26, 45), but later on he was strongly influenced by Stendhal's treatise *On Love*, which he discovered shortly after his break with Wagner (see note 50, below).

2. *SE* 5, 6. Also see *HL* 7 (which will be discussed in chapter 4).

3. *HH* 133, *D* 145, *GS* 14.

4. *HH* 291. Nietzsche counsels that the Free Spirits must trust that a word will be said in their defense if "accusing voices" claim that they are "poor in love," but since in this aphorism Nietzsche says in his own voice that the Free Spirits will not love things in all of their breadth and fullness—"having no wish to get entangled with them," and placing the quest for knowledge above love of others—Nietzsche's point seems to be that the Free Spirits should be defended notwithstanding their admittedly limited capacity for love, since that limitation is part and parcel of their determination "to live for the sake of knowledge alone." Nietzsche makes similar suggestions in later writings: for instance, in *Beyond Good and Evil*, in aphorism 41 of the chapter on "The Free Spirit," where he outlines six tests that must be passed in order to attain one's independence, the first of which is show that one is not attached to any person, "not even the most beloved"; and in the first of the 1886 prefaces for *Human, All Too Human*, he remarks in section 4 that as part of a Free Spirit's maturation, "[o]ne no longer lives in the fetters of love and hatred." So Nietzsche is consistent in maintaining that the self-disciplined heart of the Free Spirit project imposes acute limits on the cultivation of human attachments, particularly those born of love.

5. See, in particular, "Zarathustra's Prologue" 4, and the songs of Zarathustra (which will be discussed in more detail in chapter 4).

6. *A* 23; see also *KSA* 13:299–300 [1888/14/120]); *CW* 2, 3 (which will be discussed below).

7. These four essays (originally planned as part of a longer series) were all published with cover pages following the same format: the title *Untimely Meditations* appears in large print at the top of the page, and then, further down the page, in a smaller but distinctive font, one reads, "Fourth Part: *Richard Wagner in Bayreuth*" (with the number and title adjusted as appropriate for each installment in the series). So one might prefer to consider "*Richard Wagner in Bayreuth*" as a subtitle, rather than as a title proper. But the writing was originally published as an independent unit, and since Nietzsche does not use proper names in "subtitles" for any of his other works, the reference to Wagner still stands out.

8. In *Zarathustra* only one historical figure is explicitly mentioned in the text, apart from Zarathustra himself. Nevertheless, the text is full of allusions to Wagner (as is shown by Roger Hollinrake's illuminating study, *Nietzsche, Wagner, and the Philosophy of Pessimism*).

9. That Nietzsche both abhorred and admired Wagner can be made clear enough by comparing two statements from the writings of 1888: "*Parsifal* is a work of malice, of vindictiveness, of a secret attempt to poison the presuppositions of life—a *bad* work. The preaching of chastity remains an incitement to anti-nature: I despise everyone who does not experience *Parsifal* as

an attempted assassination of basic ethics" (*NCW* Wagner as an Apostle of Chastity 3); "Music as Circe. [Wagner's] last work is in this respect his greatest masterpiece. In the art of seduction, *Parsifal* will always retain its rank—as *the stroke of genius* in seduction.—I admire this work; I wish I had written it myself; failing that, *I understand it*.—Wagner never had better inspirations than at the end" (*CW* First Postscript).

10. In an unpublished note written not long after he first attended a performance of the prelude to *Parsifal*, Nietzsche remarks: "I know nothing that grasped Christianity so deeply." He adds that the prelude is "the greatest gift I have been granted for a long time" and "the greatest masterpiece of the sublime that I know" (comparing it favorably to the work of Dante and Leonardo in this respect) (*KSA* 12:198–99 [1886/5/41]). René Girard, in "Nietzsche and Contradiction," presents this text as a "smoking gun" demonstrating that Nietzsche was deeply attracted to the Christian content of Wagner's work, but sought to cover up that attraction in his published writings by adopting a posture of exaggerated hostility toward the composer. So, for Girard, Nietzsche is ultimately at odds with himself, or self-contradictory. Girard's criticism assumes that Nietzsche did not admit the "contradiction" (his simultaneous attraction to, and abhorrence of, Wagner), and address that issue, *in his published writings*. But, as I will argue in what follows, a text like *The Case of Wagner* shows a much higher degree of self-awareness on Nietzsche's part (and a correspondingly more carefully nuanced argument) than Girard recognizes. (Girard's criticism of Nietzsche is echoed by Scruton, *The Ring of Truth*, 299.)

11. *A* 30; *TI* "The 'Improvers' of Humanity" 4. See also *AOM* 95 ("The subtlest artifice which Christianity has over other religions is a word: it spoke of *love*"); and *GM* II.21 ("*Christianity's* stroke of genius . . . the creditor [God] sacrificing himself for his debtor [humankind], out of *love*"), as well as *D* 76 and *BGE* 168.

12. *Carmen* was premiered to a lukewarm reception in Paris in March 1875. Bizet died a few months after the premiere, but later in the year the opera was performed in Vienna, where it began to receive acclaim, and by the end of the decade it was being produced regularly throughout Europe. Nietzsche first attended a performance in Genoa on November 27, 1881 (he reports on the experience the next day in a letter to Heinrich Köselitz). He went on to see the opera many times, and he owned a vocal and piano score of the opera, which he learned to play and annotated in detail. Bizet's only other major work was *Les pêcheurs de perles*, but it left Nietzsche cold (see his letter to Köselitz, December 20, 1887).

13. Geuss, *Outside Ethics*, 221, says that Nietzsche's claim to prefer Bizet is disingenuous. Geuss does not elaborate, but he might have in mind a letter in which Nietzsche claims that in *CW* 1 he is employing Bizet only as an "ironic antithesis" to Wagner. Nevertheless, Nietzsche must be misleading his correspondent when he suggests that he has no serious interest in Bizet except as a literary foil to Wagner (see the letter to Carl Fuchs, December 27, 1888). Not long after first encountering *Carmen*, Nietzsche remarked: "I am near to believing that *Carmen* is the best opera there is; and for as long as we live, it will be in every repertory in Europe" (letter to Heinrich Köselitz, December 8, 1881). And in his notes on the vocal score he compares Bizet favorably to Stendhal (of whom Nietzsche always speaks in the highest terms), among other pieces of high praise. Nietzsche's numerous, and (apart from the letter to Fuchs) consistently effusive, remarks on the opera are helpfully presented by Andreas Urs Sommer, *Nietzsche-Kommentar: "Der Fall Wagner" und "Götzen-Dämmerung,"* 39–41, 49–51. The importance

of the work for Nietzsche's philosophical development is discussed by d'Iorio, "Nietzsche fra Tristano e Carmen" and Leiner, "To Overcome Oneself: Nietzsche, Bizet, Wagner." Goetz ("Nietzsche aimait-il vraiment Bizet?") also argues for the importance the opera to Nietzsche, and suggests that Nietzsche was dissembling in his letter to Fuchs, since Fuchs was a Wagnerian whose patronage Nietzsche was attempting to secure for the benefit of Köselitz.

14. Nietzsche marks off this passage by placing a long dash at both its start and its end (so that, even though there are no paragraphs breaks in the second section of the essay, the definition of love is still visually isolated on the page).

15. "Probably most of Nietzsche's interpreters have found his remarks about women simply embarrassing, hence the common effort to dismiss them from the field of inquiry by branding them just personal idiosyncrasies, lying quite apart from his philosophical thought" (Richardson, *Nietzsche's System*, 191).

16. Diethe's *Nietzsche's Women* is an informative study that presents Nietzsche as a straightforward misogynist.

17. This point is also made incisively by van Boxel, "Nietzsche in Eden"; see also Kofman, "The Psychologist of the Eternal Feminine," 185–89; Parkes, *Composing the Soul*, 205–12.

18. Apart from these two usages, *nature* only appears only twice more in *CW*: both times in section 3, and without any emphasis.

19. "Whatever is done out of love always happens beyond good and evil" (*BGE* 153).

20. Consider the early Nietzsche's characterization of Wagnerian artwork: "This music is a return to nature, while at the same being a purification and transformation of nature; for the pressing need for that return to nature arose in the souls of men filled with love, and *in their art there sounds nature transformed in love*" (*RWB* 5). Zarathustra would certainly be able to identify with the position articulated by the early Nietzsche (as we will see later in chapter 4), but *The Case of Wagner* pours cold water on that whole sensibility.

21. Consider *BGE* 230: "To translate humankind back into nature; to master the many vain and gushing interpretations and connotations that have so far been scribbled and painted over that eternal basic text of *homo natura*; to ensure that the human being henceforth stands before human beings even as it stands today, hardened by the discipline of science, before the *other* nature, with undaunted Oedipus eyes and sealed Oedipus ears, deaf to the luring songs of old metaphysical bird-catchers who have all too long fluted in their ears: 'you are more! you are higher! you are of a different descent!'—that may be a strange and insane task, but it is a *task*—who would deny it!"

22. Consider Stendhal, *On Love*, book 1, chap. 5.

23. Consider Stendhal, *On Love*, book 1, chap. 11.

24. Pippin, *Nietzsche, Psychology, and First Philosophy*, 28, 69, argues for the importance of eros to Nietzsche as the "prevolitional and prereflective" source of human attachments.

25. Quoted in Sommer, *Nietzsche-Kommentar: "Der Fall Wagner" und "Götzen-Dämmerung,"* 49. Although Nietzsche does not refer to the "Habanera" aria directly in *The Case of Wagner*, I think that we can safely presume that he expected to have readers who would be familiar with the opera. His extravagant praise certainly encourages readers to experience the work for themselves, and the opera was already quite popular when Nietzsche wrote the essay (not to mention his entirely accurate prediction that it would go on to become an enduring favorite at all opera houses).

26. As Dienstag remarks, "fate" here (that is, both for *Carmen* and for Nietzsche's interpretation of the opera) is to be understood, "as in the Greek tragedies . . . not as a particular destiny for a particular individual but simply as a general term for the forces that exceed that of the individual will" (*Pessimism: Philosophy, Ethic, Spirit*, 184). An interesting study by Pippin works with a similar understanding of fate ("as what in general makes the presumption of rational control over one's future naïve" [*Fatalism in American Film Noir*, 16]), but he appropriately highlights that in an important respect this approach contrasts with the ancient understanding, insofar as the classical view was tied to a belief in the power of the gods—something that is also notably absent from Bizet's opera (on this point, see further note 56, below).

27. "L'amour est un oiseau rebelle / Que nul ne peut apprivoiser, / Et c'est bien en vain qu'on l'appelle, / S'il lui convient de refuser. / Rien n'y fait, menace ou prière; / L'un parle bien, l'autre se tait, / Et c'est l'autre que je préfère; / Il n'a rien dit mais il me plait . . . L'amour est enfant de bohème, / Il n'a jamais, jamais connu de loi . . . tu crois le tenir, il t'évite, / tu crois l'éviter, il te tient! / L'amour!" Nietzsche once wrote as follows (in an aphorism titled "What One Can Promise"): "One can promise actions but not feelings; for the latter are involuntary. He who promises someone he will always love him or always hate him or always be faithful to him promises something that does not reside in his power; but he can certainly promise to perform actions which, though they are usually the consequences of love, hatred, faithfulness, can also derive from other motives: for several paths and motives can lead to the same action. To promise always to love someone therefore means: for as long as I love you I shall render to you the actions of love; if I cease to love you, you will continue to receive the same actions from me, though from other motives: so that in the heads of our fellow men the appearance will remain that love is still the same and unchanged.—One therefore promises the continuation of the appearance of love when one swears to someone ever-enduring love without self-deception" (*HH* 58; see also *D* 27).

28. At the end of act 2 she declares: "quand tu verras / comme c'est beau, la vie errante; / pour pays, l'univers, / et pour loi sa volonté, / et surtout, la chose enivrante: / la liberté ! la liberté!" And then, near the start of act 3: "le destin est le maître."

29. The story of *Carmen* is based on a novel by Prosper Mérimée in which she has a husband, but the opera makes many changes to the story, one of which is to free Carmen of her spouse.

30. Near the end of act 1, as he first becomes drawn to Carmen, he asks: "Carmen, je suis comme un homme ivre, / si je cède, si je me livre, / ta promesse, tu la tiendras, / ah ! si je t'aime, Carmen, tu m'aimeras?" In act 2, he returns to Carmen after having spent two months in prison, an ordeal that he explains he endured by keeping a flower of hers as a token to remember her by, along with the knowledge that he would return to her and their love.

31. At the end of act 3 he declares: "Carmen, je ne partirai pas! / Et la chaîne qui nous lie / nous liera jusqu'au trépas!"

32. José speaks in increasingly threatening tones as the opera proceeds, but he reveals his deep, abiding desire to inflict punishment most plainly near the end of act 3, when his relationship with Carmen has begun to fray, and he encounters Escamillo, who he learns also loves her. José provokes a fight, declaring twice: "*Enfin* ma colère / trouve à qui parler, / le sang, oui, le sang, je l'espère, / va bientôt couler!" In act 1 José tells Zuniga (his superior officer) that he left

his hometown and became a soldier after his spiritedness led him to get into a fight, forcing him to flee (but his mother followed after him, and he remains very much attached to her and the village where she now lives).

33. In the final scene he begins by declaring, "Je ne menace pas, j'implore, je supplie"; a little later he declares, "Je suis las de te menacer!"; shortly after, he stabs her.

34. Quoted in Sommer, *Nietzsche-Kommentar: "Der Fall Wagner" und "Götzen-Dämmerung,"* 44. Nietzsche also refers to Bizet's music as "*fatalistisch*" in *CW* 1.

35. "En vain, pour éviter les réponses amères / en vain tu mêleras! / Cela ne sert à rien, les cartes sont sincères / et ne mentiront pas! / Dans le livre d'en haut si ta page est heureuse, / mêle et coupe sans peur, / la carte sous tes doigts / se tournera joyeuse, / t'annonçant le bonheur. / Mais si tu dois mourir, si le mot redoubtable / est écrit par le sort, / recommence vingt fois, la carte impitoyable / répétera: la mort!"

36. The "Habanera" is itself preceded by the song of a group of chorus girls who represent Carmen's co-workers in a cigarette factory, and who sing: "Le doux parler des amants, / c'est fumée! / Leurs transports et leurs serments, / c'est fumée!" Nietzsche singled out this chorus for praise in his annotations on the score.

37. "To grasp the limits of reason—only *this* is truly philosophy" (*A* 55).

38. Leiner, "To Overcome Oneself," 139–42, discusses several ways in which Carmen embodies Nietzsche's ideals. Acampora, *Contesting Nietzsche*, 158, suggests that Nietzsche was impressed by Carmen's "consuming love of life." This suggestion seems to me to be on the right track, although the key to this issue turns on specifying the *way in which* life is loved, as we shall see.

39. In a notebook entry made shortly after his initial exposure to the opera, Nietzsche dwelled on the same lines, quoting them more accurately, but adding the same point of emphasis: "ja *ich* habe sie getödtet, meine Carmen, meine angebetete Carmen!" (*KSA* 9:657 [1881/15/68]).

40. An unpublished remark confirms that Nietzsche was impressed by what is *implied* about human psychology by the final scene of *Carmen* (rather than being impressed by the brutal actions depicted in the scene). In the notebook entry made shortly after his initial exposure to the opera, Nietzsche quotes Don José's concluding cry as a proof for the following proposition: "Behind every tragedy there is something funny [*Witziges*] and absurd, a pleasure in paradox" (*KSA* 9:657 [1881/15/68]). Nietzsche echoes this remark in *The Case of Wagner*, when he employs the paradoxical formula of a "tragic joke" (*tragische Witz*) to characterize José's last words. As this suggests, Nietzsche views the character of Don José from something of an ironic distance. This perspective—which, so to speak, finds the comedy in the tragedy of life—seems to be characteristic of philosophy: "there are heights of the soul from which even tragedy ceases to look tragic" (*BGE* 30; see further *HH* 628 with Plato, *Laws* 804b–c); "I would even allow myself a rank order among philosophers according to the rank of their laughter" (*BGE* 294; see also *GS* 1, 327). But whatever heights a philosopher's soul may rise up to, the philosopher is still a human being, and so must begin from the core of all too human passions represented by José, and can never hope to become detached from them entirely (consider *BGE* 36). Thus, it seems to me that the notion of a "tragic joke" indicates a duality (an abiding tension in human life), not the subsumption of one category by the other. *Carmen* is particularly well suited to

capturing this tragicomic duality because, despite its grim conclusion, the work was originally written for and premiered at the Opéra-Comique in Paris. In its original version the opera begins by depicting the playful and entertaining interplay of the passions among the major characters, and only gradually are more grave or "tragic" elements built into the work, reaching their dreadful crescendo in the final scene. Unfortunately, the opera was somewhat revised after Bizet's death to make the work more consistently melodramatic, so that it would fit more easily into the traditions of "grand opera." The work was popularized in this revised form, and it is still often performed that way today. Nietzsche would have witnessed "grand opera" performances, but with his sense for the opera's "pleasure in paradox," he seems to have grasped Bizet's intentions quite perceptively. Bizet's design for the opera can be examined thanks to a recent urtext prepared by Richard Langham Smith. This urtext was used as the basis for an excellent production that is available on DVD, filmed at the Opéra-Comique in 2009, conducted by John Eliot Gardiner, with Anna Caterina Antonnaci in the title role.

41. In this respect, José's crime of passion can be taken as prototypical, a revealing window onto a pervasive feature of human psychology: "The most common motives for homicide are moralistic: retaliation after an insult, escalation of a domestic quarrel, punishing an unfaithful or deserting romantic partner . . . Most homicides . . . are really instances of capital punishment, with a private citizen acting as judge, jury, and executioner . . . [Consequently,] those who commit murder . . . often appear to be resigned to their fate at the hands of authorities; many wait patiently for the police to arrive . . . Not unlike workers who violate a prohibition to strike—knowing they will go to jail—or others who defy the law on grounds of principle, they do what they think is right, and willingly suffer the consequences" (Pinker, *The Better Angels of Our Nature*, 83–84). This is just what Don José does with his concluding cry.

42. To clarify this point, we should note that Nietzsche believed the Old Testament was originally a basically pagan document (and to that extent praiseworthy: see *GM* III.22), but that at some point in its history more "Christian" conceptions of God were grafted onto the text (see the discussion by Beiner, *Civil Religion*, 380–82). In this respect Nietzsche inverts Schopenhauer, who thought that the admirable, world-transcending core of Christianity had been accommodated to, and compromised by, the worldliness of Judaism. Schopenhauer's argument is consistent with (and probably influenced) Wagner's anti-Semitism (see Berger, *Beyond Reason*, 346–48).

43. Goethe also employs the phrase in *Wilhelm Meister's Apprenticeship*. The relevant passages are quoted in Sommer, *Nietzsche-Kommentar: "Der Fall Wagner" und "Götzen-Dämmerung,"* 52.

44. "*Christianity's* stroke of genius: God sacrificing himself for the guilt of man, God exacting payment of himself, God as the only one who can redeem man from what has become irredeemable for man himself—the creditor sacrificing himself for his debtor, out of *love* (is that credible?—), out of love for his debtor!" (*GM* II.21). "These old philosophers were heartless: philosophizing was always a kind of vampirism. When considering such figures, including even Spinoza, don't you feel something deeply enigmatic and strange? Don't you see the spectacle unfolding, the steady *growing paler*—this ever more ideally construed desensualization? Don't you sense in the background some long-concealed bloodsucker who starts with the senses and finally leaves behind and spares only bones and rattling?—I refer to categories, formulas, words

(for, forgive me, what *remained* of Spinoza, *amor intellectualis dei*, is mere rattle, nothing more! What is *amor*; what is *deus*, when they are missing every drop of blood?)" (*GS* 372).

45. See Brusotti, "Erkenntnis als Passion."

46. See Franco, *Nietzsche's Enlightenment*, 61, 96–97.

47. Montinari, *Reading Nietzsche*, 61–62, argues that although Nietzsche during this period is determined to invest philosophy with a passionate spirit, that determination is controlled by a commitment to science, whose ability to reward the new passion he is (at least initially) uncertain of. Piazzesi, "Greed and Love," 142, argues that *D* 429 shows that a "dialectical relation, intense and unrequited, with the loved woman" as described by Stendhal "is also desirable with regard to the man of knowledge's relation with the truth he seeks, so much so that, in a sense, the stimulus to desire and further satisfaction always depends on doubt, the risk of despair, and fear."

48. Stendhal, *On Love*, book 2, chap. 59.

49. See further Campioni, *Der französische Nietzsche*, 50.

50. *D* 279, 309, 379, 479, 532; *GS* 57, 59, 62. On the echoes of Stendhal in some of these passages, see Brusotti, *Die Leidenschaft der Erkenntnis*, 375–77; Piazzesi, "Greed and Love," 122–42.

51. Lou Salome, *Nietzsche*, 80–81, remarks on the unique tension this delicate balance produces in *Daybreak* (though I disagree with her that this should be read as the prelude to a "mystical philosophy of the will"). Pippin argues that the image of the unrequited lover in *D* 429 "in effect defines Nietzsche's answer to the question of the philosophical type: it is someone who can sustain an entire lifetime of unrequited love" (*Nietzsche, Psychology, and First Philosophy*, 38). I think this is true up to a point (it is true of Nietzsche's position in *Daybreak*), and I agree that the image ought to be given more weight for the understanding of Nietzsche than it generally has been given—but it also understates the degree to which Nietzsche later sought out (and claimed to have found) a love that could be consummated, as I will now suggest—for it is not always clear that Nietzsche thought that a lifetime of unrequited love *could* be sustained, notwithstanding his regard for that ideal.

52. Lampert (*What a Philosopher Is*, 266–69) and Montinari (*Reading Nietzsche*, 64–66) both draw on Nietzsche's notebooks to argue that he only gradually came to determine that the "passion for knowledge" introduced in *D* 429 could be fulfilled through the will to power and eternal return.

53. A further, related fault-line is that *Daybreak* continues to exhibit (and exhort others to emulate) the Free Spirit's inclination for solitude (*D* 443; see also 177, 323, 441, 471, 485, 491)—but Zarathustra, although he has learned from his solitude, is shown mainly leaving it.

54. Nietzsche's critical view of the drive to possess is richly discussed by Lampert, *What a Philosopher Is*, 247–50. Nietzsche also discusses the notion of love as possession in *BGE* 194. His argument here is somewhat cryptic, but still makes plain enough that he is not an advocate of anything like the simple brute possession desperately sought after by Don José. This point is brought out in commentaries on the aphorism by Cooper, *Eros in Plato, Rousseau, and Nietzsche*, 241–43; Lampert, *Nietzsche's Task*, 163–67; Pippin, "Morality as Psychology, Psychology as Morality," 90–91. Irving Singer's history of love through the ages is not alert to Nietzsche's criticisms of the ideal of love as possession, and as a result Singer mistakenly concludes that

what Nietzsche approves of in *Carmen* is a depiction of love as "hatred" and nothing more (*The Nature of Love, Vol. 3*, 85, see also 194).

55. Or, even if that "God is dead," He has still not been replaced by a proto-pagan, life-affirming God: "God is dead; but, given the way people are, there may still for millennia be caves in which they show his shadow.—And we—we must still defeat his shadow as well!" (*GS* 108).

56. Wagner was not conventionally religious, but in his essay *Art and Religion* he famously described the task of art as "salvaging the kernel of religion," that is, re-presenting and revivifying the truths of religion in an age in which religious belief had waned. Bizet was strongly opposed to religion, and disdained religious music (see Curtiss, *Bizet and His World*, 178–79). In *Carmen* religion appears only in the following ways: in act 1, Don José mentions that he is originally from the countryside, where he trained for the priesthood, but the vocation did not suit him, and he wound up fleeing the country and becoming a soldier. Then there is the character of Micaëla, whom José's mother wishes him to marry (this character does not appear in Mérimée's novel—she is Bizet's creation). In act 1, Micaëla speaks of attending church with José's mother, and in act 3, when she journeys to call José home from the life he has made among the Gypsies, she prays to God to protect her in this strange world (and especially to protect her from Carmen, who clearly represents her antithesis). José shows an indulgent sympathy for Micaëla, but he always returns to Carmen. In these ways, Bizet makes clear that the world of the opera is one where religion has been deliberately left behind.

57. Also see the end of section 6, where Nietzsche constructs a parody of Wagner (or a "Wagnerian"), whose figure asks: "Man is corrupt: who redeems him? *what redeems him?*"

58. The mature Wagner composed ten operas, which can be counted as six if the *Ring* cycle is classified as a single unit. Nietzsche initially summarizes five of these six, alluding the motive of redemptive love in each case except the *Ring*—but in the fourth section of the essay he includes a discussion of redemption through love in the *Ring*. In his initial set of summaries he omits any mention of *Lohengrin*, even though he next lists "other lessons" to be learned from Wagner's operas (that is, lessons beyond the problem of redemption), and in that context mentions *Lohengrin* twice—claiming, in the first instance, to be discussing the opera "once more" and, in the second instance, to be mentioning it "for the third time." So there appears to be a missing reference to *Lohengrin*, and however that omission is to be explained, redemption through love is a very obvious theme of that opera.

59. See, for instance, the assessment by Young: "If there is a single theme that forms the central topic of Wagner's thought and art, both early and late, it is 'redemption'—or more expansively, 'redemption through love'" (*The Philosophies of Richard Wagner*, 91).

60. *BGE* 256; see also *HH* Second Preface 3; *GM* 3; *EH* HH 5; *NCW* "Wagner as an Apostle of Chastity" 3.

61. This point is made in a helpful way by Strong, *Friedrich Nietzsche and the Politics of Transfiguration*, 228–32.

62. Wagner's earliest works were highly derivative and mostly failures. Nietzsche does not mention any of them. Wagner's mature (or, one might say, "Wagnerian") works are: *Der fliegende Holländer*; *Tannhäuser*; *Lohengrin*; *Tristan und Isolde*; *Die Meistersinger von Nürnberg*; *Der Ring des Nibelungen* (consisting of four parts: *Das Rheingold*; *Die Walküre*; *Siegfried*;

Götterdämmerung); *Parsifal.* The operas are listed here in the order in which they were completed. However, Wagner began working on the *Ring* shortly after the first production of *Tannhäuser*, and after producing the *Ring* he wrote only one additional work, *Parsifal.*

63. See Magee, *The Tristan Chord*, 34–35; Young, *The Philosophies of Richard Wagner*, 3–9.

64. Berger, *Beyond Reason: Wagner contra Nietzsche*, 62. Also see the account of the origins of the *Ring* as a product of Wagner's reflections on the prospects for revolution by Berry, "Richard Wagner and the Politics of Music-Drama."

65. In *Die Walküre*, Act Two, Scene Two, when Wotan orders Brünnhilde to kill the lawbreaker Siegmund (the father of Siegfried), she responds: "In pity's name / take back your word! You love Siegmund: / out of love for you—/ I know—I'll shield the Wälsung". This she does, incurring Wotan's (reluctant) punishment as a result. She explains herself to Wotan in Act Three, Scene Three: "Not wise am I, / but one thing I knew—/ that you loved the Wälsung: / I knew the discord / that made you / forget this one thing altogether"; "Since, for you, I kept sight of / that one thing alone / on which, painfully torn / by the other's constraint / you helplessly turned your back!"; "Inwardly true / to the will / which inspired / this love in my heart / and which bound me to the Wälsung—/ I flouted your command." Wotan responds to her: "'you blissfully followed / the force of love / now follow him / whom you're forced to love!".

66. Brünnhilde declares: "Be gone, Valhalla's / light-bringing world! / May your proud-standing stronghold / moulder to dust! / Fare well, resplendent / pomp of the gods! / End in rapture, / you endless race!" Then, joined by Siegfried, she sings: "Siegfried's [Brünnhilde's] star / now shines upon me / He's [She's] mine forever / always mine, / my heritage and own, / my one and all: / light-bringing love / and laughing death." In a letter to August Röckel of January 25/26, 1854, Wagner explains that "[f]rom the moment that Siegfried awakens [Brünnhilde], she no longer has any other knowledge save that of love" (translated by Spencer and Millington, *Selected Letters of Richard Wagner*, 307).

67. In a letter to August Röckel, February 5, 1885, Wagner remarks: "My experience of life has brought me to a point where only Schopenhauer's philosophy could wholly satisfy me and exert a decisive influence on my whole life. By accepting unreservedly the profound truths of his teaching I was able to follow my own inner bent" (quoted in Roger Hollinrake, "Epiphany and Apocalypse," 45).

68. In a letter written not long after his discovery of Schopenhauer, Wagner comments: "let us treat the world only with contempt; for it deserves no better: but let no hopes be placed in it, that our hearts be not deluded! It is evil, *evil, fundamentally evil* . . . [The world] belongs to *Alberich* [the principal villain of the *Ring*, who renounces love for the sake of power]: to no one else!! Away with it!" (letter to Franz Liszt, October 7, 1854, translated by Spencer and Millington, *Selected Letters of Richard Wagner*, 319).

69. Letter to Franz Liszt, December 16, 1854 (translated by Spencer and Millington, *Selected Letters of Richard Wagner*, 323).

70. The various endings are presented in a bilingual edition, *Wagner's Ring of the Nibelung: A Companion*. I have quoted from Stewart Spencer's translations of the opera in this edition (which is a valuable aid for anyone beginning to study the *Ring*). A complication needs to be mentioned here: both the "Feuerbach ending" and the "Schopenhauer ending" were written as a series of verses inserted into Brünnhilde's concluding peroration, before she sets the world

aflame. But although Wagner's correspondence attests to the fact that he definitively rejected the "Feuerbach ending," and that he wrote the "Schopenhauer ending" to supplant it, he ultimately did not set the Schopenhauer verses to music, so they are not included in performances. Nevertheless, Wagner published the *Ring* as a "poem" with the Schopenhauerian verses included, which suggests that he wanted Brünnhilde's last words to be understood in light of them. When Nietzsche was completing *The Case of Wagner*, he asked his assistant, Heinrich Köselitz, to provide him with page references for the Schopenhauerian verses that Wagner had published. So, for Nietzsche, these verses were evidently essential for understanding Wagner's intentions. But even though he deploys those verses for somewhat polemical purposes in the essay, his interest in them should not be assumed to be capricious. After all, Nietzsche had appealed to these very same verses to help explain the *Ring* in the penultimate paragraph of *Richard Wagner in Bayreuth* (a piece that had delighted Wagner). Given this fact, and given how close Nietzsche was to Wagner during the period when the *Ring* was completed, there is good reason to suspect that the interpretation of the *Ring* Nietzsche offers is based on what he had been told by Wagner himself. For a detailed argument supporting Nietzsche's interpretation, see Hollinrake, *Nietzsche, Wagner, and the Philosophy of Pessimism*, chap. 4.

71. Adrian Daub observes: "As the end of *Götterdämmerung* makes clear, Wagner attaches a great deal of political importance to the concept of love . . . His frustrated political hopes were largely displaced into the erotic realm" (*Tristan's Shadow*, 9–10).

72. Nietzsche stresses this point in *GM* III.6.

73. Wagner writes to Mathilde Wesendonck: "During recent weeks I have been slowly rereading friend Schopenhauer's principal work, and this time it has inspired me, quite extraordinarily, to expand and—in certain details—even to correct his system . . . It is a question, you see, of pointing out the path to salvation, which has not been recognized by any philosopher, and especially not by Sch., but which involves a total pacification of the will through love, and not through any abstract human love, but a love engendered on the basis of sexual love, i.e., the attraction between man and woman . . . I have succeeded in demonstrating beyond doubt that in love there lies the possibility of raising oneself above the individual impulse of the will to a point where total mastery over the latter is achieved" (letter of December 1, 1858, translated by Spencer and Millington, *Selected Letters of Richard Wagner*, 432). Wagner even drafted a letter to Schopenhauer explicating this point (although the letter was never sent). Wagner's "correction" of Schopenhauer on this point has been stressed by several studies: for instance, Daub, *Tristan's Shadow*, 4–7; Hutcheon and Hutcheon, *Opera: The Art of Dying*, 60–61; Scruton, *Death-Devoted Heart*, 130–33. Tracy Strong seems to overlook this point when he comments that "in the end, Wagner is merely non-rigorous Schopenhauer" (*Friedrich Nietzsche and the Politics of Transfiguration*, 231)—but Nietzsche thought that "Wagner owes his *success* to his sensuality" (*KSA* 13:601 [1888/23/2]), which is a plausible assessment, and which could not have been said about Schopenhauer.

74. Malwida von Meysenbug attended performances of the opera with Nietzsche in 1872, reported that afterward he declared that the "drama of death" left him feeling "happy and redeemed" (cited in Hutcheon and Hutcheon, *Opera: The Art of Dying*, 70).

75. Tristan and Isolde hate the day (the world of illusion, or the world of "phenomena"), and come together only at night, as in act 2, in which Tristan declares: "So let us die, / undivided, /

eternally one, / without end" (see the fuller discussion by Hutcheon and Hutcheon, *Opera: The Art of Dying*, 58–59). In the *Ring*, Siegfried's dying words are: "Sweet extinction,—/ blissful terror–: / Brünnhild' gives me her greeting!" As Julian Young points out, death in Wagner does not appear to be "mere death" (*The Philosophies of Richard Wagner*, 92–94). Indeed, *Tristan und Isolde* concludes with a piece of music that accompanies Isolde as she declares her ecstasy while collapsing to death over Tristan's corpse, and although this piece of music has come to be called the "Liebestod" (love-death), that term does not come from Wagner, who referred to it as a "*Verklärung*" (transfiguration), and his stage directions note that when Isolde collapses, she does so "as if transfigured."

76. Nietzsche stresses the importance of Parsifal's chaste love to his redemptive capacity in the one-sentence summary of the opera that he offers in *CW* 3. The chastity of Parsifal might seem like a marked departure from the erotic passion of Wagner's earlier operas, but that is not exactly the case. There is not necessarily an opposition between erotic and chaste love (as Nietzsche once noted, *GM* III.12), insofar as in physical passion we feel liberated from our individual, physical being, and united with the beloved as part of something higher than our all too human selves. To that extent, chaste love actually seems to realize the hope or promise that is inspired by erotic love. So the love of Tristan and Isolde, if fully realized, would express itself as something closer to the chaste love of Parsifal (consider the analysis of Scruton, *Death-Devoted Heart*, 131; as well as Magee, *The Tristan Chord*, 265–70). Mere human beings cannot reliably realize this sort of chastity (which would require being redeemed from our corporeal existence), but the point of Parsifal is that he in effect transcends the human precisely in the purity of his love (as Nietzsche observes in *CW* 9, even though Parsifal is chaste, he is also supposed to be the father of Lohengrin, the hero of one of Wagner's earlier operas: "How did [Parsifal] do it?—Must one remember at this point that 'chastity works *miracles*'?"). The degree to which *Parsifal* ought to be read as a crypto-Christian work is controversial, but a compelling case in favor of such a reading is offered by Beckett, *Richard Wagner: Parsifal*.

77. As we have seen, Wagner's own remarks in his correspondence very much support the suggestion that he understood this resolution as redemptive.

78. Nietzsche could well have in mind here not only the rewriting of Brünnhilde's closing words, but also the changes that Wagner made to the character of Wotan. As Wagner revised the *Ring*, Wotan, through his striving after power, ultimately learns to renounce his own will, and deliberately sets in motion the twilight of the gods. Thus, following Wagner's discovery of Schopenhauer, Siegfried's position as the redemptive hero of the *Ring* was to some extent superseded by the figures of Wotan and Brünnhilde, each of whom gradually discovers Schopenhauerian wisdom. On this development, see Wagner's account in his letter to August Röckel, January 25/26, 1854 (in particular, see the passage quoted by Spencer and Millington, *Selected Letters of Richard Wagner*, 307).

79. See Sommer, *Nietzsche-Kommentar: "Der Fall Wagner" und "Götzen-Dämmerung,"* 74–75.

80. In an earlier notebook entry, Nietzsche quotes the motto and explicitly connects it to belief in Providence (*KSA* 8:20 [1875/3/19]). One can certainly speculate—although one cannot prove—that Nietzsche would have discussed the motto with Wagner, given their many hours

of intense conversation about Schopenhauer, along with the fact that Nietzsche was an avid reader of Diogenes Laertius.

81. Consider these passages from *CW* 10: "[Wagner] repeated a single proposition all his life long: that his music did not mean mere music. But more. But infinitely more . . ." " 'Music is always a mere means': that was his theory." "Wagner required literature to persuade all the world to take his music seriously, to take it as profound 'because its *meaning* was infinite.' " "Let us remember that Wagner was young at the time Hegel and Schelling seduced men's spirits; that he guessed, that he grasped with his very hands the only thing the Germans take seriously—'the idea,' which is to say, something that is obscure, uncertain, full of intimations." "Hegel is a *taste.*—And not merely a German but a European taste.—A taste Wagner comprehended—to which he felt equal—which he immortalized.—He merely applied it to music—he invented a system for himself charged with 'infinite meaning'—he became the *heir of Hegel.*—Music as 'idea'.—And how Wagner was understood!—The same human type that raved about Hegel, today raves about Wagner; in his school they even *write* Hegelian.—Above all, German youths understood him. The two words 'infinite' and 'meaning' were really sufficient: they induced a state of incomparable well-being in young men. It was not with his music that Wagner conquered them, it was with the 'idea.' " "In the midst of Wagner's multiplicity, abundance, and arbitrariness they feel as if justified in their own eyes—'redeemed.' "

82. "Every art, every philosophy, may be considered a remedy and aid in the service of growing or declining life: it always presupposes suffering and sufferers. But there are two kinds of sufferers: first, those who suffer from the overfullness of life and want a Dionysian art as well as a tragic insight and outlook on life—and then those who suffer from the *impoverishment* of life and demand of art and philosophy, calm, stillness, smooth seas, *or*, on the other hand, frenzy, convulsion, and anesthesia. Revenge against life itself—the most voluptuous kind of frenzy for those so impoverished! . . . Wagner responds to this dual need of the latter no less than Schopenhauer: they negate life, they slander it, hence they are my antipodes" (*NCW*, We Antipodes). This text modifies *GS* 370 (which is part of book 5 of *GS*, written in 1887), where the passage appears as a response to the question "What is Romanticism?" and the last line from the passage is given this way: "All romanticism in art and in knowledge fits the dual needs of the latter type, as did (and do) Schopenhauer and Richard Wagner, to name the most famous and prominent romantics that I *misunderstood*." This formulation emphasizes that Nietzsche rejects Wagner's entire artistic edifice, not just *Parsifal.*

83. "Every art, every philosophy . . . always presupposes suffering and sufferers." (*NCW*, We Antipodes).

84. *CW* 7. Also see *CW* 5: "Our physicians and physiologists confront their most interesting case in Wagner, at least a very complete case"; and then (echoing the preface), "Wagner is *the modern artist par excellence*."

85. Theodor Adorno states the contrast well: "In the Card Trio, as in *Carmen* as a whole, there is an absence of transcendence and meaning. . . . The contrast with Wagner, which according to the trite opinion induced Nietzsche to champion Bizet, is truly perfect. In Wagner, every sentence, every gesture, every motif and the overall interconnections—all are charged with meaning. In Bizet the inhumanity and hardness, even the violence of form, has been used to obliterate the last token of meaning, so as to forestall any illusion that anything in life could

have any meaning over and above its obvious one . . . The unsentimental, undiluted depiction of natural passion achieves what the inclusion of any consoling meaning would deny to the work . . . The prohibition on transcendence destroys the illusion that nature is anything more than mortal. This is the precise function of music in *Carmen*" ("Fantasia sopra Carmen," 61–63). As Adorno gradually makes clear, the issue of "meaning" in the contrast between Wagner and Bizet is ultimately a matter of the meaning of human mortality.

86. Nietzsche captures the difference in a striking way when he suggests that healthy music is akin to dancing, whereas Wagner's music is akin to "swimming" (*AOM* 134; this aphorism is reproduced, in modified form, in *NCW* "Wagner as a Danger" 1). One dimension of the contrast is suggested by a remark that Nietzsche makes in *D* 27: "The Greeks differed from us in their evaluation of *hope*: they felt it to be blind and deceitful; Hesiod gave the strongest expression to this attitude in a fable whose sense is so strange no more recent commentator has understood it—for it runs counter to the modern spirit, which has learned from Christianity to believe in hope as a virtue" (consider 1 Corinthians 13:13). For the fable referred to by Nietzsche, see Hesiod, *Works and Days* 50–100, which tells the story of how Zeus determined to punish human beings by creating Pandora, who is possessed of a beauty that will be appealing to humans, but also possesses a jar of evils that will wreak havoc on them once it is unleashed. One of those evils is hope, which nearly, but not quite, escapes the jar before the lid is placed back on. In his more detailed remarks on the fable in *HH* 71 and *A* 23, Nietzsche laments that modern human beings have altogether forgotten that hope *is* an evil—in fact, "the worst of evils." Wagner reflects this tendency in the extreme.

87. In *D* Preface 3 Nietzsche comments that "[m]orality does not merely have at its command every kind of means of frightening off critical hands and torture-instruments—it knows how to 'inspire'"; a few sentences later he characterizes morality as "the mistress of seduction," suggesting that morality's power of inspiration includes an erotic element.

88. Nietzsche alludes to this limitation in the writings completed immediately after *Zarathustra*: "The *pia fraus* [pious fraud] offends the taste (the 'piety') of the free spirit, who has 'the piety of the search for knowledge,' even more than the *impia fraus* [impious fraud]. Hence his profound lack of understanding for the church, a characteristic of the type 'free spirit'—*his* unfreedom" (*BGE* 105). For Nietzsche, Wagner was a sort of "pious fraud." In *GM* I.6, he acknowledges the shortcoming of Free Spirits relative to priestly classes: "The entire nature of an admittedly priestly aristocracy admittedly makes clear why it was precisely here that the valuation opposites could so soon become internalized and heightened in a dangerous manner; and indeed through them gulfs were finally torn open between man and man across which even an Achilles of free spiritedness would not be able to leap without shuddering." Thus, "with some fairness one could add that it was on the soil of this *essentially dangerous* form of human existence, the priestly form, that man first became an *interesting animal*." (See the comment on this point by Franco, *Nietzsche's Enlightenment*, 188.)

89. See the chapter of *Twilight of the Idols* on "Morality as Anti-Nature." Also see *The Antichrist*, "Law against Christianity," propositions 1 and 4.

90. "No one is free to become a Christian or not to do so; one is not 'converted' to Christianity—one must be sufficiently sick for it" (*A* 51).

91. "The Christian wishes *to be rid of himself*. Le moi est toujours *haïssable*" (The self is

always hateable). (The French quotation is from Pascal, and it is also used by Nietzsche in *D* 79). On this point, also see *GM* III.14, and *TI* Skirmishes 35: "Instead of saying '*I* am now worthless,' the moral lie in the mouth of the *decadent* says: 'Everything is worthless—life is *worthless*' . . . Such a judgment remains a great danger in the end, for it is infectious—right across the morbid soil of society it will soon shoot up into a tropical vegetation of concepts, one moment as religion (Christianity), the next as philosophy (Schopen-hauerishness)." Compare *EH* Clever 9: "I have not the slightest wish for anything to be other than it is; I myself do not want to be different."

92. Recall again: "Every art, every philosophy. . . . always presupposes suffering and sufferers" (*NCW*, We Antipodes)—and, we can now add, every religion as well.

93. Nietzsche uses the term *Glücksfall*, which has a stronger resonance than any English translation can capture since *Glück* connotes both happiness and good fortune.

94. "I do not want anything differently, not even backwards,—I was not allowed to want anything different . . . Amor fati . . . Even Christianity becomes necessary: only the highest form, the most dangerous, the one that was most tempting in its No to Life, provokes its highest affirmation—me" (*KSA* 13:641 [25/7/1888]).

95. Commenting on Nietzsche's characterization of "master morality" and "Christian morality" as "both *necessary*: they are ways of seeing," Satkunanandan suggests: "[Christianity's perspective] must be necessary because we are to see the world from as many perspectives as possible if we are to see the world richly" (*Extraordinary Responsibility*, 49). A helpful overview of Nietzsche's reflections on "seeing" the world from multiple perspectives is offered by Parkes, *Composing the Soul*, 303–5. To avoid misunderstanding, I should add that this immersion in multiple perspectives is not undertaken by Nietzsche as ecumenism for its own sake: it is conducted for the sake of ultimately finding the *richest* point of view (and rank-ordering the others on that basis). But the ecumenism is still essential to that task.

96. Satkunanandan elaborates on this point, outlining alternatives that Nietzsche's position is to be distinguished from: "[Nietzsche's] kind of inner cultivation is different from passively submitting to the value conflict within oneself, or from trying to masterfully subdue this value conflict. It is also—obviously—distinguishable from a denial of this inner conflict" (*Extraordinary Responsibility*, 48). The third alternative can be associated with the case of Wagner, that is, with the desire for redemption; the second alternative might be fairly associated with Don José, that is, with the attempt to possess or control. Since I doubt that Nietzsche would allow that total passivity is an authentic option for human beings (even though one might mistakenly believe oneself to be passive, and be comforted by that belief), I think that he would largely approve of Satkunanandan's subsequent suggestion that "the kind of greatness now available to humans could be the attainment of a civil war within the soul—how different from Plato!" (*Extraordinary Responsibility*, 48). But perhaps in very exceptional instances, thoroughgoing love of the world as it is could enable some suspension of hostilities (as will be considered in the next chapter's discussion of Zarathustra's midday happiness).

97. Recall his remark on *Parsifal*: "I admire this work; I wish I had written it myself; failing that, *I understand it*."

98. Consider *TI* Morality as Anti-Nature 6: "Reality shows us such a delightful abundance of types, the richness that comes from the extravagant play and alteration of forms: to which

some wretched loafer of a moralist says: 'no! man must be different!' . . . He even knows how man should be, this maundering miseryguts: he paints himself on the walls and says '*ecce homo*!' . . . But even when the moralist turns just to the individual and says to him: '*you* should be such and such!' he does not stop making a fool of himself. The individual is a piece of fate from top to bottom, one more necessity for all that is to come and will be. Telling him to change means that everything should change, even backwards . . . And indeed there have been consistent moralists who wanted man to be different, namely virtuous; they wanted him to be in their image, namely, a miseryguts: to which end they *denied* the world!" "We who are different, we immoralists, on the contrary have opened our hearts to all kinds of comprehending, understanding, *approving*. We do not readily deny; we seek our honor in being *affirmative*!"

99. "My formula for human greatness is *amor fati*: not wanting anything to be different, not forwards, not backwards, not for all eternity. Not just enduring what is necessary, still less concealing it—all idealism is hypocrisy in the face of what is necessary—but *loving* it . . ." (*EH* Clever 10).

100. Zarathustra often speaks of a "Great Midday" that will revolutionize the course of human existence and place it on a new foundation. In *Ecce Homo* (in the last section of the commentary on *The Birth of Tragedy*) Nietzsche says that for his younger self, Wagner's Bayreuth Festival had represented the "*great midday*" ("when the most select dedicate themselves to the greatest of all tasks")—a conceit that, he notes, "will be no mystery to those who know my *Zarathustra*."

CHAPTER 4

1. Both doctrines are also more or less introduced in this work. The eternal return was presented without being named at the conclusion to the first edition of *The Joyful Wissenschaft*, where it appears as an ingress to *Thus Spoke Zarathustra*. The will to power is prefigured in earlier works, but not articulated as such.

2. As Beiner observes: "for Nietzsche, in common with Machiavelli (*Discourses on Livy*, II.5), the highest politics consists in the founding of new religions. In fact, one might speculate that Nietzsche's whole aim in writing *Thus Spoke Zarathustra* was to prove that a single human being can sit down and write a religion. What Moses and St. Paul did *can be done again*" (*Civil Religion*, 2n3). See, similarly, the remark by Pangle and Burns: "Nietzsche intends *Thus Spoke Zarathustra* to express his own creativity, through a new form of strange and haunting writing, embodying a new synthesis of poetry and philosophy, and centered on a new kind of hero-saint" (*The Key Texts of Political Philosophy*, 402). Or see Seung, *Nietzsche's Epic of the Soul*, xxvi: "[*Zarathustra*'s] function is to announce a new religion"; or Shaw, *Nietzsche's Political Skepticism*, 55: "*Zarathustra* is testament to Nietzsche's ongoing concern, after *The Birth of Tragedy*, not just to repudiate religion but to find some substitute for it. In particular, the central idea, that of eternal recurrence, seems to be intended to offer a form of secular redemption."

3. In Robert Pippin's words, *Zarathustra* "could be both a prophetic book and a kind of send-up of a prophetic book" ("Nietzsche: Thus Spoke Zarathustra," 156). For a fuller discussion of that possibility, see Pippin, "Irony and Affirmation in Nietzsche's *Thus Spoke Zarathustra*," and also Meier, *Was ist Nietzsches Zarathustra?*

4. As Pippin, *Nietzsche, Psychology, and First Philosophy*, 61n23, points out, Nietzsche's rhetoric about "herd morality," combined with subsequent interpretations of him as a "heroic individualist," has made it difficult to understand him as a theorist of (healthy and desirable forms of) human interdependence (for instance, see the criticisms of Nietzsche by Nussbaum and MacIntyre discussed in chapter 2, note 73). But this is an authentic aspect of his thought, and the drama of Zarathustra's love drawing him repeatedly out of his solitude is the most prominent example.

5. On *Zarathustra*'s indirect (and extensive) engagements with Wagner, see Hollinrake, *Nietzsche, Wagner, and the Philosophy of Pessimism*.

6. See Blue, *The Making of Friedrich Nietzsche*, 297–301; as well as Silk and Stern, *Nietzsche on Tragedy*, 30–33. Nietzsche singled out the opera for praise later in his career as well (see *BGE* 240).

7. On the echoes of *Tristan* (and Schopenhauer more generally) in *Meistersinger*, see Dreyfus, *Wagner and the Erotic Impulse*, 112–13; Magee, *The Tristan Chord*, 251–55; Young, *The Philosophies of Richard Wagner*, 98–99.

8. Tracy Strong comments well on this problem in Wagner, remarking that in the ending to *Die Meistersinger*, "the degree of self-consciousness required for successful manipulation is such that the attained result is always seen as problematic" (*Friedrich Nietzsche and the Politics of Transfiguration*, 229). Strong argues that this difficulty is what led Wagner to turn to the "pure fool" Parsifal, that is, to make the agent of redemption into a figure who would not even realize what he was doing.

9. Gemes and Sykes, "The Culture of Myth," 65–68, explain how Wagner developed this seemingly paradoxical notion of a "*wahrster Wahn*" and made it crucial to his whole project, and note that Nietzsche picked up the notion from Wagner (rather than Schopenhauer, for whom there is only *Wahn*).

10. On this point, see Gooding-Williams, *Zarathustra's Dionysian Modernism*, 61–62; and Lemm, *Nietzsche's Animal Philosophy*, 78.

11. Lampert, *Nietzsche's Teaching*, 17, draws a contrast between the solitudes of Zarathustra and the old holy man: "Unlike the old saint, [Zarathustra] must return to mankind . . . because for him there is nothing that could bring comfort to complete solitude."

12. This point is stressed by Gillespie, *Nietzsche's Final Teaching*, 45; and Gooding-Williams, *Zarathustra's Dionysian Modernism*, 62.

13. See Meier, *Was ist Nietzsches Zarathustra?* 18–20.

14. The fourth section of the prologue elaborates on this point: "What is great in the human is that it is a bridge and not a goal: what can be loved in the human is that it is a *going-over* and a *going-under*. I love those who do not know how to live except by going under, for they are those who go over and across. I love the great despisers, for they are the great reverers and arrows of yearning for the other shore." (Also see the speech in part 1, "On the Way of the Creator": "The lover wants to create, because he despises! What does he know of love who has not had to despise precisely what he loved!")

15. See Shaw, "The 'Last Man' Problem."

16. Pippin rightly stresses that Zarathustra's failure in the prologue is not a failure to come up with a sufficiently persuasive logical argument for the assembled crowd; rather, "it is a fail-

ure of desire," that is, a failure to grasp the psychology of the great majority of human beings ("Nietzsche: Thus Spoke Zarathustra," 163, 165; compare Pippin, *Nietzsche, Psychology, and First Philosophy*, 54). In this respect, Zarathustra has more in common with an old holy man (whom he was able to understand, and even have a friendly conversation with, despite their difference stemming from one key point) than with the multitude (whom he badly misjudges and who, he realizes after his speech, hate him in addition to not comprehending him).

17. Quite a few readers with antimodern inclinations have jumped to the conclusion that Nietzsche/Zarathustra's teaching consists essentially in his initial rhetoric about the "last human," rather than in the self-critical reflection that the failure of that rhetoric induces (see the accounts of such readings by Beiner, *Dangerous Minds*, 19–20; Smith, *Modernity and Its Discontents*, 18–20, 250–51). But the most serious and significant thoughts of Nietzsche (and his Zarathustra) are contained in that self-critical reflection.

18. See Pangle, "The 'Warrior Spirit' as an Inlet to the Political Philosophy of Nietzsche's *Zarathustra*," 143.

19. For detailed accounts of how this speech serves as the culmination of part 1, see Gooding-Williams, *Zarathustra's Dionysian Modernism*, 125–27; and Lampert, *Nietzsche's Teaching*, 73–74.

20. On this point, see further Gooding-Williams, *Zarathustra's Dionysian Modernism*, 126; Pangle and Burns, *The Key Texts of Political Philosophy*, 410.

21. Gooding-Williams (*Zarathustra's Dionysian Modernism*, 51) and Lampert (*Nietzsche's Teaching*, 14–15) both helpfully elaborate on Zarathustra's understanding of the sun's neediness. On the need to "shine forth," in particular, as the core of humanity for Zarathustra, see Pangle and Burns, *The Key Texts of Political Philosophy*, 409–10.

22. See Lemm, *Nietzsche's Animal Philosophy*, 77–78 (on the sun and the bestowing virtue); and Parkes, *Composing the Soul*, 136–39 (on sun imagery in Nietzsche's thought more generally).

23. On Zarathustra's imagery here, see again Parkes, *Composing the Soul*, 139.

24. Throughout this chapter Zarathustra speaks of the love that drives him back to human beings in terms that are greatly intensified compared to his expressions in the prologue (as Pippin observes, "Nietzsche: Thus Spoke Zarathustra," 166).

25. As Pippin remarks, "[Zarathustra] seems to have realized that part of the problem with the dissemination of his teachings and writings lies with him, and not just the audience" ("Nietzsche: Thus Spoke Zarathustra," 167). Lampert, *Nietzsche's Teaching*, 83–84, outlines Zarathustra's growing distance from his disciples in part 2.

26. On the importance of reading these five chapters as a sequence, see Lampert, *Nietzsche's Teaching*, 100–120; and Newell, "Zarathustra's Dancing Dialectic," 417–18.

27. As Seung elaborates, "the free spirits are the polar opposite to the famous wise men" (*Nietzsche's Epic of the Soul*, 66; see also Lampert, *Nietzsche's Teaching*, 102).

28. On the Free Spirits and the lion-will, see Franco, *Nietzsche's Enlightenment*, 165–66; and Miner, *Nietzsche and Montaigne*, 243–44.

29. In drawing this threefold division, I am influenced by Meier (*Was ist Nietzsches Zarathustra?* 67–73), who stresses that Zarathustra uses the songs to clarify his own self-understanding (rather than to present a formal teaching for others).

30. On the problem of "sun" here, see Gooding-Williams, *Zarathustra's Dionysian Modernism*, 161–62; and Pangle, "The 'Warrior Spirit' as an Inlet to the Political Philosophy of Nietzsche's Zarathustra," 163–64.

31. "The Grave-Song" includes a quotation from *Tristan und Isolde*, and so it seems to be alluding (at least in part) to Nietzsche's wrestling with his disillusionment with Wagner (see Hollinrake, *Nietzsche, Wagner, and the Philosophy of Pessimism*, 79; Lampert, *Nietzsche's Teaching*, 328n39; Rosen, *The Mask of Enlightenment*, 157–58).

32. The German word is *unergründlich*, so Life appears as something whose *grounds* (reasons, foundations, basic elements) Zarathustra cannot grasp (see the helpful remarks on this imagery by Richardson, "Nietzsche on Life's Ends," 760–61).

33. In the third section of *The Case of Wagner*, Nietzsche stresses that men are easily seduced by the illusion of Woman's "higher" status. But, as Zarathustra will eventually make clear, if something turns out not to be "higher" in the sense that it had long been imagined to be, it by no means ought to be judged as any worse for that fact—very much to the contrary (see further Kofman, "The Psychologist of the Eternal Feminine," 185–89).

34. There is an instructive discussion of will to power as most fundamentally meaning self-overcoming for Nietzsche (rather than "*control* or *domination*," or "*ability* or *capacity*") in Reginster, *The Affirmation of Life*, 138–39.

35. This is a key point of Meier's, who argues that the will to power is primarily a diagnostic tool in the service of self-knowledge (*Was ist Nietzsches Zarathustra?* 78–79; see also 95–97, 234).

36. As Gooding-Williams comments: "the creator's responsibility for transforming humanity into a people *must fall to individuals* . . . the lovers-creators Zarathustra envisions will use the values they create to yoke the remains of previous peoples into a common way of life based on a unifying vision of good and evil" (*Zarathustra's Dionysian Modernism*, 143). Regarding the "paradoxical" new form of "oneness" that Zarathustra envisages here (paradoxical because it knows itself—as no other human consciousness heretofore knew itself—to be a deeply compelling but still essentially contestable individual creation), see Pangle and Burns, *The Key Texts of Political Philosophy*, 411–12.

37. As Lampert puts the point: "The final naming of 'will to power' is the first intimation of eternal return, not because the latter supersedes the former, but because eternal return arises out of will to power as its consequence" (*Nietzsche's Teaching*, 147).

38. This thought is pressed forcefully by Pangle: "Why is not the Free Spirit, after all, the wisest—the type which refuses to adore or let itself be adored? The primary response would seem to be, such a man lives a life of tragic incompleteness and frustration . . . But Zarathustra repeatedly exhorts us to 'become hard!' So, let us not hesitate to ask him . . . Why not interpret life as culminating in the heroic, meticulous dissection of every vision and hope?" ("The 'Warrior Spirit' as an Inlet to the Political Philosophy of Nietzsche's *Zarathustra*," 167, see also 163 and 177–79).

39. This thought is developed in different but complementary ways by Brusotti, *Die Leidenschaft der Erkenntnis*, 574; Franco, *Nietzsche's Enlightenment*, 176; Pippin, "Irony and Affirmation in Nietzsche's *Thus Spoke Zarathustra*," 54.

40. These are the words with which Zarathustra explains (in "The Convalescent," sec-

tion 2) what had repulsed him when he first encountered the doctrine (in "On the Vision and the Riddle," section 2).

41. Lampert, *Nietzsche's Teaching*, 160, observes that "at the beginning of Part III, as at the beginning of parts I and II, it is Zarathustra's love for mankind that moves him to action," but whereas before that love drove him to engage directly with the wider world, now it keeps him in solitude in order to prepare to *reengage*. More generally, as Higgins, *Nietzsche's Zarathustra*, 96–97, comments, "Part III chronicles the gradual reestablishment of harmony between Zarathustra's thinking (and consequently his doctrines) and the commotion-filled stream of life," but that begins with his being forced to recognize how much love he still has for the wider world. On the danger of a need for love that fails to be discerning about it what it loves, consider Meier, *Was ist Nietzsches Zarathustra?* 111; and Strong, *Friedrich Nietzsche and the Politics of Transfiguration*, 125–26.

42. As Gooding-Williams discusses in helpful detail, in the speech "On Old and New Tablets" Zarathustra says that before he descends from his mountain again, he must first wait for his own redemption, and this remark points us to "the final four speeches of Part Three," that is, the drama of Zarathustra's "*self-redemption*," "his redemption of his will" (*Zarathustra's Dionysian Modernism*, 248).

43. Consider Zarathustra's earlier statement in "On The Thousand Goals and One": "Pleasure in the herd is older than pleasure in the I." Zarathustra's creative activity recovers something of the pleasure that is known to the herd (but not to the "I") because that activity leads one to become lost in the new whole that one creates.

44. The animals not only address Zarathustra as "*the teacher of eternal return*," they also envision him as willing to die as a "herald" on its/their behalf—but such a death, as they indicate in the context, would (like their own deaths) be compensated for by the eternal return itself (that is, by the belief that death is not final). On this last point, consider Löwith, *Nietzsche's Philosophy of the Eternal Recurrence of the Same*, 73.

45. On the crucial differences between Zarathustra's understanding of the eternal return and his animals' understanding, see further Lampert, *Nietzsche's Task*, 212–23; and Meier, *Was ist Nietzsches Zarathustra?* 143–51.

46. Zarathustra refers to Dionysos here only as "the nameless one," but he alludes to anecdotes with which Dionysos was associated in Greek mythology. Nietzsche makes explicit the connection between Dionysos and the eternal recurrence in *Ecce Homo* ("The Birth of Tragedy," section 3; "Thus Spoke Zarathustra," section 6). On the appearance of Dionysos in Zarathustra's song, see Lampert, *Nietzsche's Teaching*, 226–29.

47. See Meier, *Was ist Nietzsches Zarathustra?* 152–53.

48. Parkes, "The Symphonic Structure of *Thus Spoke Zarathustra*," 25–26, comments well on the dynamic at play here, although I have to resist his suggestion that there are "overtones of the duets between Don José and Carmen" in the exchange between Zarathustra and his soul: Carmen and Don José's exchanges are a mixture of manipulation, frustration, and outright hostility, not affirmation and fulfillment. Moreover, Zarathustra's position at this point is precisely what Don José's position never is—a loving acceptance of the limits his will faces.

49. On this point, see also Pippin, "Irony and Affirmation in Nietzsche's *Thus Spoke Zarathustra*," 54–55.

50. I am drawing here on the fuller discussion by Meier, *Was ist Nietzsches Zarathustra?* 186–89.

51. "'*The world is perfect*'—thus speaks the instinct of the most spiritual, the affirmative instinct—: 'imperfection, everything *beneath* us, distance between man and man, the pathos of distance, the Chandala themselves, pertain to this perfection'" (*A* 57). In the speech on "Midday" Zarathustra initially asks, "Did the world not just become perfect?" but then, as he observes the world, he remarks to his soul, "The world is perfect." Immediately after this he adds: "Do not sing, you grass-wings, O my soul! Do not even whisper! Just look—still!" So here Zarathustra seems to reach a state of tranquility even beyond what he had found at the end of part 3, since he no longer needs to sing, not even to his soul—the world is perfect. When Zarathustra emerges out of this state of being, he refers back to it as "the well of eternity."

52. See Parkes, *Composing the Soul*, 412n40, 423n30; also D'Iorio, *Nietzsche's Journey to Sorrento*, 143n57.

53. See Meier, *Was ist Nietzsches Zarathustra?* 221–23; and Pippin, "Nietzsche: Thus Spoke Zarathustra," 176. This reading raises contested questions about the status of part 4 (see the case for interpreting *TSZ* without part 4 in the appendix to Lampert, *Nietzsche's Teaching*). I am skirting that controversy here, since I think that determining Zarathustra's *very* final position is not essential to the main argument I want to advance, for reasons that will now be explained.

CHAPTER 5

1. Instructive variations on this suggestion are offered by Berry, *Nietzsche and the Ancient Skeptical Tradition*, 135–36; Hutter, *Shaping the Future*, 145–46; Panaïoti, *Nietzsche and Buddhist Philosophy*, 52–54; Parkes, *Composing the Soul*, 363. However, these discussions do not focus on Nietzsche's autobiographical accounts of his health, as I will do here.

2. See Seung, *Goethe, Nietzsche, Wagner*, 282: "In *The Birth of Tragedy*, [Nietzsche] had advocated the liberation of German culture from the corrupting influence of France, namely, the culture of the French Enlightenment, which had destroyed the mythical world. Now he condemns the old-fashioned German intellectuals for fighting against the spirit of Newton and Voltaire."

3. This epigraph has a somewhat peculiar translation history in English. It was not included in the first translation of *Human, All Too Human* by Helen Zimmern, or in what is currently the most widely available translation, by R. J. Hollingdale. It is included in translations by Marion Faber and Gary Handwerk. However, Faber and Handwerk seem to have translated the passage as it appears in the original French text of Descartes's *Discourse on Method*, even though underneath the epigraph Nietzsche states that he has translated the passage into German from Descartes's later, Latin text. Here I have translated Nietzsche's German. (As for why Nietzsche might have opted to use the Latin text, see Rethy, "The Descartes Motto to the First Edition of *Menschliches, Allzumenschliches*."

4. See Campioni, *Der französische Nietzsche*, 37–38; and Franco, *Nietzsche's Enlightenment*, 18–19 (stressing that it is the "spirit" of science that Nietzsche wants to celebrate here, more than any method per se).

5. See Lampert, *The Enduring Importance of Leo Strauss*, 257. Pierre Hadot takes Nietz-

sche's thought as an attempt to revive something akin to the classical conception of philosophy as primarily constituting a way of life; see Hadot, *Philosophy as a Way of Life*, 272. A more detailed exploration of that possibility is offered by Hutter, *Shaping the Future*.

6. Plato, *Phaedo*, 96a–100a; Spinoza, *Treatise on the Emendation of the Intellect*, 1–18; Rousseau, *Reveries of the Solitary Walker*, Third Reverie.

7. Meier, *On the Happiness of the Philosophic Life*, 49.

8. "Becoming what you are presupposes that you have not the slightest inkling *what* you are. From this point of view even life's *mistakes* have their own sense and value, the temporary byways and detours, the delays, the 'modesties,' the seriousness wasted on tasks which lie beyond *the* task. Here a great ruse, even the highest ruse can be expressed: where *nosce te ipsum* [know thyself] would be the recipe for decline, then forgetting yourself, *misunderstanding* yourself, belittling, constricting, mediocritizing yourself becomes good sense itself" (*EH* Clever 9). Also consider *GS* 305: "One must be able at times to lose oneself if one wants to learn something from things that we ourselves are not." For further reflections on learning about oneself by mistaking oneself, see Pippin, "On 'Becoming Who One Is' (and Failing)," 308–10.

9. I therefore agree with Gillespie (*Nietzsche's Final Teaching*, 69) that the 1886 prefaces are designed by Nietzsche to show that "while his earlier works had been errors, each had been a necessary error, and his readers had to understand how he had overcome these errors."

10. Recall *HH* 225: "*Free spirit a relative concept.*—We call someone a free spirit who thinks differently from what we expect of him on the basis of his origin, environment, his social rank and position, or on the basis of the prevailing views of the time. He is the exception, the constrained spirits are the rule."

11. The writings from 1886 onward are rife with references to "physiology" (although Nietzsche's general interest in the subject dates back further, it becomes a leitmotif only later). A few examples (apart from *Ecce Homo*, where the theme is pervasive) include *BGE* 13, 15; *GS* 368; *GM* I.17; *CW* 7; *TI* Socrates 2; *A* 17; *NCW* "Where I Offer Objections." On philosophy as a product of physiology for Nietzsche, see further Reginster, *The Affirmation of Life*, 251.

12. There is a striking contrast suggested here between "thinking" as care for oneself, and "reading" as care for others, but although that contrast surely contains an important degree of truth, it should probably not be taken strictly categorically.

13. This is one case where Nietzsche employs hardly any exaggeration: many of Wagner's operas really do exceed five or six hours in performance (that is, when intermissions are included), and this, along with other features of Wagner's creations (their mythological settings, the atmosphere at Bayreuth that was established specifically for their performance), give Nietzsche good reason to characterize them as escapist narcotics.

14. See *WS* 170, as well as *D* 172. Also consider the self-critique implied by the following statement that Nietzsche penned shortly after leaving his philological profession: "As at all times, so now too, men are divided into the slaves and the free; for he who does not have two-thirds of his day to himself is a slave, let him be what he may be otherwise: statesman, businessman, official, scholar" (*HH* 283). During the time of his appointment at the University of Basel, Nietzsche taught for eight hours a week at the university, and six hours a week at a nearby preparatory school for students who planned to attend the university. During the time that he wrote *Human, All Too Human*, he adopted the practice of walking for six to eight hours a day, organizing his thoughts, before writing in the evening.

15. "Ignorance *in physiologicis*—that confounded 'idealism'—is the real disaster in my life"; "I count as consequences of this 'idealism' all my mistakes, all the great instinctual aberrations and 'modesties' deviating from the *task* of my life, for instance my becoming a philologist" (*EH* Clever 3).

16. "When I was almost done for—*because* I was almost done for—I started to reflect on this absurdity fundamental to my life—'idealism.' *Illness* was what made me see reason" (*EH* Clever 3).

17. For further reflections on this point, see *GS* 120, 295, 318, 326.

18. As this suggests, Nietzsche in effect distinguishes between different levels of health within an individual: "As *summa summarum*, I was healthy; as nook, as specialty, I was *decadent*" (*EH* Wise 2). For additional detail regarding the different "levels" at which Nietzsche gauges individual health, see the discussion by Jaspers, *Nietzsche*, 111–15.

19. At one point he suggests that, through such matters as "choice of nourishment, place and climate, relaxation," one can produce the "first proof that you are no accident, but a necessity" (*EH* Clever 8). These are just the sort of choices that Nietzsche began making for himself around the time of *Human, All Too Human*—but he was driven to make those choices in response to the necessity of his nature, which he had been forced to confront at that time as a result of his calamitous health (something he did not choose at all). On Nietzsche's subjection to his health (and his consequent lack of control over his own development), see further Hutter, *Shaping the Future*, 27.

20. Berry, *Nietzsche and the Ancient Skeptical Tradition*, 134, comments that "it should perhaps strike us as strange that Nietzsche's philosophy is often characterized as fundamentally *therapeutic*," and outlines some of the difficulties with such a characterization.

21. The letter (to Ernest Fritzsch, August 16, 1886) is quoted by Franco, *Nietzsche's Enlightenment*, 254n43. Regarding Nietzsche's statements to his publisher about the importance of the 1886 prefaces, also see Lampert, *What a Philosopher Is*, 7–11.

22. On this point, consider Landy, *Philosophy as Fiction*, 99; and Stern, "Nietzsche, *Amor Fati* and *The Gay Science*," 153–57.

23. Nietzsche says that he "deceived himself" in the following ways: by "knowingly-willfully closing my eyes before Schopenhauer's morality at a time when I was already sufficiently clear-sighted about morality," and by treating Wagner's Romanticism "as though it were a beginning and not an end."

24. As Lampert elaborates in helpful detail, with these remarks in the preface Nietzsche provides "an entranceway inviting his reader to be continuously aware in reading *Things Human All Too Human* that it was a start that wrongly believed that free minds already existed in Enlightenment optimists like Voltaire" (*What a Philosopher Is*, 147, also 123).

25. The same ambiguity shows up in the preface to the second volume, for instance in section 6: "Shall my experience—the history of an illness and recovery, for a recovery was what eventuated—have been my personal experience alone? And only *my* 'human, all too human'? Today I would like to believe the reverse." Conway, "Annunciation and Rebirth: The Prefaces of 1886," 43–44, attributes a kind of deadly seriousness to Nietzsche's discussion in the prefaces, which seems to me to overlook the careful ambiguity of Nietzsche's formulations.

26. On Nietzsche's plans, see Lampert, *What a Philosopher Is*, 3–7.

27. Consider *D* 96: "There are today among the various nations of Europe perhaps ten to

twenty million people who no longer 'believe in God'—is it too much to ask that they should give a sign to one another? Once they have thus come to know one another, they will also have made themselves known to others—they will at once constitute a power in Europe and, happily, a power between the nations! Between the classes! Between rich and poor! Between rulers and subjects! Between the most unpeaceable and the most peaceable, peace bringing people!" (consider also *WS* 87).

28. See Franco, *Nietzsche's Enlightenment*, 208. To my mind, Franco's judgment is confirmed by the attempts of Cohen (*Science, Culture, and Free Spirits*, 221), Miner (*Nietzsche and Montaigne*, 144–45), and More (*Nietzsche's Last Laugh*, 132–38) to divide Nietzsche's narrative into a series of precise, discrete steps: the steps that they suggest are all somewhat different, but also all plausible on the basis of the text. As a result, I think it makes most sense to conclude that Nietzsche is assuming that different individuals will have to fill out the precise details of the narrative somewhat differently, depending on their particular circumstances.

29. See Franco, *Nietzsche's Enlightenment*, 207–8.

30. Here I have in mind especially the form of self-control characteristic of *Daybreak* that I discussed earlier, in the section of chapter 3 on "Challenges for Unrequited Lovers."

31. See further my earlier discussion in the section of chapter 2 on "The Self-Disciplined Heart of the Free Spirit Project."

32. Large, "The Free Spirit and Aesthetic Self-Re-Education," 73, 80, takes the second preface as a "crucial text" because it introduces into Nietzsche's thought an "educational model" for others to follow (grounded in the *disciplina voluntatis*). According to Schacht, "Introduction," xvii, the reference to the *disciplina voluntatis* in the second preface "in part answers the question of the intended audience of these volumes": a broad audience among the younger generation who could be guided by Nietzsche's philosophy just as an earlier generation had been guided by the philosophy of the Enlightenment. Hutter, *Shaping the Future*, 9–10, also mentions the role of a *disciplina voluntatis* in training future Free Spirits.

33. Nietzsche's evasive rhetorical maneuvers here are highlighted by Conway, "Almost Everything Is Permitted," 234–36.

34. Parkes, *Composing the Soul*, 346–62, discusses in helpful detail how Nietzsche follows Plato's Socrates in looking at the organization of the soul by way of analogy to the organization of a polity, with the advocacy of hierarchy on the political level following as a consequence of hierarchy on the psychological level. Similarly, Acampora finds that Nietzsche agrees with Plato that "there is an isomorphism between forms of social, cultural, and political power and the organizations that constitute 'the household of the soul,'" but nuances the point by arguing that "agonistic economies of power" are what matter most to Nietzsche (rather than specific forms of government)—although healthy forms of self-overcoming are still the end goal here (*Contesting Nietzsche*, 161, 203–4).

35. As Higgins, "Festivals of Recognition," 86–87, points out, *GS* 353 as a whole is a text where Nietzsche outlines the dynamics of one form of communal life that he is able to approve of. Franco, *Nietzsche's Enlightenment*, 227, observes that whereas Nietzsche's early and middle writings were clearly interested in culture over politics, in the post-Zarathustra writings "it is extremely unclear at any given time whether he is talking about culture or politics." I wonder if the lines become blurred in those writings because Nietzsche's interest is in the "religion-

founder" type whose work is conceived of as laying the foundation for both "culture" and "politics."

36. See Conway, *Nietzsche and the Political*, 38–39; Kirkland, *Nietzsche's Noble Aims*, 60; Pangle and Burns, *The Key Texts of Political Philosophy*, 414–15.

37. For a sympathetic account of this crucial component of Nietzsche's understanding of religion, see Lampert, *Nietzsche's Task*, 128–36; for a critical view, see Beiner, *Civil Religion*, 377–89.

38. On the political spur to self-overcoming that Nietzsche has in mind, consider further Drochon, *Nietzsche's Great Politics*, 87, 95–96.

39. See, in particular, Lampert, *Nietzsche and Modern Times*.

40. See *BGE* 225: "The discipline of suffering, of *great* suffering—do you not know that only *this* discipline has created all enhancements of man so far?" (also see the discussion by Reginster, *The Affirmation of Life*, 186–87). It is in this light that I have to dissent from Bernard Williams when he writes that Nietzsche never arrived at "a view that offered a coherent politics . . . in the sense of a coherent set of opinions about the ways in which power should be exercised in modern societies, with what limitations and to what end" (*Shame and Necessity*, 10–11). It seems to me that Nietzsche suggests the ends that politics should be directed toward (self-overcoming), and although his proposed means for achieving those ends are radically at odds with the norms of modern societies (particularly insofar as they suggest that suffering should be embraced and even sought out, rather than prevented or ameliorated), he still has a coherent set of opinions about why they should be accepted as legitimate. Moreover, as Drochon (*Nietzsche's Great Politics*, 92–93) elaborates, Nietzsche would likely claim that notwithstanding how repellent his position would be to many modern readers, they would also find it difficult to dispose of, insofar as the modern disposition is unable to entirely eradicate suffering but also unable to justify it, whereas his position proposes to do the latter but not the former.

41. For the reading of Nietzsche's politics as discontinuous with the rest of his thought, see Warren, *Nietzsche and Political Thought*, 246.

42. To be sure, Nietzsche's interest in hierarchically imposed forms of self-discipline can be traced back to much earlier stages of his career (see Church, *Nietzsche's Culture of Humanity*, 197), but my claim here is only that when we find related arguments in later writings, they should be understood not merely as an atavistic reversion to earlier inclinations, but as consistent with considered reflections on his own personal evolution. My claim here can be contrasted with the position of Warren, who argues that Nietzsche's late writings express *unreflective* "social and political assumptions," bound up with "mere prejudices" that he never seriously attempts to justify, and which can therefore be safely disregarded by anyone interested in the more serious elements of his thought (*Nietzsche and Political Thought*, 78). Warren could still be correct that Nietzsche "lacks a politics adequate to his philosophy" (210), but a more satisfactory argument to that effect would need to take into account the degree to which Nietzsche's politics are in fact bound up with his philosophy.

43. Pippin, *Nietzsche, Psychology, and First Philosophy*, 116, argues that "despite what can seem the hortatory character of Nietzsche's rhetoric, many of the passages [in which he discusses self-overcoming] . . . do not really directly encourage readers to *do* anything" (those passages are, for Pippin, not directing anyone to overcome themselves, but simply describ-

ing what it would be like to do so, for those for whom it happened to be their fate). I think that this is largely correct, but it does not tell us why Nietzsche adopted such a "hortatory rhetoric," or address what seems to me like the most brazen example of that rhetoric in the second of the prefaces written for *Human, All Too Human*. My position, therefore, falls somewhere in between that of Pippin and Large (see note 32 in this chapter): I agree with Large that (particularly in the aforementioned preface) Nietzsche presents what can easily read like an "educational model," and therefore he must have wanted readers to consider seriously the possibility that he was proposing something like a program of self-overcoming; but I agree with Pippin that Nietzsche sprinkles cold water over the expectations that can easily be engendered by his own rhetoric (which therefore should not be taken as the ultimate *raison d'être* of his writings).

44. See further *EH* HH 4: "I have never been so happy with myself as in my life's periods of greatest illness and pain: you need only take a look at *Daybreak* or *The Wanderer and His Shadow* to understand what this 'return *to myself*' was: the highest kind of *recuperation*! . . . The other kind simply followed on from this." This means that a no-saying work of Nietzsche's greatest sickness and solitude (*WS*) is only a short step from his recovery and yes-saying work (*D*). So while the Free Spirit's emergence in the "great liberation" may be represented as a relatively clear break in Nietzsche's career, subsequent stages may be better thought of in terms of shadings.

45. "Is there a more holy condition than that of pregnancy? To do all we do in the unspoken belief that it has somehow to benefit that which is coming to be within us!" "And if what is expected is an idea, a deed—toward all that we bring forth we have essentially no other relationship than that of pregnancy and ought to let blow in the wind all presumptuous talk of 'willing' and 'creating'!" (*D* 552; see also *GS* 72). Nietzsche's metaphors of pregnancy are discussed insightfully by Hough, *Nietzsche's Noontide Friend*, 142–48; see also Acampora, *Contesting Nietzsche*, 176–78; Parkes, *Composing the Soul*, 239–43.

46. Note Nietzsche's language in section 4 of the second preface: "That concealed and imperious something for which we for long have no name until it finally proves to be our *task*."

47. Especially important is a reference in section 4 to "the great health," a notion closely connected to *Zarathustra* (as we will see later in this chapter); the reference to "midday" in section 6 calls to mind the same work, and "the problem of order of rank" resonates with the post-*Zarathustra* writings more generally (on these connections, see further Franco, *Nietzsche's Enlightenment*, 180, 207, 226).

48. On this point, see further Lampert, *What a Philosopher Is*, 145–47; and More, *Nietzsche's Last Laugh*, 135–36.

49. I am, therefore, compelled to dissent from Daniel Conway's suggestion ("Annunciation and Rebirth," 43–44) that Nietzsche's self-criticism in these prefaces amounts to a form of "self-mutilation," the gruesomeness of which Nietzsche ("bleeding from a wound that will never heal") hopes will be impressive enough to convince readers with a taste for "ritual bloodletting" to go endure "a similar rite of initiation." Conway thinks that this spectacle is a desperate gambit to finally win a few fellow travelers over to Nietzsche's side. In contrast to Conway, Nicholas More (*Nietzsche's Last Laugh*, 138) emphasizes the more ironic and lighthearted aspects of Nietzsche's self-presentation, and I think that as a result he gives a more accurate esti-

mate of Nietzsche's situation. The situation as I see it is this: Nietzsche's self-criticisms do not reflect frustration over his failure—they reflect a *fulfillment* of the Free Spirit project that brings that project to fruition in a manner that leaves him *in no dependence on anyone else.*

50. See the comment by More, *Nietzsche's Last Laugh*, 131, on this passage as "Nietzsche interpreting Nietzsche," that is, Nietzsche interpreting the meaning of one of his early texts in light of his subsequent development (in effect identifying that text as reflecting his task's germination at the early stage of "unconscious pregnancy").

51. On this point, see further Lampert, *What a Philosopher Is*, 220–21.

52. On Nietzsche's identification of his task with that of his character, see further Lampert, *Nietzsche's Teaching*, 354n8.

53. Zarathustra is "the most affirmative of all spirits" (EH *TSZ* 6), "he is *yes-saying* to the point of justifying, redeeming even all that is past" (EH *TSZ* 8). The previous subchapter had begun with the words: "*Daybreak* is a yes-saying book, profound but bright and generous. The same is true once again and to the highest degree of the *gaya scienza*." *Nietzsche* does not directly describe *Human, All Too Human* as a "no-saying" work, but its primarily critical, destructive thrust fits the category—and, notably, the first work that Nietzsche calls "no-saying" is *Beyond Good and Evil*, which was originally planned as a second edition of *Human, All Too Human* (this connection explains why the Free Spirit is the main character in each work).

54. See the comments on Nietzsche's formulation by Gillespie, *Nietzsche's Final Teaching*, 5–7. Nietzsche seems to have used similar formulations privately to allude to his changed and unusual state of mind around the time when the "basic conception" occurred to him (see Bishop and Stephenson, *Friedrich Nietzsche and Weimar Classicism*, 65–69).

55. "Type" here is *Typus*, which could have the sense of "prototype," and "ambushed" is *überfiel*, which can connote a violent assault, but can also have the sense of something that falls onto or into one. Nietzsche uses *überfiel* in *D* 551 to refer to the experience of being overcome by a kind of awed or reverential faith "in the presence of everything unknown and mysterious." In *TSZ* ("On the Free Death") he uses it to characterize the experience of Jesus, "overcome by a yearning for death." In *EH* Wise 4 he notes that in Zarathustra IV "a great cry of distress reaches [Zarathustra] and compassion, like one last sin, wants to ambush [*überfallen*] him and lure him away from himself."

56. See, in particular, sections 1 and 7 of that work (Duncan Large, in the notes to his translation of *Ecce Homo*, observes that its description of being-outside-yourself recalls these passages of *BT*). Also see the remark by Pippin: "From the beginning of his publishing career to near the end, the creative state is always understood as Dionysean, a dissolution of boundaries and not their Apollonian establishment, a state of reverie and intoxication" (*Nietzsche, Psychology, and First Philosophy*, 110–11).

57. On these writings, and the "being-outside-yourself" that they discuss, see Parkes, *Composing the Soul*, 61–64.

58. Consider *D* 172: "*Tragedy and Music.*—Men whose disposition is fundamentally warlike, as for example the Greeks of the age of Aeschylus, are *hard to move*, and when pity does for once overbear their severity it seizes them like a frenzy and as through a 'demonic force'—they then feel themselves under constraint and are excited by a shudder of religious awe. Afterwards

they have doubts about their condition; but for as long as they are in it they enjoy the delight of the miraculous and of being-outside-themselves." Franco, "Becoming Who You Are," 72–74, argues that for Nietzsche one must periodically loosen the bonds of self-mastery in order to learn what one is most fully, and that *GS* IV discusses this possibility in a way that goes beyond what is suggested by earlier texts, prefiguring the notion of "self-overcoming" in *TSZ*. My suggestion here (which will be elaborated in the next section) is that self-forgetting as part of the process of self-overcoming is a notion to be found not only in the texts of *GS* IV and *TSZ*, but also (according to *EH*) in *the creation of the text* of *TSZ* (which would be fitting, since *GS* IV is designed as a kind of prelude to *TSZ*).

59. Parkes, *Composing the Soul*, 358–59, sees *Zarathustra* as distancing itself from any ideal of self-mastery on the basis of a newfound recognition that the boundaries between one's self and what lies outside oneself are essentially permeable, and that Zarathustra welcomes their dissolution.

60. The "great health" is a theme discussed instructively by Panaïoti, *Nietzsche and Buddhist Philosophy*, but his treatment has the shortcoming that it declines to consider this theme in relation to *Thus Spoke Zarathustra*, justifying that choice by claiming that there is an "ironic relation" between "Nietzsche's thought" and "the world of Zarathustra's wisdom" (14n36). This is too hasty, because, as we will now see, Nietzsche himself ties "the great health" tightly to *Zarathustra* (although he does so in a way that turns out to offer support for Panaïoti's identification of an "ironic relation" between Nietzsche and Zarathustra, but without thereby suggesting that the latter figure can be disregarded).

61. See further Faustino, "Philosophy as a 'Misunderstanding of the Body' and the 'Great Health,'" 213–15; and Lemm, *Nietzsche's Animal Philosophy*, 150–51.

62. More, *Nietzsche's Last Laugh*, 173, highlights the trials and tribulations that Nietzsche alludes to as part of this process.

63. Faustino, "Philosophy as a 'Misunderstanding of the Body' and the 'Great Health,'" 213, observes that with regard to a number of key concepts Nietzsche uses the adjective "great" in an "almost 'technical' sense," in order to indicate that these concepts are "elevated, reinforced, and enhanced precisely by their apparent opposites," so that "great health" refers not to health simply, but to the productive interaction between health and illness (see further Jaspers, *Nietzsche*, 115: the "great health" has "in a manner of speaking, incorporated illness"). Also see Glenn, "The Great Health," 104–9; and Richardson, *Nietzsche's System*, 138, on the dynamic of health and illness in Nietzsche's broader thought (beyond the autobiographical writings).

64. Consider *GS* 120 (on "*Health of the Soul*"): "Finally, the great question would still remain whether we can *do without* illness, even for the development of our virtue; and whether especially our thirst for knowledge and self-knowledge do not need the sick soul as much as the healthy."

65. As Glenn, "The Great Health," 110, comments: "Sickness serves a positive function by presenting a mighty opponent against which one must struggle." Miner, *Nietzsche and Montaigne*, 277, contrasts Nietzsche's dynamic or restless understanding of health with Montaigne's understanding that "[h]ealth for me is maintaining my accustomed state without disturbance" (Montaigne makes this statement in his essay "Of Experience").

66. "A philosopher—alas, a being that often runs away from itself, often is afraid of itself—

but is too inquisitive not to 'come to' again—always back to himself" (*BGE* 292; consider further 80–81).

CONCLUDING REMARKS

1. See *D* Preface 2.
2. See *BGE* 42.

WORKS CITED

Abbey, Ruth. *Nietzsche's Middle Period*. New York: Oxford University Press, 2000.

Acampora, Christa Davis. "Being Unattached: Freedom and Nietzsche's Free Spirits." In *Nietzsche's Free Spirit Philosophy*, edited by Rebecca Bamford. New York: Rowman & Littlefield International, 2015.

Acampora, Christa Davis. *Contesting Nietzsche*. Chicago: University of Chicago Press, 2013.

Adorno, Theodor W. "Fantasia sopra *Carmen*." In Adorno, *Quasi una Fantasia: Essays on Modern Music*, translated by Rodney Livingstone. London: Verso, 1992.

Anderson, R. Lanier, and Joshua Landy. "Philosophy as Self-Fashioning: Alexander Nehamas's Art of Living." *Diacritics* 31, no. 1 (2001): 25–54.

Ansell-Pearson, Keith. *Nietzsche's Search for Philosophy: On the Middle Writings*. London: New York: Bloomsbury, 2018.

Arnhart, Larry. *Political Questions: Political Philosophy from Plato to Pinker*. Long Grove, IL: Waveland Press.

Aschheim, Steven E. *The Nietzsche Legacy in Germany, 1890–1990*. Berkeley: University of California Press, 1992.

Barney, Rachel. "Callicles and Thrasymachus." In *The Stanford Encyclopedia of Philosophy*, edited by Edward N. Zalta. Fall 2017 edition, https://plato.stanford.edu/archives/fall2017/entries/callicles-thrasymachus.

Beauvoir, Simone de. *The Ethics of Ambiguity*. Translated by Bernard Frechtman. New York: Citadel Press, 1976.

Beckett, Lucy. *Richard Wagner: Parsifal*. Cambridge: Cambridge University Press, 1981.

Behler, Ernest. "Nietzsche in the Twentieth Century." In *The Cambridge Companion to Nietzsche*, edited by Bernd Magnus and Kathleen M. Higgins. Cambridge: Cambridge University Press, 1996.

Beiner, Ronald. *Civil Religion; A Dialogue in the History of Political Philosophy*. Cambridge; New York: Cambridge University Press, 2011.

Beiner, Ronald. *Dangerous Minds: Nietzsche, Heidegger, and the Return of the Far Right.* Philadelphia: University of Pennsylvania Press, 2018.

Berger, Karol. *Beyond Reason: Wagner contra Nietzsche.* Oakland: University of California Press, 2017.

Berry, Jessica. *Nietzsche and the Ancient Skeptical Tradition.* Oxford: Oxford University Press, 2011.

Berry, Mark. "Richard Wagner and the Politics of Music-Drama." *Historical Journal* 47, no. 3 (2004): 663–83.

Bishop, Paul, and R. H. Stephenson. *Friedrich Nietzsche and Weimar Classicism.* Rochester, NY: Camden House, 2005.

Bizet, Georges. *Carmen: Opéra-Comique in Four Acts.* Edited by Richard Langham Smith. London: Peters, 2013.

Blue, Daniel. *The Making of Friedrich Nietzsche: The Quest for Identity, 1844–1869.* Cambridge: Cambridge University Press, 2016.

Brobjer, Thomas. "The Absence of Political Ideals in Nietzsche's Writings." *Nietzsche-Studien* 27 (1998): 300–318.

Brobjer, Thomas. *Nietzsche's Philosophical Context: An Intellectual Biography.* Urbana: University of Illinois Press, 2008.

Brusotti, Marco. "Erkenntnis als Passion: Nietzsches Denkweg zwischen Morgenröthe und der Fröhlichen Wissenschaft." *Nietzsche Studien* 26 (1997): 199–225.

Brusotti, Marco. *Die Leidenschaft der Erkenntnis: Philosophie und ästhetische Lebensgestaltung bei Nietzsche von Morgenröthe bis Also sprach Zarathustra.* New York: Walter de Gruyter, 1997.

Campioni, Giuliano. *Der französische Nietzsche.* Berlin: Walter de Gruyter, 2009.

Carnegy, Patrick. *Wagner and the Art of the Theatre.* New Haven, CT: Yale University Press, 2006.

Caro, Adrian del. *Grounding the Nietzsche Rhetoric of Earth.* New York: Walter de Gruyter, 2004.

Church, Jeffrey. *Infinite Autonomy: The Divided Individual in the Thought of G. W. F. Hegel and Friedrich Nietzsche.* University Park: Pennsylvania State University Press, 2012.

Church, Jeffrey. *Nietzsche's Culture of Humanity: Beyond Democracy and Aristocracy in the Early Period.* New York: Cambridge University Press, 2015.

Church, Jeffrey. "Two Concepts of Culture in the Early Nietzsche." *European Journal of Political Theory* 10, no. 3 (2011): 327–49.

Clark, Maudemarie, and David Dundrick. *The Soul of Nietzsche's "Beyond Good and Evil."* New York: Cambridge University Press, 2012.

Cohen, Jonathan R. *Science, Culture, and Free Spirits: A Study of Nietzsche's Human, All-Too-Human.* New York: Humanity Books, 2010.

Conway, Daniel W. "Almost Everything Is Permitted: Nietzsche's Not-So-Free Spirits." In *Nietzsche's Free Spirit Philosophy*, edited by Rebecca Bamford. New York: Rowman & Littlefield International, 2015.

Conway, Daniel W. "Annunciation and Rebirth: The Prefaces of 1886." In *Nietzsche's Futures*, edited by John Lippitt. New York: St. Martin's Press, 1999.

Conway, Daniel W. *Nietzsche and the Political*. London: Routledge, 1997.

Conway, Daniel W. *Nietzsche's "On the Genealogy of Morals": A Reader's Guide*. London: Bloomsbury, 2006.

Cooper, Laurence. *Eros in Plato, Rousseau, and Nietzsche: The Politics of Infinity*. University Park: Pennsylvania State University Press, 2008.

Crowley, Monica. *Nixon in Winter: His Final Revelations about Diplomacy, Watergate, and Life Out of the Arena*. New York: Random House, 1998.

Curtiss, Mina. *Bizet and His World*. New York: Knopf, 1958.

Dannhauser, Werner. *Nietzsche's View of Socrates*. Ithaca, NY: Cornell University Press, 1974.

Daub, Adrian. *Tristan's Shadow: Sexuality and the Total Work of Art after Wagner*. Chicago: University of Chicago Press, 2014.

Davis, Michael. *The Autobiography of Philosophy*. Lanham, MD: Rowman & Littlefield, 1999.

Deleuze, Gilles. *Nietzsche and Philosophy*. Translated by Hugh Tomlinson. New York: Columbia University Press, 1983.

Detwiler, Bruce. *Nietzsche and the Politics of Aristocratic Radicalism*. Chicago: University of Chicago Press, 1990.

Dienstag, Joshua Foa. *Pessimism: Philosophy, Ethic, Spirit*. Princeton, NJ: Princeton University Press, 2006.

Diethe, Carol. *Nietzsche's Sister and "The Will to Power": A Biography of Elisabeth Förster-Nietzsche*. Urbana: University of Illinois Press, 2003.

Diethe, Carol. *Nietzsche's Women: Beyond the Whip*. New York: Walter de Gruyter, 1996.

D'Iorio, Paolo. "Nietzsche fra Tristano e Carmen." In *Filosofia e musica*, edited by Carlo Tatasciore. Turin: Bruno Mondadori, 2008.

D'Iorio, Paolo. *Nietzsche's Journey to Sorrento: Genesis of the Philosophy of the Free Spirit*. Translated by Sylvia Mae Gorelick. Chicago: University of Chicago Press, 2016.

Dodds, E. R. *Plato's "Gorgias."* Revised text with introduction and commentary. Oxford: Clarendon Press, 1959.

Dreyfus, Laurence. *Wagner and the Erotic Impulse*. Cambridge, MA: Harvard University Press, 2010.

Drochon, Hugo. *Nietzsche's Great Politics*. Princeton, NJ: Princeton University Press, 2016.

Faustino, Marta. "Philosophy as a 'Misunderstanding of the Body' and the 'Great Health.'" In *Nietzsche on Instinct and Language*, edited by João Constâncio and Maria João Mayer Branco. Berlin: Walter de Gruyter, 2015.

Ferguson, Kathy. *Emma Goldman: Political Thinking in the Streets*. Lanham, MD: Rowman & Littlefield, 2011.

Flanagan, Owen. *The Geography of Morals: Varieties of Moral Possibility*. New York: Oxford University Press, 2017.

Foot, Philippa. *Moral Dilemmas: And Other Topics in Moral Philosophy*. Oxford: Oxford University Press, 2002.

Foucault, Michel. *The Courage of Truth (The Government of Self and Others II): Lectures at the Collège de France, 1983–1984*. Translated by Graham Burchell. New York: Palgrave Macmillan, 2012.

Foucault, Michel. *The History of Sexuality, Vol. 2: The Use of Pleasure*. Translated by Robert Hurley. New York: Vintage Books, 1985.

Foucault, Michel. "Nietzsche, History, Genealogy." In *The Foucault Reader*, edited by Paul Rabinow. New York: Pantheon Books, 1984.

Franco, Paul. "Becoming Who You Are: Nietzsche on Self Creation." *Journal of Nietzsche Studies* 49 (2018): 52–77.

Franco, Paul. *Nietzsche's Enlightenment: The Free Spirit Trilogy of the Middle Period*. Chicago: University of Chicago Press, 2011.

Franco, Paul. "Tocqueville and Nietzsche on the Problem of Human Greatness in Democracy." *Review of Politics* 76 (2014): 461–63.

Fukuyama, Francis. *The End of History and the Last Man*. New York: Free Press, 1992.

Gemes, Ken. "'We Remain of Necessity Strangers to Ourselves': The Key Message of Nietzsche's *Genealogy*." In *Nietzsche's Genealogy of Morals: Critical Essays*, edited by Christa Davis Acampora. Lanham, MD: Rowman & Littlefield, 2006.

Gemes, Ken, and Chris Sykes. "The Culture of Myth and the Myth of Culture." In *Individual and Community in Nietzsche's Philosophy*, edited by Julian Young. Cambridge: Cambridge University Press, 2015.

Geuss, Raymond. *Changing the Subject: Philosophy from Socrates to Adorno*. Cambridge, MA: Harvard University Press, 2017.

Geuss, Raymond. *Outside Ethics*. Princeton, NJ: Princeton University Press, 2005.

Gillespie, Michael Allen. *Nietzsche's Final Teaching*. Chicago: University of Chicago Press, 2017.

Gillespie, Michael Allen. *Nihilism before Nietzsche*. Chicago: University of Chicago Press, 1996.

Girard, René. "Nietzsche and Contradiction." *Stanford Italian Review* 6, nos.1–2 (1986): 53–65.

Glenn, Paul E. "The Great Health: Spiritual Disease and the Health of the Higher Man." *Philosophy & Social Criticism* 27, no. 2 (2001): 100–117.

Goetz, Benoît. "Nietzsche aimait-il vraiment Bizet?" *La portique* 8 (2001), https://leportique.revues.org/209.

Goldhill, Simon. "The Seductions of the Gaze: Socrates and His Girlfriends." In *Kosmos: Essays in Order, Conflict and Community in Classical Athens*, edited by Paul Cartledge, Paul Millett, and Sitta von Reden. New York: Cambridge University Press, 1998.

Golomb, Jacob. "Will-to-Power: Does It Lead to the 'Coldest of All Cold Monsters'?" In *The Oxford Handbook of Nietzsche*, edited by Ken Gemes and John Richardson. Oxford: Oxford University Press, 2013.

Gooding-Williams, Robert. *Zarathustra's Dionysian Modernism*. Stanford, CA: Stanford University Press, 2001.

Hadot, Pierre. *Philosophy as a Way of Life: Spiritual Exercises from Socrates to Foucault*. Translated by Michael Chase. Oxford: Blackwell, 1995.

Hadot, Pierre. *What Is Ancient Philosophy*? Translated by Michael Chase. Cambridge, MA: Belknap Press of Harvard University Press, 2002.

Hatab, Lawrence J. *Nietzsche's "On the Genealogy of Morality": An Introduction.* New York: Cambridge University Press, 2008.

Hayek, F. A. *The Road to Serfdom: Fiftieth Anniversary Edition.* Chicago: University of Chicago Press, 1994.

Heidegger, Martin. *Basic Concepts of Aristotelian Philosophy.* Translated by Robert D. Metcalf and Mark B. Tanzer. Bloomington: Indiana University Press, 2009.

Heidegger, Martin. *Nietzsche.* Translated by David Farrell Krell. San Francisco: Harper & Row, 1979.

Henrich, Joseph. *The Secret of Our Success: How Culture Is Driving Evolution, Domesticating Our Species, and Making Us Smarter.* Princeton, NJ: Princeton University Press, 2015.

Higgins, Kathleen. "Festivals of Recognition." In *Individual and Community in Nietzsche's Philosophy*, edited by Julian Young. New York: Cambridge University Press, 2014.

Higgins, Kathleen Marie. *Nietzsche's Zarathustra.* Revised edition. Lanham, MD: Lexington Books, 2010.

Hobbs, Angela. *Plato and the Hero.* New York: Cambridge University Press, 2000.

Hollinrake, Roger. "Epiphany and Apocalypse." In *Wagner's Ring of the Nibelung: A Companion, with the Full German Text*, translated by Stewart Spencer, with commentaries by Barry Millington et al. London: Thames & Hudson, 1993.

Hollinrake, Roger. *Nietzsche, Wagner, and the Philosophy of Pessimism.* London: George Allen & Unwin, 1982.

Hough, Sheridan. *Nietzsche's Noontide Friend: The Self as Metaphoric Double.* University Park: Pennsylvania State University Press, 1997.

Huss, Bernhard. "The Dancing Sokrates and the Laughing Xenophon, or the Other 'Symposium.'" *American Journal of Philology* 120, no. 3 (1999): 381–409.

Hutcheon, Linda, and Michael Hutcheon. *Opera: The Art of Dying.* Cambridge, MA: Harvard University Press, 2004.

Hutter, Horst. *Shaping the Future: Nietzsche's New Regime of the Soul and Its Ascetic Practices.* Lanham, MD: Lexington Books, 2006.

Janaway, Christopher. *Beyond Selflessness: Reading Nietzsche's Genealogy.* Oxford: Oxford University Press, 2007.

Jaspers, Karl. *Nietzsche: An Introduction to the Understanding of His Philosophical Activity.* Translated by Charles F. Wallraff and Frederick J. Schmitz. Tucson: University of Arizona Press, 1965.

Kaag, John. *Hiking with Nietzsche: On Becoming Who You Are.* New York: Farrar, Straus & Giroux, 2018.

Kaufmann, Walter. *Nietzsche: Philosopher, Psychologist, Antichrist.* 5th edition. Princeton, NJ: Princeton University Press, 2013.

Kirkland, Paul. *Nietzsche's Noble Aims: Affirming Life, Contesting Modernity.* Lanham, MD: Lexington Books, 2009.

Kofman, Sarah. "The Psychologist of the Eternal Feminine (Why I Write Such Good Books, 5)." Translated by Madeleine Dobie. *Yale French Studies* 87 (1995): 173–89.

Lampert, Laurence. *The Enduring Importance of Leo Strauss.* Chicago: University of Chicago Press, 2013.

Lampert, Laurence. *How Philosophy Became Socratic: A Study of Plato's "Protagoras," "Charmides," and "Republic."* Chicago: University of Chicago Press, 2010.

Lampert, Laurence. *Nietzsche and Modern Times: A Study of Bacon, Descartes and Nietzsche.* New Haven, CT: Yale University Press, 1993.

Lampert, Laurence. *Nietzsche's Task: An Interpretation of "Beyond Good and Evil."* New Haven, CT: Yale University Press, 2001.

Lampert, Laurence. *Nietzsche's Teaching: An Interpretation of "Thus Spoke Zarathustra."* New Haven, CT: Yale University Press, 1986.

Lampert, Laurence. "Thus Spoke Zarathustra." In *A Companion to Nietzsche: Life and Works*, edited by Paul Bishop. Rochester, NY: Camden House, 2012.

Lampert, Laurence. *What a Philosopher Is: Becoming Nietzsche.* Chicago: University of Chicago Press, 2018.

Landy, Joshua. *Philosophy as Fiction: Self, Deception, and Knowledge in Proust.* Oxford: Oxford University Press, 2004.

Large, Duncan. "The Free Spirit and Aesthetic Self-Re-Education." In *Nietzsche's Free Spirit Philosophy*, edited by Rebecca Bamford. New York: Rowman & Littlefield International, 2015.

Large, Duncan. "Nietzsche's *Helmbrecht*; Or, How to Philosophise with a Ploughshare." *Journal of Nietzsche Studies* 13 (1997): 3–22.

Leibowitz, David. *The Ironic Defense of Socrates.* Cambridge: Cambridge University Press, 2010.

Leiner, George H. "To Overcome Oneself: Nietzsche, Bizet, Wagner." *Journal of Nietzsche Studies* 9–10 (1995): 132–47.

Lemm, Vanessa. *Nietzsche's Animal Philosophy: Culture, Politics, and the Animality of the Human Being.* New York: Fordham University Press, 2009.

Löwith, Karl. *Nietzsche's Philosophy of Eternal Recurrence of the Same.* Translated by J. Harvey Lomax. Berkeley: University of California Press, 1997.

MacIntyre, Alasdair. *Dependent Rational Animals.* Chicago: Carus Publishing, 1999.

Magee, Bryan. *The Tristan Chord: Wagner and Philosophy.* New York: Metropolitan Books, 2000.

McCloskey, Deirdre. *The Bourgeois Virtues: Ethics for an Age of Commerce.* Chicago: University of Chicago Press, 2006.

Meier, Heinrich. *On the Happiness of the Philosophic Life: Reflections on Rousseau's Reveries.* Translated by Robert Berman. Chicago: University of Chicago Press, 2016.

Meier, Heinrich. *Was ist Nietzsches Zarathustra?* Munich: C. H. Beck, 2017.

Miner, Robert. *Nietzsche and Montaigne.* New York: Palgrave Macmillan, 2017.

Montinari, Mazzino. *Reading Nietzsche.* Translated by Greg Whitlock. Urbana: University of Illinois Press, 2003.

More, Nicholas D. *Nietzsche's Last Laugh: "Ecce Homo" as Satire.* Cambridge: Cambridge University Press, 2014.

Morrison, Donald R. "Xenophon's Socrates as a Teacher." In *The Socratic Movement*, edited by Paul A. Vander Waerdt. Ithaca, NY: Cornell University Press, 1994.

Mullin, Amy. "Nietzsche's Free Spirit." *Journal of the History of Philosophy* 38, no. 3 (2000): 382–405.

Nehamas, Alexander. *The Art of Living: Socratic Reflections from Plato to Foucault*. Berkeley: University of California Press, 1998.

Nehamas, Alexander. *Nietzsche, Life as Literature*. Cambridge, MA: Harvard University Press, 1985.

Nehamas, Alexander. *Virtues of Authenticity: Essays on Plato and Socrates*. Princeton, NJ: Princeton University Press, 1999.

Newell, Waller. "Zarathustra's Dancing Dialectic." *Interpretation* 17, no. 3 (1990): 416–32.

Nussbaum, Martha. "Pity and Mercy: Nietzsche's Stoicism." In *Nietzsche, Genealogy, Morality: Essays on Nietzsche's "Genealogy of Morals,"* edited by Richard Schacht. Berkeley: University of California Press, 1994.

Panaïoti, Antoine. *Nietzsche and Buddhist Philosophy*. Cambridge: Cambridge University Press, 2013.

Pangle, Thomas L. "The Roots of Contemporary Nihilism and Its Political Consequences according to Nietzsche." *Review of Politics* 45 (1983): 45–70.

Pangle, Thomas L. "The 'Warrior Spirit' as an Inlet to the Political Philosophy of Nietzsche's *Zarathustra*." *Nietzsche-Studien* 15 (1986): 140–79.

Pangle, Thomas L., and Timothy W. Burns. *The Key Texts of Political Philosophy: An Introduction*. Cambridge: Cambridge University Press, 2014.

Parkes, Graham. *Composing the Soul: Reaches of Nietzsche's Psychology*. Chicago: University of Chicago Press, 1994.

Parkes, Graham. "Nietzsche and East Asian Thought." In *The Cambridge Companion to Nietzsche*, edited by Bernd Magnus and Kathleen M. Higgins. Cambridge: Cambridge University Press, 1996.

Parkes, Graham. "The Symphonic Structure of *Thus Spoke Zarathustra*: A Preliminary Outline." In *Nietzsche's "Thus Spoke Zarathustra": Before Sunrise*, edited by James Luchte. London: Continuum, 2008.

Piazzesi, Chiara. "Greed and Love: Genealogy, Dissolution and Therapeutic Effects of a Linguistic Difference in FW 14." In *Nietzsche on Instinct and Language*, edited by João Constâncio and Maria João Mayer Branco. Berlin: Walter de Gruyter, 2015.

Pinker, Steven. *The Better Angels of Our Nature: Why Violence Has Declined*. New York: Penguin Books, 2012.

Pinker, Steven. *Enlightenment Now: The Case for Reason, Science, Humanism, and Progress*. New York: Viking, 2018.

Pippin, Robert B. *Fatalism in American Film Noir: Some Cinematic Philosophy*. Charlottesville: University of Virginia Press, 2012.

Pippin, Robert B. *Hegel on Self-Consciousness: Desire and Death in the Phenomenology of Spirit*. Princeton, NJ: Princeton University Press, 2010.

Pippin, Robert B. *Interanimations: Receiving German Philosophy*. Chicago: University of Chicago Press, 2015.

Pippin, Robert B. "Irony and Affirmation in Nietzsche's *Thus Spoke Zarathustra*." In

Nietzsche's New Seas, edited by Michael Allen Gillespie and Tracy B. Strong. Chicago: University of Chicago Press, 1988.

Pippin, Robert B. "Morality as Psychology, Psychology as Morality: Nietzsche, Eros, and Clumsy Lovers." In *Nietzsche's Postmoralism: Essays on Nietzsche's Prelude to Philosophy's Future*, edited by Richard Schacht. Urbana-Champaign: University of Illinois Press, 2000.

Pippin, Robert B. "Nietzsche: Thus Spoke Zarathustra." In Nietzsche, *Introductions to Nietzsche*, edited by Robert B. Pippin. Cambridge: Cambridge University Press, 2011.

Pippin, Robert B. *Nietzsche, Psychology, and First Philosophy*. Chicago: University of Chicago Press, 2010.

Pippin, Robert B. "On 'Becoming Who One Is' (and Failing): Proust's Problematic Selves." In Pippin, *The Persistence of Subjectivity: On the Kantian Aftermath*. Cambridge: Cambridge University Press, 2005.

Ratner-Rosenhagen, Jennifer. *American Nietzsche: A History of an Icon and His Ideas*. Chicago: University of Chicago Press, 2012.

Reginster, Bernard. *The Affirmation of Life: Nietzsche on Overcoming Nihilism*. Cambridge, MA: Harvard University Press, 2006.

Rethy, Robert A. "The Descartes Motto to the First Edition of *Menschliches, Allzumenschliches*." *Nietzsche-Studien* 5 (1976): 289–97.

Richardson, John. "Nietzsche, Language, Community." In *Individual and Community in Nietzsche's Philosophy*, edited by Julian Young. Cambridge: Cambridge University Press, 2015.

Richardson, John. "Nietzsche on Life's Ends." In *The Oxford Handbook of Nietzsche*. Edited by John Richardson and Julian Young. Oxford: Oxford University Press, 2013.

Richardson, John. *Nietzsche's New Darwinism*. Oxford: Oxford University Press, 2004.

Richardson, John. *Nietzsche's System*. Oxford: Oxford University Press, 1996.

Rosen, Stanley. *The Mask of Enlightenment: Nietzsche's Zarathustra*. Cambridge: Cambridge University Press, 1995.

Rosenthal, Bernice Glatzer. *New Myth, New World: From Nietzsche to Stalinism*. University Park: Pennsylvania State University Press, 2002.

Russell, Bertrand. *Power: A New Social Analysis*. London: Routledge, 2004.

Ryan, Alan. *On Politics: A History of Political Thought from Herodotus to the Present*. New York: Liveright, 2012.

Salome, Lou. *Nietzsche*. Translated by Siegfried Mandel. Redding Ridge, CT: Black Swan Books, 1988.

Satkunanandan, Shalini. *Extraordinary Responsibility: Politics beyond the Moral Calculus*. Cambridge: Cambridge University Press, 2015.

Schaberg, William. *The Nietzsche Canon: A Publication History and Bibliography*. Chicago: University of Chicago Press, 1995.

Schacht, Richard. "Introduction." In Nietzsche, *Human, All Too Human*, translated by R. J. Hollingdale. Cambridge: Cambridge University Press, 1996.

Schacht, Richard. *Making Sense of Nietzsche: Reflections Timely and Untimely*. Urbana: University of Illinois Press, 1995.

Schacht, Richard. "Translating Nietzsche: The Case of Kaufmann." *Journal of Nietzsche Studies* 43, no. 1 (2012): 68–86.

Scruton, Roger. *Death-Devoted Heart: Sex and the Sacred in Wagner's "Tristan and Isolde."* New York: Oxford University Press, 2004.

Scruton, Roger. *The Ring of Truth: The Wisdom of Wagner's "Ring of the Nibelung."* London: Allen Lane, 2016.

Seung, T. K. *Goethe, Nietzsche, Wagner: Their Spinozan Epics of Love and Power*. Lanham, MD: Lexington Books, 2006.

Seung, T. K. *Nietzsche's Epic of the Soul: "Thus Spoke Zarathustra."* Lanham, MD: Lexington Books, 2005.

Sevea, Iqbal Singh. *The Political Philosophy of Muhammad Iqbal: Islam and Nationalism in Late Colonial India*. Cambridge: Cambridge University Press, 2002.

Shapiro, Gary. *Archaeologies of Vision: Foucault and Nietzsche on Seeing and Saying*. Chicago: University of Chicago Press, 2003.

Shaw, Tamsin. "The 'Last Man' Problem: Nietzsche and Weber on Political Attitudes to Suffering." In *Nietzsche as a Political Philosopher*, edited by Manuel Knoll and Barry Stocker. Berlin: De Gruyter, 2014.

Shaw, Tamsin. *Nietzsche's Political Skepticism*. Princeton, NJ: Princeton University Press, 2007.

Silk, M. S., and J. P. Stern. *Nietzsche on Tragedy*. New York: Cambridge University Press, 1981.

Singer, Irving. *The Nature of Love, Vol. 3: The Modern World*. Chicago: University of Chicago Press, 1987.

Smith, Steven B. *Modernity and Its Discontents: Making and Unmaking the Bourgeois from Machiavelli to Bellow*. New Haven, CT: Yale University Press, 2016.

Sommer, Andreas Urs. *Kommentar zu Nietzsches: "Der Fall Wagner" und "Götzen-Dämmerung."* Boston: De Gruyter, 2012.

Stern, Tom, ed. *The New Cambridge Companion to Nietzsche*. New York: Cambridge University Press, 2019.

Stern, Tom. "Nietzsche, *Amor Fati* and *The Gay Science*." *Proceedings of the Aristotelian Society* 113, no. 2, pt. 2 (2013): 146–62.

Stern, Tom. "'Some Third Thing': Nietzsche's Words and the Principle of Charity." *Journal of Nietzsche Studies* 47, no. 2 (2016): 287–302.

Strong, Tracy B. *Friedrich Nietzsche and the Politics of Transfiguration*. Expanded edition. Berkeley: University of California Press, 1988.

Strong, Tracy B. *Politics without Vision: Thinking without a Bannister in the Twentieth Century*. Chicago: University of Chicago Press, 2012.

Taylor, A. E. *Plato: The Man and His Work*. London: Routledge, 2013.

Taylor, Charles. *The Ethics of Authenticity*. Cambridge, MA: Harvard University Press, 1981.

Trivers, Robert. *The Folly of Fools: The Logic of Deceit and Self-Deception in Human Life*. New York: Basic Books, 2011.

Van Boxel, Lise. "Nietzsche in Eden." In *The Pious Sex: Essays on Women and Religion in the History of Political Thought*, edited by Andrea Radasanu. Lanham, MD: Lexington Books, 2010.

Velkley, Richard. *Being after Rousseau: Philosophy and Culture in Question*. Chicago: University of Chicago Press, 2002.

Villa, Dana. *Socratic Citizenship*. Princeton, NJ: Princeton University Press, 2001.

Von Hippel, William, and Robert Trivers. "The Evolution and Psychology of Self-Deception." *Behavioral and Brain Sciences* 34, no. 1 (2011): 1–56.

Wagner, Richard. *Selected Letters of Richard Wagner*. Translated and selected by Steward Spencer and Barry Millington. New York: W. W. Norton, 1988.

Wagner, Richard. *Wagner's "Ring of the Nibelung": A Companion*. Translated by Stewart Spencer, with commentaries by Barry Millington et al. London: Thames & Hudson, 1993.

Warren, Mark. *Nietzsche and Political Thought*. Cambridge, MA: MIT Press, 1988.

Williams, Bernard. *Shame and Necessity*. Berkeley: University of California Press, 1993.

Wolin, Richard. *The Seductions of Unreason: The Intellectual Romance with Fascism, from Nietzsche to Postmodernism*. Princeton, NJ: Princeton University Press, 2004.

Young, Julian. *Friedrich Nietzsche: A Philosophical Biography*. Cambridge: Cambridge University Press, 2010.

Young, Julian. *The Philosophies of Richard Wagner*. Lanham, MD: Lexington Books, 2014.

INDEX